Comparative Employment Relations

Comparative Employment Relations

K.D. Brahma Datt

AKHAND

AKHAND PUBLISHING HOUSE

NEW DELHI (INDIA)

Published by
AKHAND PUBLISHING HOUSE
L-9 A, IST FLOOR, STREET NO. 42
SADATPUR EXTENSION
DELHI-110094 (INDIA)
CELL- 0-9013387535, 0-9968628081

Comparative Employment Relations

Edition 2010
ISBN 978-81-910525-5-8

Printed in India
at Asian Offset Printers, Delhi

Preface

As we move into the 21st century it is becoming clear that no country is immune from the globalisation process and/or its impact. As a result of this process there is an increasing need for organisations operating in the global environment to increase their competitiveness. In doing so they are looking to the people within those organisations and, in particular, the development of their human resources to give them this competitive edge. This search for competitiveness has meant that employers are seeking larger degrees of flexibility in the recruitment, selection, remuneration and deployment of staff.

The new global economy places stresses on industrial relations because the large transnational or global firms tending to dwarf the power and influence of the labour unions. There has been opposition to core labour rights in many countries because of the issue of free trade and the need for developing economies, in particular, to maintain their competitive edge. The challenge facing organisations will be to understand various business systems and processes at a macro- level, rather than a purely organisational one. The use of comparative studies can provide a perspective and greater insight into domestic issues in one's own country by contrasting its industrial relations institutions and practices with those in other countries.

This book provides a concise introduction to employment and industrial relations. It adopts a comparative approach, examining the changing nature of employment practices in relation to the processes of globalisation. By equipping students with a set of useful concepts and perspectives, this book will give them the confidence to explore the now extensive international literature on employment management, and to utilise the methods of comparative analysis in their own work.

Author

Contents

1

Introduction to Employment Relations

As we move into the 21st century it is becoming clear that no country is immune from the globalisation process and/or its impact. As a result of this process there is an increasing need for organisations operating in the global environment to increase their competitiveness. In doing so they are looking to the people within those organisations and, in particular, the development of their human resources to give them this competitive edge.

The challenge facing organisations will be to understand various business systems and processes at a macro- level, rather than a purely organisational one. Bean believed that the use of comparative studies can provide a perspective and greater insight into domestic issues in one's own country by contrasting its industrial relations institutions and practices with those in other countries. By placing one's own country in context by the use of comparative studies, then one's own system may be fully understood.

The new global economy places stresses on industrial relations because the large transnational or global firms tending to dwarf the power and influence of the labour unions. There has been opposition to core labour rights in many countries because of the issue of free trade and the need for developing economies, in particular, to maintain their competitive edge. Governments in many countries have enacted liberalised employment legislation, which in turn has impacted upon the power of unions. This liberalisation has been designed to increase the attractiveness of various countries for Foreign Direct Investment (FDI) and the accumulation of capital by those countries and companies involved in this investment.

By encouraging FDI, many countries, especially those that can be considered to be newly industrialising, hope to increase the level of productive employment thereby decreasing poverty and inequity. The United Nations World Summit for Social Development recognised that the generation of productive employment is the most effective means of alleviating poverty, inequity and social exclusion.

The three countries, New Zealand, Malaysia and Thailand were chosen for study for the following reasons:

1. To provide a context, in order to understand New Zealand's employment relations environment.
2. All three countries are dependent on Foreign Direct Investment (FDI) to sustain growth.
3. All three countries have had governments that have utilised industrial relations policies to encourage this foreign direct investment.
4. As is typical in the Asia Pacific region all three have very different cultural and historical features and the 'one size fits all' approach does not work.

The Asia-Pacific is a region of stark contrasts: Asia contains more unemployment and poverty than any other region with almost two-thirds of the world's 1.1 billion poor mostly in South Asia.

New Zealand is a parliamentary democracy and currently still retains close links with its former colonial power, Britain. New Zealand still acknowledges the Queen of England as its Head of State. The Privy Council based in London is the ultimate Appeal Court for the New Zealand legal system. An appreciation and understanding of this colonial past is essential in understanding employment relations in New Zealand. Laws based in the British legal system have been transplanted to the New Zealand legal system, for example, the concept of 'master' and 'servant' in terms of the law of contract becoming embedded in the New Zealand workplace.

New Zealand is a predominately Christian country and has a population that is predominately European. One of the major challenges facing the country is how to balance the demands of the indigenous people for economic power, sovereignty and self-determination and the demands of other ethnic groups living in the country.

Malaysia was also a colony of Britain and as such has a parliamentary democracy modelled after the British system. The presence of three main ethnic groups has been the cause of ethnic tension and Malaysia has developed a number of social and economic policies to ensure the continued prosperity and power for the indigenous Malay people.

Thailand is the only country of the three that has not been colonised — the word *Thai* meaning *free*. Until 1932 Thailand had a system of absolute monarchy subsequently replaced by a constitutional monarchy. However, despite Thailand being a constitutional monarchy the military has considerable influence on Thai political life. 'Military governments have ruled 80 percent of the time since 1932, either directly or through surrogates appointed by military leaders'. Thailand does not appear to have had a high level of disagreement between the various ethnic groups. Thailand and Malaysia are considered to be Newly Industrialising Countries (NICs) and, as such, have a need for capital accumulation to provide for this industrial expansion. Both countries are amongst the wealthier of the NICs in the Asia Pacific region and have birth and death rates that are comparable with New Zealand, which is considered to be a fully industrialised country.

Both Thailand and Malaysia were amongst the fastest growing in the region. New Zealand, similarly, after low levels of economic growth during an intense restructuring period has experienced strong growth especially in 1993 and 1994. Since then the economy has settled into a lower, more stable, growth trajectory.

All countries have experienced a negative GDP growth in 1999, this being attributed to the continuing effects of the economic downturn experienced in Asia. All three countries, however, have a need for FDI. New Zealand, while considered fully industrialised, is moving from dependence upon agricultural exports and requires investment for expansion of the service and manufacturing sectors. Countries at different stages of structural transformation towards industrialisation have different types of requirements for capital accumulation. Therefore, it could be suggested that New Zealand should differ significantly in its approach to employment relations than Thailand and Malaysia given that it is at a different stage of industrialisation and, therefore, has different capital accumulation needs.

GOVERNANCE

All three countries have a tripartite system of employment relationshowever, the power balance with this tripartite system is far from what could be considered equal in any of the three countries. New Zealand, Malaysia and Thailand, whilst at different stages of this industrial transformation, all wish to attract foreign investment and, consequently, their respective political systems have worked to control unions and maintain labour participation at a level that will encourage this investment.

This need for FDI has meant that in many countries a framework of laws has been introduced aimed at restraining union power. Epstein wrote that the employment relationship is best governed by 'freedom of contract where individuals are free to make whatever bargains they please with whomever they please'. New Zealand developed the Employment Contracts Act of 1991 based upon this principle. This has meant that New Zealand operated, until the year 2000, under a legal system that has favoured individualism over collectivism. The ECA also abolished compulsory unionism and restricted the power of union groups in the workplace.

In Thailand, a number of governmental and non-governmental institutions make up the framework for the relationship between labour, employment and the government. Thailand has one of the lowest levels of unionisation in the region and the organised labour movement has remained fragmented and fractionalised. In addition, Thailand's military has played a unique role in Thailand's political life by asserting itself when domestic economic policies not favoured by the military leaders are enacted. This includes a number of occasions when civilian efforts to enact labour law reform, which extended entitlements to workers, incurred military disfavour.

Similarly, in Malaysia government policy has been to subordinate the labour movement and guide trade unionism to the broader consideration of national economic development as defined by the ruling elite. The Malaysian system of industrial relations in the private sector are closely controlled by the state: the freedom of unions to organise and bargain are severely restricted and the industrial relations rules and regulations clearly reflect the state's efforts to contain industrial conflict in the interests of economic development.

WORK ORGANISATION

Work organisation according to Verma et al.'s model equates to the level of union participation in the workplace. That is, the extent and nature of employee participation and/or involvement in decision-making. New Zealand is a country that has moved to a strategy of higher value-added export oriented industrialisation. The IR/HR policy goals under this form of strategy shift from one of cost containment to one of work- force flexibility and skills development. The government introduced the Employment Contracts Act (ECA) in an effort to achieve more labour market flexibility. Prior to the ECA 1991, workplace organisation in New Zealand focussed upon narrow job descriptions and clear lines of demarcation between individual jobs. Union membership in New Zealand has decreased since the advent of the Employment Contracts Act 1991 and the removal of compulsory union membership.

Since the advent of the ECA there has been a corresponding increase in the number of individual contracts in an attempt to provide employers with the flexibility they require. The new environment encouraged new work practices and remuneration structures that can be built around new technology and process innovations. A NZIER survey showed that there is increased experimentation with more flexible work practices, such as multi-skilling and team-based work units.

Malaysia is in transition from a low cost exporting oriented country to one focussing on advanced export orientated industrialisation. The workplace organisation policies reflect the desire of the Malaysian government to control labour costs. This took the form of government controls on union membership, how and when unions are recognised, the definition of issues subject to bargaining, and freedom to strike and dispute recognition. As a result of these measures Malaysian union membership decreased from 11 percent of total employment to 9.4 percent in 1990. The organised labour movement in Thailand is fragmented and fractionalised with comparatively low levels of union membership.

Work place environments are becoming more diverse as all three countries look to migrant labour to fill vacancies created by skill shortages. In addition, all three countries are experiencing an increase of females in the workplace. The International Labour Office reported: 'a striking phenomenon is the feminisation of Asian labour and labour migration'. In New Zealand female participation in the workforce has grown to 47.7 percent. This is resulting in changing demands of workers, for example, childcare and flexible working hours. The first national Childcare Survey, conducted on behalf of Statistics New Zealand, reported that an estimated 60 percent of New Zealand children under the age of five and approximately 20 percent of school-age children have childcare or early childhood education arrangements.

Part-time work has increased in New Zealand in the last decade by 42.8 percent as compared to a full-time employment increase of 7.9 percent. Whilst part-time work can offer distinct advantages in terms of workers being better able to balance home, family and work responsibilities, there are drawbacks. The International Labour Organisation reports that part-time workers are very often at a disadvantage in comparison with full-time colleagues. Typically their wages are lower, they are ineligible for certain social security benefits and their career prospects are more limited.

Employment Security

Kurnvilla & Arudsothy in Verma noted that job security is not well established in Malaysia, the predominant strategy being to reduce the core labour force during economic downturn. Malaysia has enacted a number of laws that are designed to protect the employment security and tenure for the indigenous Malay population.

As Verma et al. stated, these types of contractual arrangements, especially the use of oral contracts where the contract can be modified from day to day or week to week, are incredibly precarious and do nothing to encourage high levels of worker loyalty, innovation, productivity and commitment.

The unemployment rate increased to 3.9 percent in 1998 as a result of an economic downturn. Total employment declined by 3 percent to 8.5 million in 1998 as the number of retrenched workers reported increased sharply in 1998. A similar situation exists in Thailand where during the recent economic downturn workers were terminated or had their working hours reduced. Owing to the economic crisis, the labour market saw a reduction in employment in 1998. Total employment recorded at 30.8 million reflected a decline of 812,000 or 2.6 percent from the previous year. A 1997 UNICEF Report on the HIV epidemic highlighted the spread of the infection as casual workers, including those in the entertainment industry no longer required in Thailand, were being sent home to countries such as Myanmar.

The report raised concerns regarding employment security and occupational safety and health protection for migrant workers throughout Asia. The Bangkok Post reported on 20/07/00 'that many labour-protection programmes in Thailand have small population coverage. Because of implementation and enforcement problems, these programmes are biased in favour of formal-sector employees, who tend to be better off than informal sector employees. Low-wage and disadvantaged workers who most need protection during economic downturns fall beyond the purview of these programmes'. In theory a casual workforce would give the employer the freedom to tailor the workforce daily — or hourly — to the needs of the business so as to provide maximum efficiency.

Skill formation: New Zealand is currently grappling with shortages of skilled labour in a number of areas. A Lampen Group survey conducted in 1999 reported employers' concerns regarding a shortage of IT/technical skills, accounting, sales, and call centre and customer service people. Research conducted in 1999 on the New Zealand finance sector indicated that career development, if done at all, was focused upon managing people out of the business. Anecdotal evidence sourced from various HR professionals working in the IT industry suggests that the sector is attempting to recruit for this skill shortage from countries such as Bangladesh, Pakistan, Sri Lanka, Malaysia and Thailand.

The New Zealand government is currently attempting to address these issues with training programmes that are focussed on science and technology and the introduction of an apprenticeship scheme focussing upon the more traditional trade areas. Many politicians have expressed concern about the 'brain drain' of well-qualified people attracted by more attractive salaries that can be earned internationally.

The newly emerging economies (NIEs) of which Malaysia and Thailand are considered to be part of are finding that they are beginning to experience labour and skill shortages. Malaysia since the 1980s has experienced shortages of technical workers in manufacturing and of unskilled workers in rubber and oil-palm plantations. Malaysia is attempting to solve this labour shortage by recruiting migrant workers; there are currently half a million 'documented' foreign workers in the country. In Thailand the market for unskilled workers is becoming tighter and there are shortages of semi-skilled and highly skilled workers especially in engineering and management sectors. It is believed that educational institutes should focus upon producing properly qualified graduates, while companies should have continuous programmes for staff development.

Compensation

The central debate over compensation according to Verma et al. \involves whether or not it is becoming more flexible or contingent that is related in some way to variations in performance. Therefore, compensation systems that reward productivity and performance can become a critical success factor in organisational competitiveness. Bailey wrote that the additional challenge in compensation design is the requirement that excessive costs are avoided and, at the same time, employee morale be maintained at high levels. Bailey argued 'as people move from business to business, market to market and country to country, organisations will increasingly be tested by the need to bring multinational and multicultural perspectives and practices to the human resource management function'.

The Act allowed employers, if they chose, to restructure the level of wage bargaining and to reshape its focus through direct negotiations with employees. Employers took advantage of this power and in 1997, 75 percent of employees were employed on individual contracts and there is evidence of a greater incidence of performance related pay and of workers being able to negotiate more flexible remuneration packages than was possible under the previous regime.

Harbridge reported dramatic changes to working time arrangements with changes to what days of the week ordinary hours can be worked, for example, Saturday and Sunday. Important changes have also been introduced in the application of penalty and overtime rates and such things as triple time rates have virtually disappeared.

Unlike New Zealand that has given employers flexibility to negotiate, Malaysia appears to have more traditional forms of wage and salary payment systems. These systems that include predetermined, automatic adjustment systems and non-adjustable bonuses only serve to constrain employer flexibility.

Whilst Thailand has the legal means to enable workers to negotiate, often it is difficult for them to effect change. Violence is often used in an effort to prevent unions from negotiating improvements in conditions. The Thai national press has reported incidents of violence perpetrated against striking workers who were attempting to gain improved conditions.

The processes and pressures caused by globalisation appear to demand cheap labour if MNCs and FDI are to remain in the various countries.

'Foreign investors first poured money into Thailand to take advantage of its cheap labour and when countries like China and Vietnam opened up with even cheaper labour they started moving out in droves, creating conditions for an overall loss of international confidence and *the subsequent financial crisis*'.

Managing with Trade Unions

A belief in managerial prerogative, or the right to manage, underpins management behaviour in employment relations. Historically, although managements vigorously attempted to exclude trade unions from their workplaces, in practice the strength of union organisation in many areas of the economy obliged them to try to sustain their prerogative by accommodating workers' demands. During the twentieth century, employers often recognised unions for collective bargaining so as to mitigate disruption, and foster order and stability. This was, however, in large part a reaction by employers to the pressure coming from workers themselves to organise unions. Attempts to exclude unions caused too much disruption, given the collective power that workers were able to wield. Thus employers took a pragmatic approach, recognising unions, but doing so in a way that disturbed managerial prerogatives as little as possible. During the 1960s and 1970s, in a context of growing union power, companies that had hitherto not recognised a union found it advantageous to do so, in order to quell workplace militancy. For example, management in the biscuit works studied by Scott were aware of a growing union presence within the factory and chose to accommodate it by means of a centralised negotiating relationship with union full-time officers, from which workplace union activists were distanced. The company embraced collective bargaining with a recognised union, but did so in a way that upheld managerial rights and secured workplace order. For much of the twentieth century, many employers chose to try to exclude unions from their workplaces by dealing with them through employers' associations. However, the growth of workplace bargaining prompted employers to look for more sophisticated ways of managing employment relations in unionised environments.

Rise and Fall of Employers' Associations

Employers tried to externalise their employment relations activity, and thus uphold managerial prerogative in the workplace, by bargaining with trade unions through employers' associations. The origins of employers' associations in Britain can be traced to the late eighteenth and early nineteenth centuries; although these early organisations were local and transient in character, employers often combined to challenge the efforts of the nascent trade unions to organise workers. The 1890s and 1900s saw the emergence of permanent national federations of employers, such as the Engineering Employers' Federation (EEF).

The development of employers' associations during this period is ascribed to three factors. First, growing state intervention in employment relations was seen to necessitate a more coordinated response by employers. Second, employers were better able to cope with increasing competitive pressures by combining for collective bargaining purposes. Multi-employer bargaining over pay meant that firms did not have to compete on wage costs, removing a potential source of destructive competition. Third, most importantly, multi-employer bargaining, through the offices of employers' associations, helped to negate the growing power of workplace trade unionism in a number of important sectors of the economy, in particular the building, engineering, and printing industries. In matters that went unregulated by collective agreements, particularly those pertaining to the organisation and pace of work, the assumption was that management prerogative would predominate.

Although the structure and policies of employers' associations often varied considerably, the development of permanent, national bodies between the 1890s and 1920s reflected the concern of employers that union power be accommodated and contained within the institution of collective bargaining. Many employers' associations also operated disputes procedures. These helped to resolve disputes between a union and one or more of its member firms. It is important, then, not to understate the influence of employers' associations on the development of employment relations in Britain.

Nevertheless, during the late 1960s and the 1970s there was a major trend away from multi-employer bargaining as an increasing number of firms, especially larger ones, chose to develop organisation-specific procedures. By the late 1970s, although multi-employer bargaining remained important in some parts of the private sector, particularly over matters like working hours, bargaining activity was increasingly conducted at company level. In 1980, just 30 per cent of private sector employees had their pay determined largely by multi-employer bargaining, compared to 40 per cent by single-employer bargaining. Only about one in twenty employees in the private sector now have their pay determined by multi-employer bargaining.

Given these developments, it is hardly surprising that the membership of employers' associations has diminished, although they are increasingly focusing their activities on commercial matters, and the provision of employment relations advice. Data from successive Workplace Employee Relations Surveys show that, in 1990, just 13 per cent of private sector workplaces reported that they were in organisations that were members of an employers' association.

Managerial Innovation in Employment Relations

Attempts to bargain with unions by means of employers' associations contributed to the widespread neglect of employment relations management in many firms, or what Hyman refers to as the 'tradition of unscientific management'. The historical weakness of the personnel management function in Britain has long been acknowledged. Writers point to the history of unsophisticated managerial control systems, the lack of complex managerial hierarchies within firms, and the slow, and indeed relatively late, diffusion of scientific management techniques. Employers exhibited a preference for *ad hoc*, informal, and unsophisticated ways of managing their workforces, such as a reliance on simple payment by results techniques. What factors contributed to managerial neglect of employment relations matters? Clearly the externalisation of relations with trade unions was one influence. Three other elements were also important: first, the process of industrialisation in Britain, which started earlier than in other competitor economies, delayed the emergence of the modern corporate firm; second, diverse and fluctuating product markets, and an ample labour supply were obstacles to modernisation; and third, in some industries, a pre-industrial craft ethos, in which workers enjoyed a degree of control over the content of their jobs, prevailed.

During the 1940s and 1950s, there was a marked growth in the incidence of workplace bargaining in Britain, particularly in the engineering sector. Not only did this reflect the increasing difficulty employers had in upholding managerial rights in the workplace, but the weakness of agreements reached by means of multi-employer bargaining, and a tight labour market created by full employment, which enhanced workers' bargaining power, were also contributory factors. The reluctance of senior managers to take control over their own employment relations during this period in a resolute and strategic way, and to come to terms with, and accommodate the growth of, workplace unionism, rather than see it as a threat to be nullified, was seen by the pluralists as a major error, contributing to industrial disputes and workplace disorder.

Employers were encouraged to secure greater control over employment relations within the workplace by recognising, formally, the legitimacy of shop-floor unionism rather than by trying to extinguish it, something that would only cause greater disruption. It was set up to examine the system of employment relations in Britain, and to make proposals for its reform, given the detrimental effect aspects of it were held to have on British economic performance, in particular, 'wage drift', inflationary increases in earnings caused by workplace bargaining, and the associated high level of industrial conflict. Influenced by prominent pluralist writers such as Allan Flanders, Donovan identified managerial weakness as a prime source of Britain's employment relations problems and strongly recommended that, in order to rectify them, managers should secure greater control over workplace employment relations.

During the 1960s and 1970s, in a context of growing union militancy, managers adopted a notably more interventionist approach in respect of workplace employment relations anyway, in order to contain and accommodate trade union power, and thus exercise greater control. Employers were increasingly the 'main instigators in reshaping the system of industrial relations in Britain'. Perhaps the most significant managerial intervention during this period was the rise of 'productivity bargaining', heralded as a major managerial initiative in the reform of employment relations. Not only was it held to be important as a pioneering attempt to resolve some of the problems caused by unregulated workplace bargaining, but it was also deemed significant as an example of managerial initiative in employment relations.

What, then, were the features of the Blue Book deal struck between management and unions at Fawley? Its major targets were the perceived 'under-utilisation' of labour and excessive overtime working. The high level of overtime allowed workers to supplement low basic wages with premium payments for doing the extra work. This not only contributed to wage drift, since earnings became increasingly distant from formally negotiated pay rates, but it also encouraged workplace bargaining over overtime rates and allocation. Furthermore, the prospect of supplementing earnings through opportunities for overtime was detrimental to productivity since it gave workers an incentive to reduce their effort during their normal working time in the hope that this would make overtime necessary. It was envisaged that such an approach would encourage order and stability, as well as generating productivity improvements.

Over and above the features of the agreement itself, the deal struck at Fawley was held to be significant in two important respects. First, it was an example of managerial innovation in employment relations, standing out from the hitherto *ad hoc*, unsophisticated, and reactive approach to employment relations exhibited within most British firms. Second, the agreement appeared to possess a 'higher order function', being the 'very embodiment of pluralist industrial relations'.

The Fawley experiment, then, appeared not only to be beneficial for the employer, in that it led to improved economic performance, but it also seemed to secure, and legitimise, the interests of employees through the establishment of a cooperative relationship with the unions. Ensuing productivity gains, though, were limited and largely the result of staffing cuts, rather than the more efficient utilisation of labour, and overtime working remained commonplace. Managers, moreover, never eschewed their unitary beliefs; indeed, they used productivity agreements to undermine union power in the workplace, part of a long-term strategy to manage without unions altogether.

During the late 1960s and early 1970s, there was a marked increase in the popularity of productivity agreements, though they varied considerably in their scope, detail, and outcomes. In particular, employers increasingly sought to gain control of their own employment relations, encouraged by a process of corporate restructuring and rationalisation which stimulated demand for greater managerial expertise and professionalism. Personnel policies were reformed. More sophisticated payment systems were introduced, for example, involving the introduction of new job evaluation techniques.

Moreover, workplace trade unionism, particularly the role of shop stewards became increasingly formalised as managers encouraged, or 'sponsored', them in an attempt to accommodate union power. In the Cadbury's confectionery plant at Bourneville, for example, managers acceded to the operation of a closed shop arrangement as part of an attempt to contain and accommodate the growing influence of the shop stewards, and to direct it in a 'responsible and realistic' direction. During the 1970s, shop steward structures were extended into areas, such as the public sector, where the presence of formal workplace unionism had hitherto been rare. One should not disregard the extent to which the development of workplace union organisation derived from the efforts of workers themselves to secure change. Union activity was not always amenable to management objectives. In Cadbury's, for example, the Transport and General Workers' Union (TGWU) became rather more powerful in the workplace than managers considered desirable.

From this overview of how employment relations was managed in Britain before the 1980s, it should be clear that while employers accepted trade unionism, this reflected a pragmatic response to circumstances, notably union power, rather than a genuine belief in the virtues of a pluralist approach. If managers had to deal with trade unions, they tried to do so in such a way that it contained workplace militancy. Managers may have been obliged to respond constructively to the implications of growing union power, but their fundamentally unitary values generally remained constant.

DEVELOPMENT OF TRADE UNIONISM

There is an imbalance of power in the employment relationship in favour of the employer. The main way in which workers have attempted to challenge this power differential is to combine in collective organisations, trade unions, so that they can influence the terms of their employment relationships from a position of greater strength. Thus one of the earliest and most well-known definitions of a trade union, dating from the end of the nineteenth century, refers to it as 'a continuous association of wage earners for the purpose of maintaining or improving the conditions of their working lives'. A more sophisticated definition should, however, be more specific about the means by which unions seek to improve the conditions of people's working lives. It does so by providing workers with protection from the arbitrary exercise of managerial prerogative, bargaining with management over the terms and conditions of their employment, giving them influence over decisions that affect them at work, and by providing them with a means of effecting political changes that are favourable to their interests.

While one can trace their ancestry further back in time to the trade clubs and friendly societies of the eighteenth century, in Britain the trade unions originated in the nineteenth century during a period of sustained and rapid industrialisation. Although there were attempts to form workers into unions during the early nineteenth century, these were generally transient bodies that either lacked formal organisational arrangements or were local affairs. The first stable and permanent national bodies date from around the middle of the nineteenth century and were mainly combinations of local organisations in industries such as engineering, construction, and printing. Two related developments during this period, the emergence of large-scale production enterprises, or the factory system, in industries like cotton manufacture, and the increasing prevalence of the capitalist system of wage labour, would, given their potentially exploitative effects, appear to have generated the necessary conditions for the emergence of trade unionism.

To what extent, though, is the emphasis on the factory system, which was specific to the Lancashire cotton industry at this time, an accurate representation of the industrialisation process during the nineteenth century? Samuel argues that much industrial production continued to be concentrated in small workshops. Moreover, there was a marked reluctance among the nascent industrial capitalists to abandon aspects of the tried and tested craft production system. Thus rather than subjugate all their workers to the rigours of new and more intensive production techniques, as suggested by Marx, employers came to depend upon the expertise of skilled, generally male workers who exercised considerable discretion over the production process. Indeed, in what came to be known as the process of 'internal sub-contracting' employers actually ceded a considerable amount of control over the manufacture of goods to key groups of skilled craft-workers, many of whom employed their own helpers and assistants. Rather, union organisation developed as a means of maintaining craft control, and of regulating the terms and conditions of the trade.

Indeed, many 'of the early British trade unions were primarily associations of internal contractors and they often used the union to develop a set of rules regulating the work done by helpers and underhands'. A major function of these early trade unions was to provide their skilled craft-worker members with 'friendly benefits' such as unemployment and sick pay. These workers aimed to defend and maintain their customary working practices and pay rates, and thus control, through the principle of unilateral regulation, their conditions of employment.

The existence of strict apprenticeship rules, which prevented employers from recruiting outside the trade, and the provision of friendly benefits, which enabled workers to refuse jobs unless they were paid at the customary rate, helped them to do so. Increasingly, though, friendly benefits came to be used not just as a means of defending customary practices, but as a way of establishing, and then enforcing, common terms and conditions of employment, or the 'common rule'. From the 1860s onwards, moreover, trade unionism began to take root in industries such as coal mining, the railways, and steel making where craft practices, while evident, were much less deep-rooted, something that placed a greater onus on collective bargaining as a means of regulating pay and employment conditions.

The period between 1880 and 1920 saw a major expansion of trade unionism in Britain. The development of 'general' unions, in industries such as the docks, transport, and gas for example, in two waves, first during the 1880s, and second, during the 1910s, demonstrates how, under the influence of prominent leaders, many of whom were imbued with a socialist outlook, increasing numbers of semi- and unskilled workers became organised. This has been described as 'the most radical alteration in union structure and the most explosive lasting extension of union coverage of any period of labour history'.

Unlike their skilled craft counterparts, most of the workers who unionised in this period looked to secure improvements in their pay and conditions through widespread collective organisation, and a readiness to use strikes and political activity, including the formation of a dedicated parliamentary party to represent the labour interest. These were industries in which trade unionism had secured a foothold before the 1880s. The most sizeable occupation, domestic service, was almost entirely unorganised however.

Between 1910 and 1914, there was a sustained period of major industrial unrest in Britain, particularly in the coal mining and transport industries, a function of increasing union membership and a reluctance on the part of some employers to concede moderate wage demands. In turn, the disputes stimulated further union growth which continued during the First World War (1914–18) and its immediate aftermath, a period of further industrial unrest that even included a police strike, and was in part stimulated by the quasi-revolutionary conditions that characterised the post-war years. By 1921, trade union membership in Britain had risen to more than 8 million. Most of the inter-war period, however, saw a considerable erosion in the level of union membership and organisation. Employment in some of the large, staple industries in which there was a robust union presence, such as cotton and coal mining for example, declined because increased international competition eroded export markets.

Moreover, the government's concern with maintaining tight control over the supply of money also challenged the competitiveness of British industry and further encouraged employers to examine ways in which they could institute cost savings and roll back the influence of trade unionism. Although employers in the engineering industry won a notable victory over the main engineering union in 1922, the major arena of conflict was the coal industry.Union leaderships, though, worried about the constitutionality of the strike, called it off after nine days, leaving the miners to suffer a heavy defeat.

In the early 1930s, the trade unions were further weakened by the onset of a major economic recession and the resulting mass unemployment it created, especially in the major industrial regions of north-east England and South Wales. In places dominated by a single industry, such as shipbuilding in the north-eastern town of Jarrow for example, industrial closure had devastating consequences. In respect of industry, then, 'Britain was turning into two nations'.

One of the most notable aspects of employment relations in the new factories was the attempt to introduce more sophisticated and rigorous systems of managerial control, based on scientific management techniques. Although there was some union opposition to the imposition of such practices, overall it was rather limited. Many of the jobs in the new factories were taken by women. There is evidence that the unions, however, were reluctant to recruit such workers. While union membership started to recover as the economy picked up in the second half of the 1930s, it was still only three-quarters of what it had been in 1921.

Although trade union membership had started to increase again during the late 1930s, the Second World War and the political and economic climate of the post-war period, in which full employment predominated, were major sources of union growth. Trade union membership reached 13 million by the 1970s. The development of trade unionism in Britain during this period was marked by a number of distinctive features, including the growing significance of shop stewards, the spread of unionisation beyond its manual worker origins, and the increasing influence of the Trades Union Congress (TUC). To start with, the traditional basis of trade unionism in the old, staple industries of the nineteenth century, such as coal mining, continued to be eroded as a result of employment contraction.

The post-war economic boom was predicated upon the growth of manufacturing industry, the mass production of electrical goods and other standardised products such as motor vehicles, based on a narrow division of labour. Moreover, the rather monotonous nature of the assembly-line work in largescale factory environments, allied with the more vigorous exercise of managerial prerogative, generated increasingly adversarial and 'low-trust' relations between managers and workers.

Growth of hop Stewards

The role of shop stewards, unpaid union representatives based in the workplace, attracted greater attention. Although the shop steward position originated in the first two decades of the twentieth century, the growth of workplace bargaining saw a massive rise in their numbers, particularly in engineering and parts of manufacturing industry, thus generating a 'shift in authority' within the trade unions away from the salaried cadre of full-time professional officials. By the end of the 1970s, shop stewards had spread to the public sector, and there may have been as many as 250,000 of them active in Britain. Shop stewards, or workplace, or office, representatives as they are sometimes called, are often the first point of contact for union members. Shop stewards bargain with management on behalf of their members and represent their interests, supporting, advising, and standing up for them in the workplace. Stewards, then, provide workers with protection at work that they are less able to secure for themselves as individuals.

Stewards derive much of their authority and legitimacy from their closeness to the members they represent in the workplace. But their role can often be a thankless one. They are frequently at the beck and call of their members, receive little gratitude for their achievements, but are the target of complaints should they make a mistake. Stewards can also be the target of criticism that they are only 'in it for themselves'; that the job is a way of shirking work, or used as a vehicle for self-advancement. In the manufacturing plant studied by Batstone, Frenkel, and Boraston, stewards who had used their position as a stepping-stone to a supervisor's job came in for criticism from their erstwhile colleagues. They do not just represent the interests of their members, but actively determine what a legitimate interest is, how it will be handled by the union, and whether or not it will be put to managers.

A further challenge for stewards is to forge a constructive relationship with managers, while at the same time having to oppose them, and thus fulfil the sometimes unrealistic expectations of their members. Indeed 1970s legislation, which obliges employers to give shop stewards of recognised unions reasonable paid time off work to attend to their union duties, reflected the prevailing pluralist policy assumption that by accepting and integrating workplace unionism, rather than challenging it, managers could effectively contain industrial conflict.

Rise of White-collar Unionism

During the 1960s and 1970s, the development of trade unionism in Britain was characterised by two notable trends. First, union membership and organisation became more commonplace among non-manual, so-called 'white-collar' workers in both the private and public sectors. Much of the rapid acceleration in union membership during this period – by 1979 over half the British workforce were unionised – reflected the increased unionisation of workers in office-based occupations in sectors such as central and local government administration. Much was made of the success of the Association of Supervisory, Technical and Managerial Staff (ASTMS), now part of the Amicus trade union, in recruiting scientific, professional, and quasi-professional workers. By 'the end of the 1970s nearly 40 per cent of all trade unionists were in white-collar jobs'. An alternative explanation for this growth, however, attributes it to employment restructuring and the development of large-scale enterprises employing non-manual labour, the greater propensity of employers to recognise trade unions, and a supportive public policy environment.

How can the character of these white-collar unions be understood? It seems that unions of white-collar workers were prepared to act militantly, and take industrial action, but in pursuit of their own material interests, rather than as an expression of collective solidarity. Thus trade unionism 'is viewed in this light as a means of keeping ahead of manual workers rather than as an expression of unity with them in fighting for a common cause'.

The second development concerns the increasingly prominent role enjoyed by the Trades Union Congress (TUC) in British employment relations. As a trade union confederation, which represented the interests of its union affiliates, provided them with services, like education and training for example, and also attempted to regulate their behaviour, the TUC originated in the nineteenth century. During the 1960s and 1970s, however, the growth of state intervention in employment relations enhanced the stature of the TUC as a conduit to government.

By the end of the 1970s, perhaps the most striking feature of employment relations in Britain was the strength of trade unionism. For example, the aggregate level of trade union membership, and membership density, a term that is used to refer to the proportion of the workforce who are union members, peaked in the late 1970s.

State and Employment Relations

Although management and unions are the principal parties in employment relations, it is also important to emphasize the strong, or 'pervasive', influence of the state and its bodies. It is conventional to understand the effects of state activity on employment relations in four ways. First, employment in the state, or public, sector is a major element of contemporary employment relations.

Second, states enact legislation in the area of employment relations, such as that designed to regulate trade union behaviour, or establish minimum wages. The European Union is also a source of employment legislation. Third, states operate arrangements to assist employers and unions to resolve disputes, notably arbitration and conciliation machinery. Fourth, the economic and political programmes followed by the governments of national states also have important implications for employment relations.

How, though, can the state be defined, since it can be a rather slippery concept? One of the most popular approaches is that of the German sociologist Max Weber, who understood the state in terms of the monopoly it enjoys over the legitimate use of physical force within certain defined territorial limits. According to one prominent contemporary political scientist, the state is 'a system of relationships which defines the territory and membership of a community, regulates its internal affairs, conducts relations with other states and provides it with identity and cohesion'.

Liberal-pluralist approaches have long dominated attempts to understand the way in which groups mobilise and accrue power, and thus come to have their interests represented by the state. As a result, 'the making of public policy by governments is the end-product of a process of negotiation and accommodation in which citizens organised in groups to represent their interests exert pressure to realise their ambitions'. While the liberal-pluralist perspective encompasses a variety of distinctive strands, in respect of employment relations the state's role is generally seen to involve maintaining a balance between the competing interests of capital and labour, and accommodating the demands of both. There are two fundamental problems with liberal-pluralist perspectives. First, they fail to account for the marked tendency of state policy to favour the interests of employers. Second, they assume that state intervention produces an equivalence of power between capital and labour when in reality the odds remain stacked against the latter.

However, a rather different assumption underpins new right, or neo-liberal, perspectives, as exemplified by the work of writers such as Hayek that became more prominent during the 1970s and 1980s. Whereas liberal-pluralist approaches consider state intervention in the area of employment relations as a largely progressive development, helping to ameliorate the imbalance of power between capital and labour, from a neo-liberal perspective, laws that make it easier for unions to operate endanger the liberties of individual workers and their employers to conduct their affairs in a manner of their own choosing. State regulation is desirable only in so far as it helps to protect and support free markets.

For a critical, and more sophisticated, appreciation of the role of the state in employment relations it is appropriate to draw upon Marxist perspectives. Although Marx himself did not develop an explicit theory of the state under capitalism, two distinct approaches to understanding its role can be inferred from his work. In his early writings, the state is treated as an instrument of class rule by the dominant capitalist interest. In this approach, the emphasis is on the coercive, repressive role of the state, and the way in which its offices and policies are designed to undermine trade unions and the interests of labour in general in order to further those of capital.

Yet state policy is not just characterised by the repression of the labour interest. Thus the second broad approach to understanding the role of the state under capitalism that can be inferred from Marx's writings, and that is particularly associated with the Italian Marxist theorist Antonio Gramsci, suggests that in order to maintain the long-term viability of capitalism, states need to win the favour, or consent, of those they govern. This provides a stable and ordered environment within which the capitalist order can flourish. From this perspective, then, policies and legislation ostensibly designed to favour the labour interest, such as the nineteenth-century laws restricting the working hours of women and children, in fact benefit capital in the long term. Thus in order to maintain the long-term viability of capitalism, states adopt policies or enact legislation that runs counter to the short-term interests of business.

Although Marxism offers a rather sophisticated understanding of the influence of the state on employment relations, suggesting that its approach is characterised by a mixture of coercion and consent, the extent to which state policies necessarily support the interests of capital has been questioned. Edwards contends that it is oversimplistic to view the state as the servant of one class and that state managers, policy-makers, and government officials have to accommodate the interests of both capital and labour. The state does not just respond to demands from capital. Nevertheless, the state must still operate within a capitalist order, something that shapes, but does not determine, the character of its policies. This is even more pronounced given the imperatives of globalisation.

Voluntarism and Employment Relations

An appreciation of the importance of voluntarism is crucial to understanding the nature of employment relations in Britain. What, then, is meant by the term 'voluntarism'? In essence, it refers to the general absence of direct state intervention in employment relations and a preference for the terms of the employment relationship to be determined voluntarily by employers and trade unions, without state interference. During the seventeenth and eighteenth centuries the development of capitalism in Britain was informed by the complementary ideologies of economic *laissez-faire* and market individualism within which the recognition of private property interests predominated.

Nascent capitalist entrepreneurs were resistant to state intervention in their affairs and preferred, wherever possible, to handle their own affairs. Under the common law, with its emphasis on individual rights, the trade unions, as collective organisations of workers, were treated as criminal conspiracies acting in 'restraint of trade'.

The dominance of market individualism and *laisses-faire* ideologies provided the foundation for the development of 'collective *laissez-faire*' as the dominant state approach to employment relations in Britain, a preference that employers should deal with employment relations matters, and with unions, themselves, without direct intervention by the state. The existing legal framework enabled employers to deal with union activities in ways that did not threaten their interests too severely, and thus obviated the need for more explicit measures.

Why, though, did the trade unions come to place so much faith in voluntarism? They were disinclined to look to the state for legislation that would enhance the labour interest and, given their suspicion of state organs, especially the judiciary, were to develop a considerable attachment to the principle of 'free collective bargaining', based on the strength of their collective organisation, as the most effective means of regulating the employment relationship.

To a large degree, therefore, the development of employment relations in nineteenthcentury Britain was characterised by an abstentionist role on the part of the state, something that was to have a pronounced and longstanding influence during the twentieth century. Moreover, du ing the late nineteenth and early twentieth centuries, the British state sought to accommodate trade unionism and encourage the development of moderate trade unions, by enabling them to organise strikes and industrial action without breaching the common law.

Unlike many other countries, then, the regulation of the employment relationship in Britain came to be determined largely by a combination of collective bargaining and managerial prerogative, without the development of a comprehensive system of statutory employment rights. While direct state intervention in employment relations may have been marginal, one should not assume that the British state therefore exercised neutrality in employment relations matters. Moreover, ongoing judicial hostility to trade unions – laws were interpreted in ways that benefited employers for example – frequently undermined unions' legitimacy.

The system of collective *laissez-faire* that developed in Britain did not mean that intervention by the state in employment relations was entirely absent. Rather, the aim was, so far as possible, to reduce the likelihood of judicial interference. Moreover, during periods of sustained industrial unrest, such as in the years immediately following the conclusion of the 1914–18 war, the state acted promptly in taking measures designed to repress trade unions and their ability to undertake strike action. During the Second World War, strikes were forbidden by the government lest they disrupted the war effort.

These examples serve to illustrate how the state's role in employment relations is far removed from that of a neutral, disinterested observer. Rather, it is largely concerned with providing an environment in which businesses can thrive, something that in Britain has, for the reasons we have outlined above, generally implied limited direct state intervention in employment relations, but does not rule out a more coercive approach should it be dictated by circumstances.

State Intervention and Employment Relations

In the post-war period, there was a notable accentuation in the degree of state intervention in employment relations, something that posed a considerable challenge to the established voluntaristic system. For one thing, both Labour and Conservative governments supported full employment as the principal goal of economic policy. As part of the socialdemocratic post-war 'consensus', active government intervention to achieve this goal was deemed desirable. However, full employment caused upward pressure on wages, generated inflationary pressures in the economy, and consequently damaged economic competitiveness.

By the time of the 1964–70 Labour governments, these voluntary 'incomes policies' had developed from relatively short-term and *ad hoc* interventions designed to overcome short-term economic difficulties, becoming a characteristic feature of attempts to manage the economy. Given that they posed a major challenge to the principle of 'free collective bargaining', the development of incomes policies, which for a period of time during the late 1960s even had statutory force, helped to erode the hitherto dominant voluntarist system. Nevertheless, prompted by growing membership discontent, during the late 1960s the unions became more hostile to incomes policies, particularly statutory ones, something that impeded the ability of governments to incorporate and integrate the unions in processes of state economic management.

Alongside the development of incomes policies, during the 1960s and 1970s the development and evolution of tripartite arrangements for economic and industrial policy formulation was further evidence not only of greater state involvement in economic planning and management, but also of government efforts to incorporate, with business representatives, union leaderships and the TUC into state policy-making processes. Thus 'tripartism' refers to the participation of unions, employers, and government representatives in operating state institutions. While it is important not to overstate the level of union influence during this period, the trade union movement came to be characterised as a 'governing institution', or as an 'estate of the realm'.

Voluntarism was further eroded during the 1960s and 1970s by the growing statutory regulation of the employment relationship in areas such as redundancy payments, the dismissal of employees, equal pay, and sex and race discrimination. For a number of reasons, including economic efficiency, social change, and pressure from workers for improved rights, this period saw a substantial growth, which continues in the present period, in the 'juridification', that is the regulation of social and economic activity by statute, of the employment relationship.

The involvement of union leaderships and the TUC in the formulation of state policy marked a clear attempt to control the behaviour of the trade unions by involving and incorporating them into the machinery of the state. At a time of considerable economic instability, the capacity of workers 'to disrupt government economic policy inspired a strategy of enmeshing unions in its formulation and administration'. The success of such a strategy depended, however, upon the willingness of workers to accept it, something that could not be assumed.

In the area of employment relations policy, the 1974–79 Labour government was dominated by the experience of the so-called 'social contract'. In exchange for legislation designed to promote genuine social reforms, the TUC accepted the need for voluntary wage restraint as a means of reducing inflation and securing improvements in economic competitiveness. To what extent did the social contract resemble the corporatist arrangements characteristic of other European countries? By corporatism, or neo-corporatism as it is referred to in some accounts, we are referring to the way in which government intervention to manage the economy is achieved by integrating, or incorporating, employers' associations and trade unions into state policy-making processes.

To a crucial extent, though, the British experience fell well short of genuine corporatism, although it is fair to suggest that corporatist 'tendencies' or 'pressures' were present during this period. The ethos of voluntarism proved to be rather too resilient to enable corporatism to prosper in Britain, not least because of the reluctance of the TUC and employers' groups to commit themselves to change, as well as their inability to control their affiliates and members. The extent of corporatism in Britain, then, was largely restricted to the institution of *ad hoc*, short-term efforts designed to relieve immediate economic crises, or as a means of conflict avoidance, for which the term 'bargained corporatism' has been deemed appropriate.

Despite its ambitious intentions, in practice the social contract ended up as little more than a conventional incomes policy since, after 1976, the government came under increasing pressure, not least from the International Monetary Fund, which made it a loan condition, to scale back its social policies in order to pursue austerity measures. Union support for wage restraint fell away, largely because of the discontent voiced by workers, particularly in the public sector, who were unhappy at the relative decline in their standard of living.

The development of corporatist 'tendencies' in the 1970s was part of an attempt by the state to accommodate trade union power, to shape and control it, in order to sustain economic growth and the long-term viability of the capitalist market economy. But it is important to acknowledge the repressive basis of this attempt to incorporate the union interest. Importantly, though, union leaders were also influenced by pressure from their members, which inevitably limited the extent to which a whole-hearted strategy of incorporation could ever be realised.

COLLECTIVE BARGAINING

Collective bargaining is an important means of regulating the employment relationship. But what is collective bargaining? It can be considered in both narrow and broad terms. In its narrow sense, collective bargaining is simply a means of determining pay and conditions of employment. Beatrice and Sidney Webb, its first serious students, suggested that it is largely an economic process, the collective equivalent of individual bargaining.

Collective bargaining, however, is more than just a means of determining employment terms. It also fulfils a broader, political function. Flanders stressed that collective bargaining is a rule-making process. Not only does it set the terms and conditions on which labour is hired, but it also gives workers, through their unions, rights to challenge and influence managerial decisions over such things as the organisation of work. The American writers Chamberlain and Kuhn identified two strands of this political aspect of collective bargaining. It is a rule-making process, allowing workers collectively to influence the terms of their employment, and also a system of industrial governance, in that it establishes a procedure that enables managements to reach decisions jointly with trade unions. It is inappropriate, therefore, to view collective bargaining simply as a device for determining pay and conditions. Rather, it 'is generally more useful to use the term to cover a broader set of joint regulatory behaviour, embracing all activity whereby employers deliberately permit representatives of employee collectivities to be involved in the management of the employment relationship'.

For pluralist writers, collective bargaining is the most effective means of regulating the employment relationship. For one thing, it enables workers to exercise influence over decisions that affect them at work. This was a particularly strong theme of the 1960s Donovan Royal Commission which, heavily imbued by the dominant pluralist thinking of the time, stated that where it was properly undertaken 'collective bargaining is the most effective means of giving workers the right to representation in decisions affecting their working lives, a right which is or should be the prerogative of every worker in a democratic society'.

For the pluralists, though, collective bargaining not only gives workers a voice over matters that affect them at work, but is also an important means by which the inherent conflict in the employment relationship can be accommodated or, as it is often put, institutionalised.

The principal radical critique of collective bargaining is that it contains workers' militancy within boundaries that are acceptable to employers. By institutionalising conflict, it runs counter to the real interests of workers. It is suggested, moreover, that by becoming enmeshed in the process of bargaining with management, unions come to adopt a fundamentally conservative ethos, concerned with the procedural details of negotiations and agreements, rather than with advancing the substantive interests of their members.

In practice, however, one cannot readily distinguish between union leaders' concern with stable and secure bargaining relationships and the desire of their members for improved pay and conditions. Workers have a concern with the security and survival of their union because, without it, they have no means of winning better employment terms.

Collective bargaining in Britain emerged during the nineteenth century as craft societies, the forerunners of the trade unions, in industries such as printing and engineering for example, eschewed their traditional reliance on trying to regulate employment conditions unilaterally in favour of joint regulation with employers. Initially, bargaining took place at a local or district level but, by 1910, following the path-setting 1898 national agreement in engineering, unions in the shipbuilding, printing, building, and footwear industries, among others, secured national recognition agreements, frequently as a result of industrial action.In general, collective bargaining found favour among employers, as well as among cautious union leaders, in that it enabled industrial conflict to become 'institutionalised', accommodated and contained within the bargaining relationship. The alternative was continuing instability and disorder as unions struggled to secure a presence. Thus the decision to recognise and bargain with unions reflected an acceptance on the part of employers that a union presence was inevitable: the 'lesser of two evils'.

The implications of the 1914–18 war, in particular the growth of union bargaining power, compelled the British government to intervene in employment relations.Its remit, part of broader governmental concern with the conditions for post-war reconstruction, was to examine ways in which relationships between managers and workers could be improved. The most well-known recommendation was that collective bargaining arrangements, in the form of Joint Industry Councils (JICs), should be established at a national level across all industries, supplemented by joint committees at lower levels.

Even though many of the new JICs soon became moribund, government intervention had nonetheless accentuated the trend towards industry-wide bargaining. During the inter-war years, economic depression meant that the development of collective bargaining was gradual, but the 1939–45 war provided a further stimulus.

Collective Bargaining in the Public Sector

The development of national-level, multi-employer collective bargaining was a particularly noteworthy feature of employment relations in the public sector. For example, in 1919 the Burnham committee was established. Based on Whitley principles, it provided a forum within which schoolteachers' pay could be negotiated between representatives of the local authority employers and the teaching unions, and conflicts between them resolved, without the need for disruptive strikes and industrial action.

There are three further things to bear in mind about the implementation of Whitleyism in the public sector. First, its spread was somewhat piecemeal and haphazard. Although in some occupations, such as schoolteaching, Whitley-style arrangements were implemented at a fairly early stage, elsewhere their diffusion was gradual. Whitley arrangements were extended to the health sector following the establishment of the National Health Service (NHS) in 1948, and Whitleyism only really became 'entrenched' in the public sector during the 1950s. Second, national collective bargaining machinery, since it set standardised rates of pay and was thus seen to be fair, can be presented as a central feature of the 'model employer' tradition in public sector employment. However, this concealed significant problems of low pay in some parts of the public sector, particularly among women.

Third, it would be a mistake to see harmonious employment relations as the outcome of the development of Whitleyism in the public sector.In practice, managers were reluctant to accept the legitimacy of trade unions and collective bargaining.

Rise of Workplace Bargaining

By the 1950s, multi-employer, industry-wide bargaining arrangements dominated the formal system of employment relations in Britain. Of the estimated 80 per cent of employees whose pay was set by collective bargaining, three-quarters were covered by multi-employer agreements either at national or sometimes regional level. It was always improbable that employers could effectively exclude union influence from the workplace, not least because of the inadequacies of industry agreements.

During the 1950s and 1960s, in a climate of full employment, shop stewards in the engineering industry were able to negotiate with local managers over bonuses, overtime arrangements and incentive payments, and reach settlements that were outside, and in addition to, the industry agreements. Thus 'many managements tended increasingly to settle matters in their own workplace by negotiating through shop stewards rather than through multi-employer bargaining involving their employers' organisation'.

The influence of multi-employer bargaining was inevitably eroded, and there were concerns about the consequences. The increasing gap between the rates agreed by means of industry-level bargaining and the actual earnings of workers, augmented by locally negotiated supplements, or 'wage drift' as it became known, was perceived to have inflationary consequences. Added to this, informal workplace bargaining tended to 'sap management control over work', and generated a multitude of small-scale, often short industrial disputes which, taken together, were deemed by policy-makers to be detrimental to British economic performance.

Although dominated by the experience of the engineering sector, the Donovan Royal Commission found, as we have already observed, that much of the blame for the problems outlined above could be laid at the door of management who, it was asserted, should take a greater degree of responsibiiity for shaping their own employment relations arrangements.

A study of manufacturing industry undertaken in the late 1970s revealed that while multi-employer agreements continued to be commonplace, in textile production for example, their effectiveness was much diminished. While singleemployer bargaining had grown rapidly in significance, it had come about not as a result of the 'deliberate rejection of established multi-employer arrangements' but as a 'largely unplanned consequence of piecemeal reform'.

By the early 1980s, collective bargaining remained the predominant method of pay determination in Britain, with over 70 per cent of employees covered by collective agreements. Although single-employer bargaining had become more common, particularly in manufacturing industry, in large parts of the economy, including the food retail and banking sectors, multi-employer arrangements prevailed. Though some criticism of these latter arrangements had been expressed, no fundamental reforms were advocated, and generally single-employer bargaining was restricted to a small number of local authorities. Nevertheless, since the 1980s the coverage of collective bargaining has declined markedly, and, outside the public sector, multi-employer bargaining is virtually extinct.

WORKPLACE PARTICIPATION

In so far as it allows workers to influence decisions that affect their employment conditions and working environment, collective bargaining may be viewed as a form of participation and involvement. Generally, though, we use terms such as employee involvement and worker participation to refer to other arrangements that enable workers to exercise influence over organisational or workplace decisions, or that allow managers to communicate with their staff. A major problem, however, concerns the diversity of practices that can be accommodated under these labels. Thus, 'participation and involvement are somewhat elastic terms and are amenable to a range of definitions'.

There are five areas where the potential for differing interpretations and conceptual misunderstandings exist. First, what is the purpose of participation? Is it driven largely by managers, with the aim of eliciting improved worker commitment and thus more output? Or is participation driven from the bottom up, through the collective organisation and mobilisation of workers, and designed to restrict the exercise of managerial prerogative? Thus it is important to recognise that terms like 'participation' and 'involvement' are often used in an imprecise way that invites confusion over their real meaning.

Nevertheless, some scope for clarity does exist. The term 'participation', for example, may be used to refer to arrangements that give workers some degree of influence over organisational and workplace decisions. The term 'employee involvement' (EI) is more usefully applied to managerial initiatives that are designed to further the flow of communication at work as a means of enhancing the organisational commitment of employees. Second, it is important to recognise differences over the subject matter, or scope, covered by participation.

Third, following on from this, it is evident that the level at which participation takes place may vary. It can occur at the level of the organisation, the workplace or, particularly in respect of teamworking initiatives, the work group. Fourth, participation may be undertaken directly between management and the workforce, or indirectly, by means of workers' representatives, who may, or may not, be trade unionists. Fifth, perhaps the greatest potential for ambiguity concerns the depth, or degree, of participation and involvement. There is a distinction to be drawn between those arrangements that enable workers, or their representatives, to exercise influence over organisational or workplace decisions, and those that simply allow managers to communicate information with their staff.

The most pronounced form of participation, and by far the rarest, is control over the business by workers themselves. Demands for workers' control and industrial democracy were a prominent feature of employment relations in the late nineteenth and early twentieth centuries. During the 1960s and 1970s, though, there was a revival of interest in such matters. Workers and shop stewards occupied the yard for a period of time in order to prevent its closure.

There was also much interest evinced in how workers' interests could be represented on company boards of directors. A government committee of inquiry recommended that union representatives should have equal parity with shareholders on the boards of large companies, with an 'intermediary' group of ostensibly independent directors appointed by mutual consent maintaining a balance between the two sides. Employer opposition and the hostility of influential union leaders, who were concerned about the threat to the primacy of collective bargaining, ensured that the proposals came to nothing. Nevertheless, in 1978–79 union representation was established on the board of the Post Office. Not only did the so-called 'independent' directors tend to side with management, but also the union representatives themselves were weakened by internal differences and by their acceptance of the expertise and authority demonstrated by managers.

Development of Joint Consultation

Having outlined the meanings of, and conceptual difficulties associated with, participation and involvement at work, we now focus on one important aspect, the development of joint consultation arrangements in Britain. Joint consultation has long been a feature, albeit not always a prominent one, of Britain's employment relations landscape. It is a form of participation that is particularly amenable to managers since it renders their prerogatives relatively untouched in as much as they can secure employees' views without being bound by them. Workers 'influence but in no way determine managerial policy and practice'. In theory, joint consultation committees (JCCs) are seen to be appropriate forums for matters where there is a supposed greater propensity for cooperation and a commonality of interests between management and workers, such as health, safety, and welfare issues, as opposed to the more explicitly conflate collective bargaining relationship. Moreover, as we will consider shortly, the practice of joint consultation varies considerably, something that renders a simple association between JCCs and the regulation of employment conditions where there is a commonality of interest problematic.

Although instances of consultation arrangements can be traced as far back as the nineteenth century, the area 'first became a problem of general importance during the 1914–18 war', given the priority accorded to maintaining wartime production in a context of growing industrial unrest and union militancy. Hence, the Whitley Committee and its reports were concerned to establish formal means by which this conflict could be accommodated and contained. By 1921, some seventy-three Joint Industry Councils, and over 1,000 local committees had become established with the purpose of promoting greater industrial cooperation without ceding too much control to the workers and their unions.

During the 1920s and 1930s, though, with the exception of a few major companies, such as ICI for example, the Whitley-based arrangements for joint consultation fell into disuse, not least because, given the less amenable climate for trade unionism, employers were less interested in securing cooperation. Once again, however, wartime circumstances, in this case the Second World War, and official backing from the government, stimulated greater efforts to build cooperative relations between managers and workers in the shape of formal workplace consultation arrangements that came to be known as joint production committees (JPCs). By the mid-1940s, some 4,000 JPCs existed in the engineering industry alone: 'their agendas covered items relating to production, efficiency, productivity and the like, but excluded anything to do with negotiable issues such as pay'.

Although the industries that were taken into state ownership following the war were obliged to establish joint consultation machinery, the incidence of consultation arrangements appears to have declined fairly substantially during the late 1940s and the 1950s. According to one influential interpretation, this was an inevitable function of the development of workplace bargaining. Although some writers argue that the incidence of joint consultation remained relatively stable between the 1950s and 1980s, a significant revival in joint consultation activity appears to have occurred during the 1970s. It is important, therefore, to emphasize the diversity of joint consultation arrangements;

Marchington identifies four ideal types. First, they can be operated as an alternative to collective bargaining machinery, particularly in firms where there is no recognised trade union. Second, joint consultation can operate in such a way that it is marginal to the process of collective bargaining, covering relatively trivial welfare issues such as the state of the car parking and canteen facilities.

Third, it can be used as a way of competing with, or undermining, the collective bargaining process. In these cases managers will seek to consult, rather than bargain, with a union over as many issues as they can given that, with consultation, as opposed to bargaining, they reserve the right to make the final decisions. Fourth, joint consultation can be operated in conjunction with, or as an adjunct to, the collective bargaining process, encompassing matters on which common interests appear to be more readily apparent.

What, though, explains the waxing and waning of employer interest in participation initiatives such as joint consultation? Ramsay proposes the existence of cycles of participation. At particular times, such as 1918–21, and in the 1960s and 1970s, employers foster participation as a means of containing and moderating worker militancy. Participation is embraced as a means of defusing industrial conflict and accommodating workers' demands as part of a more cooperative ethos to managing the employment relationship. The main problem with this approach, however, is that it assumes that the incidence of worker participation has a single causal factor when, in practice, participation initiatives are more likely the outcome of a number of considerations, of which accommodating worker militancy is just one.

Thus the concept of 'waves of interest' in participation has been developed in order to provide a more influenced explanation of trends in employee involvement and worker participation. According to this approach, participation may take different forms and be driven by a variety of motives. Thus 'rather than viewing EI or participation as either absent or present, as some absolute or unidimensional concept, we can analyse a number of different forms or aspects of participation'.

A further advantage of the 'waves of interest' approach is that it does not assume that historical patterns of participation repeat themselves in an overly mechanical way. Rather, 'waves come in different shapes and sizes, and last for different lengths of time in different organisations'.

REFERENCES

Adams, R.J. 1991. 'An International Survey of Courses in Comparative Industrial Relations', in M. Bray (ed.), *Teaching Comparative Industrial Relations,* ACIRRT Monograph No 2 University of Sydney, Sydney.

Boxall, P. & Deeks J. 1992. 'New Zealand' in M. Rothman, D. Briscoe & R. Nacamulli (eds.), *Industrial Relations Around the World: Labour Relations for Multinational Companies,* De Gruyter & Co., Berlin.

McNally, B. 1999. *Global Managers? An investigation into transnational competencies in the New Zealand Finance Sector',* unpublished dissertation completed in partial fulfilment of the requirements for an MBA Henley Management College.

Shenkar, O. 1995. *Global Perspectives of Human Resource Management,* Prentice Hall, New Jersey.

2

Globalisation and Employment Relations

The diversity presented by globalisation converts it into a complex, multi-faceted and dynamic event; yet, beyond its varied aspects and expressions, it may be reduced, in its innermost basic nature, to the expansion and deepening of capitalist economy and its theoretical postulates, such as free competition, market, free trade, export growth, etc. The expiration of the bipolar world, which had distinguished the largest part of the XX century, accelerated and intensified such expansion.

This globalising process implies at least three dramas for workers and for all those concerned with social problems: a) a relative lack of interest in the domestic market; b) the limitations of state power to govern economic variables; and c) the dominance of ideologies that do not favour labour as a factor of production. Let us analyse briefly these "three dramas".

During the prevailing economic system previous to globalisation—the "import substitution" scheme—beyond the sincere and altruistic social concerns of governments and employers with respect to the living and working conditions of the population in general, and of workers in particular, both held a selfish interest to retain some of the population's purchasing power. Production was focused on those consumers; workers and the domestic population were the national industry's "market" which intended— with the aid of the government—to replace imports. Trade union power and the dominant ideological and political conceptions reinforced this implicit pact, this incidental, relative and critical alliance between domestic capital. Each day its population is less important as its own market, which is increasingly replaced by markets outside its borders.

Concurrently, the globalisation of the economy gradually withdraws the innermost means of power from the national government and from any other structure limited by national boundaries. In a globalised world, to be local is a handiçap. The mobility of capital and communications have brought about such a degree of time-space compression, that it might be referred to as the end of geography, with quite more appropriateness and less frivolity than the presumed end of history.

Nowadays, in the globalised world, either élites are movable and have instant communications or they are not élites. All this has given a huge advantage to capital over State and labour, since the almost instant mobility enjoyed today by capital is in contrast with the necessary localisation of the national State and the cultural localisation of labour as a factor of production. Thus, globalisation contributes to the fact that each day political power becomes less autonomous and that, on the whole, national counterbalances lose part of their efficiency; among them, labour Law and trade union action.

Indeed, this process is accompanied by a legitimating ideology aimed to favour capital over labour. The enterprise's competitiveness within the global market becomes the supreme goodness to which all others are subordinated. Individual interests are more valued than previously, while collective interests are likely to lose prestige. Solidarity is no longer in fashion, and selfishness tends to be regarded as an engine for progress.

Business efficiency justifies the means. The welfare State, which had played the role of restraining communism and of promoting national consumption, is no longer considered necessary. Labour Law and trade union action may now be regarded as barriers to free enterprise development. At any rate, it is surprising that the entrepreneur is exalted, precisely at a moment when he fails to accomplish his social function: employment creation. It should be recalled that the term employer, which identifies the entrepreneurial party in working relations, means somebody who provides employment, who employs another individual, that is, a provider of employment.

Traditional Labour Relations System

Within the framework just outlined, the traditional labour relations system is experimenting diverse questionings and changes. It is not easy to distinguish those stemming directly from globalisation, and those due to other more or less autonomous but coinciding causes.

The axis of that traditional system was the working relation connecting the worker with the same employer for an indefinite period of time. In effect, the entrance to the classic working relation has a vocation for continuity. Likewise, such entrance was aimed to perform a given task, clearly defined and in exchange of a predominantly fixed remuneration. This relation is regulated by the State and the trade union, with the purpose to protect the weaker party: the worker.

It should be added that this traditional labour relations system occurs in a society where work takes up a central place. Actually work is, in part and in the first instance, the livelihood of the worker and of his family; thus, the importance of salary, its stability and its suitability. But besides, in that society, work is the chief means of the individual's social identification and inclusion. This is so true that one of the first questions made regarding an unknown person, in addition to his name and eventually his approximate age, are "and what does he do?", "what's his activity? ", or "what's his job?". Certainly, social identification. But it also means inclusion, since from salary and work depend all the social protection network, which converts the worker into a citizen in the political and social meaning of the term: a member of society and of the nation. Likewise, some enterprises and trade unions provide social services to their workers and affiliates.

Globalisation ranks at the front place the concern for the enterprise's international competitiveness, and the enterprise challenges the cost of the traditional system. For that purpose, neo-liberal postulates on labour affairs are just the thing needed to serve the enterprise's interests.

1) non-intervention of the State in individual relations, so that each worker may negotiate his work's rate at freedom with the employer, without being subject to minimum limits; and
2) State intervention in collective relations in order to limit, restrain and, if politically possible, eliminate trade union action, collective bargaining and strike;

This program of methodic destruction of the collective sphere focuses on the objective to bring about the complete individualisation of labour relations. In its maximum expression, the neo-liberal project would establish, between worker and employer, an individual and deregulated relation, without trade unions, without collective bargaining, without the right to strike, without special legislation, without Labour Inspection and without a specialised system of Justice.

Why? What for? Theoretically, to lower the cost of labour and thus contribute to raise the company's competitiveness and increase entrepreneurial profits. This would bring about investments, which would in turn generate new jobs and, therefore, by "spurting" or "dripping", the concentration of income would finally benefit everybody.

It is evident that should this program be fully implemented—which never happened, as it is usual with any theoretical project—it would not only affect labour relations, but also it would make them disappear. Labour Law would be replaced by civil or business Law ; ikewise, instead of labour relations, there would be civil or business relations.

And though this project has not been completely implemented, as just remarked, it has subsisted along with other trends which reinforce its weakening effects upon the traditional labour relations system: in particular, technological innovation, replacing manpower and generating flexibility in work organisation, all of which has set up an economic system that destroys employment and fragments existing employment.

Paradigm of Post-modern Labour Relations

Along these lines, the neo-liberal model, spurred by globalisation and combined with the effects of technological change, is outlining a kind of paradigm for postmodern labour relations.

As already stated, the pure theoretical model would be the dissolution of labour relations in individual, civil or business relationships. Since this has not taken place in practice—in fact, there still exist trade unions, collective negotiations and strikes, labour Codes, public labour Administration and a labour system of Justice—for the time being, the resulting pattern remains "halfway".

Some of the features of these post-modern labour relations would be as follows. In the first instance, the "off-centering" of labour. Due to the priority consideration of capital over labour and the growing replacement of manpower by technology, it is ever possible to produce more and better with fewer workers. The obvious and natural consequences are the increase of unemployment and social exclusion. Since current economy destroys jobs, but society keeps considering work as the foundation for social citizenship and inclusion.

In the second place, the segmentation of the workforce. Productive flexibility encourages decentralisation of work organisation, which is facilitated by the deregulation or flexibilisation of labour Law. There is an increase in informality and outsourcing, and enterprises tend to organise themselves on the basis of two clearly separate groups of workers: a) a focal group of stable, protected workers, with good remuneration and qualifications, and b) an unstable, precarious, rotating, outsourcing or informal "periphery".

Thirdly, employment instability, not only in that precarious and rotating periphery, but also in the overall system, taking into account the flexibilisation or deregulation of labour recruitment and dismissal, as well as a higher sensitivity of the enterprise to the shifts of international competition and external variables, such as 'hot' capital flows.

In the fourth place, the individualisation of labour relations, in varied dimensions. On one hand, a greater individualisation emerges as a result of labour Law's deregulation or flexibilisation, which expands the scope of the employer's will for autonomy and even gets to tolerate the retreat, from labour legislation to private Law, of relations that formerly were regulated without discussion by the latter. In short, decentralisation of collective bargaining becomes part of a continuum that is aimed at the individualisation of working relations. This does not imply disregarding the principle that it should be possible to negotiate collectively at all levels; nor to deny that decentralised collective bargaining may have advantages in dealing with specific given issues in each enterprise, which are not common to a given sector of activities.

In the fifth place, and as a result of all the above, labour cost cutting. If there is less employment and more unemployed people, if employment tends to become precarious except for a relatively reduced group, if protective legislation is abated and those measures are not offset by the action of a weakened trade union, the consequence is a decrease in real salary, wealth concentration and a decline of salaries' share in national income. This salary reduction is strengthened by the introduction of salary modalities more linked to performance, by the flexibilisation of working hours depending on productive needs, and by the promotion of functional mobility. No doubt, they are helpful in certain circumstances; yet their depreciating effect on employment may also be suspected, since they tend to be used by the employer to optimise labour.

This is approximately the labour relations model being designed. However, many doubts still remain. One of them is whether we are before a model of relative historical stability or just before a transition stage toward the dissolution of labour relations, a topic related, in addition, to the issue concerning "the end of labour".

Alternative Labour Relations Model

The present objective is not to predict the future. The speculation on an eventual alternative model of labour relations is justified in the light of what seems to be an insurmountable malfunction of the post-modern paradigm. Actually, the future projection of that model makes us doubt about its feasibility.

The first unanswered question is: which is the exclusion threshold admitted by society, without bringing about the outburst of a new social issue and the breach of the democratic system? Which is the short- and long-term stability of a model that excludes a higher number of people than those that it includes?

The second issue consists that labour deregulation has not proved to be efficient to create employment nor to stop growing unemployment but, in return, it did produce a rise in the precariousness of existing employment. Additional employment is not created—because the origin of unemployment does not lie on labour standards—and the quality of the remaining employment is downgraded.

Neither it is evident that the abatement of labour costs ascertains, by itself, a greater competitiveness for the enterprise. Among other reasons, because the enterprise's competitiveness not only depends upon the competitiveness of labour, principally when labour costs usually account—specially in Latin America—for a much lower share than total production costs and the sale price of products or services. In addition, the precariousness and rotation of the workforce would be openly in contradiction with two axioms of modern personnel management. And it is not reasonable to pretend that an employer would invest in training a worker that he knows soon will be out of the enterprise, nor it is reasonable to pretend that the worker may feel involved with the objectives of a company, knowing that it will oust him shortly.

Thus, it seems it is the moment to start thinking that a feasible labour relations model should be based on the promotion of continuity and not on the rotation and precariousness of the payroll.

Continuity or stability would allow—and should be necessarily accompanied by— initial and ongoing vocational training. Ongoing training, based on initial training, can adapt and develop permanently the worker's competencies and translate them to his own benefit, allowing him to maintain his job even if its contents may change.

The worker's permanence and qualification will indeed allow his involvement with the objectives of the enterprise and, furthermore, will permit and favour his multifunctionality.

At the same time, this will allow the permanence and non-replacement of the worker vis-à-vis technological or organisational changes. This also implies admitting a given degree of internal flexibility—the counterpart of stability, permanence or continuity—which may permit the employer to benefit from the worker's multi-functionality and keep him on the payroll. This internal flexibility could include too the flexibility of the working day, which may allow the employer to adapt the work's pace to production needs, but also as a counterpart of the inexorable reduction of working time, in view of the necessity to move on to a certain measure of distribution of the work available. In that aspect, it becomes a measure of social inclusion or, at least, of curbing or alleviating exclusion.

A model with such purpose might not operate without trade unions and collective bargaining. In the first place—and this would be sufficient—because they are core human rights. But, in addition, because they are important instruments to help adapt labour rights and relations to the needs of the enterprise and the worker. The neo-liberal and post-modern model overlooked the role that trade unions and collective bargaining play in governing the labour relations system.

Yet up to this stage, this scheme has operated within the national framework: and even if globalisation is not the only root of the present state of affairs in the working world, it is actually one of the main concurring elements. The internationalisation of the economy, the extra-nationalisation of the main sources of power, the globalisation or regionalisation of production are generating two processes which should be highlighted: a) the emergence of an international labour relations system; and b) the call for "international re-regulation".

INTERNATIONAL LABOUR RELATIONS

It has already been asserted that the globalisation of production, trade and finances tends to locate the focal points of the decision-making processes beyond the territorial scope of the nation-State and that it is accompanied by space-time compression, to such a degree that those who make decisions and exert influence should have mobility and the possibility of instant communications. At the same time, one of the answers to the globalising process has been, in certain places, economic regionalisation, that is, setting up regional economic integration blocs aimed to expand the internal market and to build a larger unit, enabling members to compete better in international trading with the rest of the world. Both processes—globalisation and regional integration—are conducive to require the re-scaling of the labour relations system. In effect, the national labour relations system—like the national State—seems increasingly powerless to have a bearing on a domain that is beyond its physical boundaries.

Globalisation and regionalisation imply the internationalisation of the labour relations context. And the internationalisation of its context requires the internationalisation of stakeholders and of their relationships.

In other words: globalisation and regional integration set up a new scene, which is no longer national; this scene is now overlapped by another multinational setting. And in this new larger and different scene, old national partners, designed for the previous model, can no longer perform. It is necessary to restructure those partners or to create new partners suited for the dimension of the new setting and relationships—no longer exclusively national—which will inevitably emerge in the new context.

The internationalisation of the partners' structures did not take place distinctly within the frame of globalisation, though international structures exist from the past, both representing labour and employers (OIE). But it has occurred more conspicuously in two regional economic integration blocs: the European Union and Mercosur. In the European Union, since long ago the ETUC and its employers' counterpart, UNICE are in operation.

Within Mercosur, workers were the first who perceived the need to create a regional structure. Simultaneously, with the negotiation and adoption of the Asuncion Treaty, trade unions from Argentina, Brazil, Paraguay and Uruguay seized a preexisting institution: the Trade Union Federations Coordinator of the Southern Cone, which had been established in 1986 to support the Latin American democratisation process, still pending, at that time, in Bolivia and Chile.

At the beginning of the 1990s, this Southern Cone's Trade Union Federations Coordinator had accomplished its duty and it was then revitalised so as to operate as the labour structure of and within Mercosur. To this end, Mercosur's Trade Union Commission was created within its framework and from 1991 to date it has displayed a permanent, intense and relatively successful participation in all matters relative to building Mercosur's social space. It is likely that the Southern Cone's Trade Union Federations Coordinator—acting through Mercosur's Trade Union Commission—might have been the chief engine for the recognition of the existence of a social dimension in Mercosur, at first, and for the gradual setting up of Mercosur's social space, later. In this sense, Mercosur's employers reacted more belatedly.In general, the presence and action of these institutions, as such, have been much lower than that of the unions Coordinator; employers' participation has been permanent, but the above mentioned regional structures did not have institutional intervention.

International social dialogue, including multinational collective bargaining, have also had a certain degree of recognition and practical commitment in these two regional integration blocs, despite their scarce or non-existent implementation at an actually universal level.

In the European Union, ETUC and UNICE have undertaken an important process of European international social dialogue, despite comings and goings and different appraisals on the part of various observers. At any rate, it has produced, on one hand, the establishment of regional social dialogue, and on the other, a number of agreements, joint standpoints or common judgments on a wide range of labour issues. In a parallel fashion, several cases of collective agreements of European multinational enterprises cover the different sites that these companies control in the region. Meanwhile, in Mercosur, the recent Socio-Labour Declaration recognises, among collective rights, the right of "national and regional" social dialogue, which Party States agree to promote. Likewise, even more recently, the first regional or multinational collective agreement ever known in Latin America was formalised.

Conceived as a collective agreement "within Mercosur", this agreement is expressly based, as set forth en one of its "preambular paragraphs", on "the need to extend agreements concerning relations between capital and labour to the scope of Mercosur". In that framework, it provides for information exchange; holding a joint annual meeting between enterprises, trade unions and plants' internal commissions; the commitment to avoid conflicts by means of permanent dialogue and the settlement of differences through negotiation, as far as possible.

Finally, this agreement contains provisions of interest regarding vocational training. It provides for the "standardisation" of training programs, the cooperation of trade unions and internal commissions in the elaboration of programs, and the automatic recognition of courses held at any of the company's sites within Mercosur. Workers' participation in the enterprise spread importantly in Europe, in contrast with its non-existent development in Mercosur, with the exception of the pioneer provisions contained in Volkswagen's collective contract just mentioned.

The practice undertaken in Europe to set up multinational mechanisms for information and consultation had its formal embodiment, and hopefully a new boost, through the adoption of Directive 94/45/CE by the European Council, on 22 September 1994. It establishes an information and consultation procedure with workers in community-wide enterprises or groups of enterprises.

International conflict arose in various circumstances, both in Europe and in North America, in the latter case, involving workers and enterprises from Canada and the USA. In Mercosur, only some regional drives took place which, for the time being, could be labelled as experimental.

Finally, with respect to institutional participation in globalisation and regionalisation processes, it should be underlined that, at world level, the International Labour Organisation has provided, throughout this century, the best and largest experience from its own tripartite structure. It even represents the only example of global, universal or worldwide participation.

At regional level, the Economic and Social Committee of the European Union and the Committee of the Regions are the bodies designed to make possible such participation. In Mercosur, the Economic and Social Consulting Forum is the only permanent body, envisaged in the founding treaties, designed to facilitate the organised representation and participation of stakeholders. However, Working Subgroup No. 10, a three-party operating commission competent on labour affairs, has been of great importance too. Significant initiatives have arisen within its framework, such as the proposal calling on the four Mercosur member countries to ratify a common set of international labour conventions. It should be recorded that, as far as institutional participation is concerned, the Andean Pact has also given rise to different bodies and resorts: the Economic and Social Advisory Council, the entrepreneurial Consulting Council and the labour Consulting Council.

International Re-regulation

If globalisation is generating a certain emptiness in national labour relations systems and, in particular, of its regulatory network; if national legislations are becoming less efficient to regulate events which take place or originate at another level; if these events — together with other coincident factors—tend to breed undesirable or malfunctioning situations of exclusion and precariousness; and if, in addition, there is a trend toward the emergence or development of supranational labour relations, the proposal made by some authors to advance toward an "international re-regulation" of labour relations seems evidently valid.

International labour conventions, the main Pacts and Declarations on human rights, social Charters, social clauses and some unilateral substitute instruments of the latter are some of the forms adopted, available or proposed, at the moment, for such "international re-regulation", designed to place the standards network at the same level of development of those events that it should rule.

The international labour conventions issued by the ILO are the first and most developed efforts to generate a universal regulatory network. Furthermore, so far, they are the only instruments that have reached global or worldwide proportions. They aim to establish minimum standards for working conditions and labour relations, on the basis of four foundations: social justice, the proof that peace is impossible without equity, the principle that labour cannot be treated as a commodity, and concern for "social dumping".

When much later, already in the 1990s, globalisation poses again the problem of linking international trade expansion and the observance of certain minimum labour standards, the ILO launches a campaign for the universal ratification of a limited number of conventions considered "fundamental", relative to trade union freedom and collective bargaining non discrimination forced labour, and child labour.

Simultaneously, in 1998, the International Labour Conference adopted the Declaration on Fundamental Principles and Rights at work. According to it, any country, by the sole fact of being an ILO member, commits itself to comply with the principles contained in those conventions, even though it may not have ratified them.

As observed, from a certain viewpoint, the aim is a qualitative jump, striving to universalise or "globalise" the principles contained in a given number of conventions, setting their effectiveness free from the national ratification procedure. From another perspective, rather pessimist, it has been affirmed that the ILO has adopted a minimalist option, responding to the demands of deregulation and flexibilisation, and limiting its efforts to the compliance of a reduced set of conventions, which would tacitly imply unconcern for the rest of them.

The main Human Rights Pacts and Declarations, in particular those issued by the UN, also have a universal vocation. This is the case of the Universal Declaration of Human Rights of 1948, the International Pact of Civil and Political Rights of 1966, and the International Pact of Economic, Social and Cultural Rights of the same year. With respect to those pacts subject to State ratification, its actual juridical effectiveness at national level depends, for some people, from the standpoint that may be sustained regarding the existence of unity or duality between international juridical order and domestic juridical orders, as well as from the hierarchical position that international order may have on each of the latter. It can also be asserted, however, and it seems this is a growing trend that, as part of "jus cogens", human rights recognised as such by the international community in those ample Declarations and Pacts integrate the international public order and, therefore, benefit from imperium beyond any national act of ratification, validation or reception. The same applies to American Declarations and Charters, though limited to the hemispheric scope.

Supranational labour standards are in force in the European Union. This is the only truly supranational entity to which member States have transferred their sovereignty, including the labour sphere. This is specially so since the Justice Tribunal decided the direct application of Directives whenever their provisions are clear, precise and self-executable, and ever since the Amsterdam Treaty incorporated the Charters to the founding Treaties.

Social Charters, despite the variety they usually display, may be defined tentatively and generically as solemn declarations in which States proclaim certain rights and/or recognise particular labour or social common goals or objectives. They aim to build up a social space in a group of countries, on the basis of a minimum common stand of social rights, in general within a set of nations which consider to have a common profile and specially in those which make up a regional economic integration bloc.

Their main objective is social: to guarantee the recognition of particular principles and rights considered important in the signatory countries. This objective may be limited to member countries or extend to their relationship with third countries. Thus: 1) inside the bloc, the Social Charter proposes to grant those basic rights which members commit themselves to respect in equal manner; and 2) outside the bloc, the Charter may make partners' trade with third countries dependent upon the observance of social conditions respected inside the bloc.

But as far as Social Charters are concerned, what is essential is their internal goal and not the external objective. Thus, for example, the European Social Charter of 1961 and the Community Charter of Fundamental Rights of workers of 1989 do not contain any reference to foreign or domestic trade. Likewise, Mercosur's Socio-Labour Declaration of 1998 recognises a set of rights common to the bloc's countries, independently from intra-regional trade, and makes no reference to any requirement of compliance by third countries that conduct trade with Mercosur.

In addition, non-observance penalties of a Social Charter—if any—may be commercial or not. They may be political, moral or even not exist; and should economic penalties be set up, these may be connected or not with international trade.

Actually, the content of a Social Charter may be entirely declarative or programmatic and lack penalties. Whenever its provisions are binding, they may be accompanied by penalties. At any rate, those penalties may consist of observations or recommendations, fines, cancellation or suppression of tariff preferences, or declarative or constitutive judgments, in case there is a tribunal or an international or supranational court.

At all events, Social Charters may also pose the question regarding the effectiveness of Declarations and Pacts on human rights: do they comprise "mankind's juridical heritage", as expressed in one of the Preambular paragraphs of Mercosur's Socio-Labour Declaration and, therefore, may be considered part of "jus cogens", or are they simply ethical declarations of principles or good intentions?

Social clauses—unlike Social Charters, Declarations and Pacts on human rights and international labour standards—only have sense within international trade or in connection with it. The term itself of "clause" indicates that, essentially, in its original and purely conceptual form, the social clause is a clause within a treaty, convention or trade agreement, in which parties commit to respect and eventually enforce certain social rights. In case of infringement of those social rights, they agree to drop preferences mutually recognised or those granted to third parties, or even resort to simple termination due to the lack of observance of the entire agreement.

Therefore, the objective of the social clause is to make tariff preferences or other trade advantages offered to partners (effective inside the agreement) or to third countries (effective outside the agreement) dependent upon the observance of rights established in such clause.

Indeed, there are connective or linking elements between the Social Charter and the social clause.

A Social Charter may operate as a social clause if its non-compliance produces penalties relevant to international trade. Not otherwise; in which case they will continue to be different.

On its part, the social clause may refer to a Social Charter: a trade agreement may contain a clause which establishes penalties or its termination in case the social rights contained in a Social Charter or in an international labour convention or in any another autonomous instrument are not respected. Those rights can be defined in the same clause or in an attached listing or refer to an independent instrument.

On its part, the social clause may also refer to monitoring the agreed commitments in the entirety or in part of the national legislations. This may be a different mechanism from a Social Charter and from a social clause, but it may also be regarded as a modality of any of them.

The possibility of making international trade dependent upon the observance of labour rights through social clauses has given rise to an intense debate. This is not the moment to enter into such a discussion, which would require a specific essay devoted exclusively to this issue. It is just sufficient to point out here the inevitability of the social clause or of alternative mechanisms. If the effective implementation and observance of international labour conventions, Declarations, Pacts and Social Charters are not achieved, certain countries will feel prone to impose social clauses in their trade agreements or to apply unilateral measures with the purpose or pretext of promoting the compliance of those instruments and avoid "social dumping", something that is already beginning to happen.

Among the unilateral substitute systems of social clauses, there are national, regional and private-voluntary schemes. The Generalised System of tariff Preferences of the United States of North America illustrates the first kind of system.

The "labour clause" envisaged in E. C. Rule No. 1154/98 of 25 May 1998, of the European Union, is an example of the second type of system: a substitute measure of the social clause, imposed unilaterally no longer by a State, but by a regional bloc. It establishes 10% to 35% tariff cuts in favour of industrial products from developing countries having legislation and practices that apply the principles contained in international labour conventions Nos. 87, 98 and 138, on labour freedom, collective bargaining and minimum age for employment admission. However, their unilaterality and willful nature limit their effectiveness and affect their credibility, almost as much as the doubts concerning their own objective: respect for social rights or just publicity and image campaigns?

Globalisation: Impact on Labour in India

Globalisation is shaping a new system of international economic relations – be it in the fields of investment, production, trade, finance or technology. The canvas of globalisation, however, is very vast as it means different things to different people. The wider view equals globalisation with the notion of Vasudhaiv Kutumbakam and the narrower economic interpretation with increasing the ratio of foreign trade and investment in a country's output. On a philosophical plane, India has been a votary of globalisation since ages. It is reflected in hymns like Aa no bhadra rutavo yantu viswatah.

Manusmriti says: *Sarve bhavantu sukhinah, sarve santu niramayah, sarve bhadrani pashyantu, maa kaschit dukhabhag bhavet*. The Saints and seers in ancient India had a global view of mankind in which all human beings could lead a happy life, nobody practised deceit, everybody wished happiness for others, and nobody suffered hardship. Globalisation, however, refers to a process of deepening economic integration, increasing economic openness and growing economic interdependence between countries in the world economy. This process is driven by the lure of profit, and the threat of competition in the market.

The definition of globalisation with intellectual rigour notwithstanding globalisation has been viewed quite differently from the individual perspective. A few such opinions recorded during the dialogue on Social Dimension of Globalisation provide interesting insights :

— "We were sleeping on the shore when a big wave came," said a participant.
— A participant in the Philippines said, "There is no point to a globalisation that reduces the prices of a child's shoes but costs the father his job."
— A participant from Poland gave an analogy of a force which could be harnessed : "If globalisation is a river, we must build dams to generate power."

In other words, globalisation in its scope, content and application has become quite controversial. According to Stiglitz globalisation has the potential to enrich everyone in the world, particularly the poor. But the way globalisation has been managed, including the international trade agreements that have played such a large role in removing barriers, and the policies that have been imposed on the developing countries in the process of globalisation, need to be carefully and critically scanned.

Current Scenario

Globalisation is a complex phenomenon that has had far-reaching effects. Not surprisingly, therefore, the term "globalisation" has acquired many emotive connotations and become a hotly contested issue in current political discourse. At one extreme, globalisation is seen as an irresistible and benign force for delivering economic prosperity to people throughout the world. At the other, it is blamed as a source of all contemporary ills.

The social impact of globalisation is not confined just to countries that have been marginalised from the process or have been less successful in their attempts to integrate themselves into the global economy. Even in the relatively successful countries significant social costs are involved in the form of transitional adjustment costs. Similarly, as evidenced by the Asian financial crisis, even countries with exemplary positive records of economic performance can suffer heavy social costs.

The fallouts of growth have also been unevenly distributed across countries, among both industrialised and developing countries. In terms of per capita income growth, only 16 developing countries grew at more than 3 per cent per annum between 1985 and 2000. In contrast, 55 developing countries grew at less than 2 per cent per annum, and of these, 23 suffered negative growth. At the same time, the income gap between the richest and poorest countries increased significantly.

This uneven pattern of growth is shaping a new global economic geography. The most striking is the rapid economic growth in China over the last two decades, together with a more gradual but significant improvement in the economic growth performance of India and two countries which together account for more than one-third of the world's population.

Though some countries have benefited from globalisation, in several countries there has been a phenomenal reduction in the growth of employment opportunities. Many workers in the organised sectors lost their jobs.

The official line from the former Prime Minister Atal Behari Vajpayee's Economic Advisory Council is unequivocal, arguing, "Globalisation is an unavoidable process which is taking place independent of us. It forces us to cope with it. There is no room in a globalised world for an economy delinked from world trade and foreign investment." There is no divine dispensation that gives India alone the power to survive and prosper as an isolationist island in a globalised world."

Under the new Prime Minister Mr. Manmohan Singh that conviction is undiminished. Nonetheless, universal consensus on this view is far from apparent.

In India economic reform process got accelerated after 1991. In 1991, the country's GDP growth rate had dipped to a snaillike 1.1 per cent. In the years of Rao's Prime Ministership, India has witnessed an average growth of 5.5%. Today, successive prime ministers have started calling for 7-8 per cent growth.

Other comparisons of the situation in 1991 and 2004 are more dramatic. In the early 90's, inflation was at 17%. Now the Government is worried when it crosses 7%. Foreign Direct Investment then was $133 million; it annually measures about $4 billion today. Forex reserves were $1 billion then; today, they stand at $130 billion and many experts perceive a crisis of abundance. The market capitalisation of Indian bourses has increased from Rs.1,103 billion to Rs. 15,560 billion; and exports from $18 million to $64 billion during the same period.

The 1991 crisis forced the Indian political establishment to embrace reforms quite simply because the status quo was not viable. While the first emphasis was to tackle the macro-economic crisis, success in that arena also paved the way for reforms of domestic industrial investment policy, foreign investment regulations, and foreign trade.

Since the dark days of 1991, India has come a long way. It has healthy foreign exchange reserves, a booming software and services export market, and a burgeoning knowledge economy.

India remains handicapped by enormous infrastructure and institutional constraints. The question is not whether India has not begun to produce an impressive record in growth, employment, and poverty reduction, but rather how to overcome the obstacles impeding even faster progress, as the global economic system becomes increasingly competitive. According to the Report of the 2nd National Commission on Labour, the perceived benefits of globalisation are as follows:

— Sustained economic growth, as measured by gross national product is the path to human progress.
— Free markets, with little or no intervention from government, generally result in the most efficient and socially optimal allocation of resources.
— Economic globalisation, achieved by removing barriers to the free flow of goods and money anywhere in the world, spins competition, increases economic efficiency, creates jobs, lowers consumer prices, increases economic growth and is generally beneficial to everyone.
— Privatisation, which shifts functions and assets from government to the private sector, improves efficiency.
— The primary responsibility of the government is to provide the infrastructure necessary to advance commerce and enforce rule of law with respect to property rights and contracts.

However, there is a growing realisation that globalisation is not an unmixed blessing. It can at best be an outcome, not a prerequisite for successful growth strategy. The following are among the several demerits or pitfalls of globalisation:

— The process of globalisation seems to be driven by a few in a uni-polar world whereby it is benefiting few and hurting many.

— It is another form of imperialism.

— It is leading to growing inequalities between the rich and the poor, both at the level of individuals and among countries.

— It is destroying jobs and local communities.

— It is ruthless, root less, jobless, fruitless....

Changes in Labour Market Structure

Globalisation has resulted in global division of labour. The huge expansion in cross border capital, trade technology and information flows have become a defining feature of globalisation. The advent of WTO coupled with the lending policies of IMF and the World Bank have resulted in globalisation and privatisation.

Unemployment weakens the bargaining position of the workers and enables employers to hire workers on terms and conditions of work they dictate. Some of the emerging flexible labour categories are – casual and temporary workers, consultants, agency workers, home workers, daily workers, part-time workers and 'badli' workers.

Also come to advent of liberalisation, privatisation and globalisation. Policies of privatisation and disinvestment are being pursued as part of economic reforms in India. The objectives of disinvestment basically are:

— To enhance budgetary receipts.

— To minimise budgetary support towards loss making units.

— To improve performance by bringing out changes in ownership and performance

— To ensure long term viability and sustainable levels of employment in public sector enterprises.

— Broad based dispersal of shares, especially in the profit-making public sector enterprises among investors.

Three broad reasons why privatisation is being pursued are greater economic democracy through increased private initiatives in economic activities, achieving higher levels of economic growth and employment, and reducing budgetary deficits.

Whatever form it takes, social effects of privatisation or restructuring will be as follows :

— Initial overstaffing will lead to rationalisation, retrenchment and displacement of labour
— Informalisation of the economy
— Stagnation of employment in organised sector
— Growing casualisation of labour

In dealing with the redundant workers, several options are available though not all are equally attractive in solving the problem of unemployment. These are :

— Voluntary retirement scheme (VRS)
— Cash compensation or golden handshake
— Retraining of workers
— Redeployment
— Counselling
— Eventual Rehabilitation
— Creation of unemployment benefit and social security.

Small scale Industries

So far as India is concerned, the small scale industrial sector accounts for about 28 million units, 16 million employment and production of over 7500 items with export share of about 34%. The New Economic Policy pursued since 1991 has brought this sector face to face with competition through delicensing, reduction in customs and excise duties. Several small scale units have withered away but those who have adopted modern production practices like auto ancillary sectors have benefited substantially.

This brings us to the benefits of globalisation. The global economy is undergoing a major change-shift towards knowledge-based growth. India is preparing for and participating in the emerging knowledge-based economy. The new economy and high-tech sectors are exhibiting openness, competitiveness and knowledge intensity.

Using its intellectual manpower India has developed an expertise in producing generic drugs and has been able to increase its exports in a highly competitive market. The international capital market is providing increased opportunities to India to attract FDI. Further, textiles and garment industry will expand with the phasing down of quantitative restrictions under Multi Fibre Agreement (MFA).

Internationalisation of Production Chains

India is emerging as a major hub in the pharmaceutical sector. There are global alliances and acquisitions.

There is emergence of a buoyant private sector with industries like Tatas, Ranbaxy, Mahindra & Mahindra etc. becoming conglomerates. Such companies not only assimilate foreign capital and know-how but also display the ability to withstand MNC competition and becoming global players themselves.

India has produced global players in software like TCS, Wipro, Infosys, Iflex, Satyam, HCL Tech and Mphasis. NRIs are also marching ahead; after its American acquisition of Wilbur Ross's International Steel Group, Lakshmi Mittal's newly named Mittal Steel Company straddles four continents and fourteen countries to become the largest steel producer in the world with a 70 million tonne capacity. ONGC, GAIL and Indian Oil have investments in countries like Angola, Iran, Iraq, Libya, Myanmar, Russia, Sudan, Syria, Vietnam, Sri Lanka and Mauritius.

India has been a beneficiary of sub-contracting and outsourcing arrangements, thereby becoming an integral part of the global production chain. Outsourcing particularly, the increasing trend of offshoring has prompted many to suggest that the phenomenon is leading to a re-allocation of jobs from developed to developing economies.

Impact on Trade Union Organisations

Verification of membership strength of Central Trade Union Organisations is conducted by the Chief Labour Commissioner from time to time. BMS, INTUC, CITU, HMS and AITUC have emerged as the biggest five. They control the workers in coal, mining, ports and docks, railways, textiles, iron and steel, engineering and power sectors. The new entrant is Self-Employed Women's Organisation (SEWA) which is a registered trade union and whose membership strength will be verified by the Chief Labour Commissioner as per a court directive. Several CTUOs like NLO, HMKP have lost their all India character.

Due to globalisation, contractualisation and casualisation and as a result of the entry of several multinationals, the unions have been losing strength and power ever since the reform process has begun. The public sector industries no longer can price their products on cost plus basis.

The mandays lost due to strikes and lockouts are very high compared to most other countries. Percentage of women members in trade unions that submit returns has increased but the figure is not a satisfactory one as a substantial section of women workers are engaged as 'home workers'. Less than two per cent of the workers in formal and informal sectors of India are covered by collective bargaining agreements.

New Actors and the Emerging Dynamics. The industrial relations system comprises certain actors in a certain context. The actors are a hierarchy of managers or of workers and trade unions. Then, there are governmental agencies. In the post-liberalisation, globalisation era, consumers and community have begun to assert themselves and take a significant role. When the rights of consumers and community are affected, the rights of workers/unions and managers/employers are taking a back seat.

The court rulings are borne by the realisation that wider public good matters most in preference to the narrow self interest of a minority. Workers and unions, in particular are asked to assert their rights without impinging on the rights of others, particularly the consumers and the community. Increasingly, trade unions are getting isolated and see a future for themselves and their members only when they align themselves with the interests of the wider society.

World over, when the State assumed a welfare role and adopted pro-labour policies, trade unions have grown in strength and power. When the State is neutral, trade union movement gets stagnant. When the State adopts pro-investor policies, trade unions are declining in power and influence, if not in number. In these circumstances, unless trade unions forge broader and wider alliances with the society – consumers and community and various civil society institutions, including non-governmental institutions –they find their power base dwindling.

Declining trade union density: In the traditional strongholds of trade union membership – government and public sector – the workforce is declining due to non-filling of vacancies and the introduction of voluntary/early separation schemes. New employment opportunities are shrinking in these sectors. In the private sector, particularly the service and the soft ware sectors, the new, young and female workers are generally less eager to join the unions. Trade unions are still to conceive and implement meaningful strategies to make unionism relevant and appealing to these new and diverse workgroups. Here too, trade unions are finding an adversary in someone who is otherwise considered an ally: the non-governmental organisations operating under the guise of or as virtual trade unions.

The sickness, closure and non-viability of industries have forced the trade unions to re-orient their role to ensure survival of the industry. The workers appear to be willing to overlook their grievances as they are more concerned with retention of employment. Hence, they are not reporting grievances to unions. Issues such as survival of industry, maintaining competitive edge and productivity dominate collective bargaining. There appears to be a growing realisation of the futility of a confrontationist attitude in the unions.

The threat of privatisation and withdrawal of budgetary support looming large over the Ordnance Factories Board, with its nearly 40 factories manufacturing mainly defence equipment and ammunition, adopted strategies such as diversification of production for civilian market, marketing these products in domestic and international markets, stopping all recruitments, cutting over-time payment bills and going for I.S.O. certification. The federations/unions operating in Ordnance Factories have not opposed these strategies. More and more stress is given on R&D. TISCO has completely overhauled its production unit at Jamshedpur bringing in new technology. SAIL has modernised its plants at Durgapur and Rourkela.

Worker militancy replaced by Employer Militancy? Economic reforms introduced in India in 1991 signify India's quest for global economic integration. If during the decade 1981-90, India lost 402. This does not mean that the industrial relations situation has actually or substantially improved.

Workers are reluctant to go on strike because of fear of job insecurity, concern about the futility of strikes and recognition of the imperative need to consider the survival of enterprise as a prerequisite for job and income security. Further, trade unions are hesitant in giving a call for a strike because it may lead to loss of jobs or closure of the unit. What is even more striking is that over 60 per cent of the man-days lost in the post-reform period was due to lockouts and less than 40 per cent due to strikes. It must be added that quite a few lockouts may have been preceded by strikes.

One measure of trade unions becoming more defensive than being on a more offensive and collision course with employers is seen from the shift in their actions from strikes to litigation. Also, instead of pressing for higher wages and improved benefits, trade unions are pressing for maintenance of existing benefits and protection and claims over non-payment of agreed wages and benefits.

Collective bargaining. Trade unions' bargaining power is shrinking. Also, there is a gradual movement from parity to disparity.

Other Methods of Dispute Resolution

The conciliators both at the central and at the State level have started appreciating the impact of globalisation on industrial relations and labour market institutions in the new perspective and are very sympathetic to the needs of the employer who has to face competition around the globe for their products. Accordingly, they have to make changes in the product design which entail changes in the working conditions. The workers have to retrain and improve their skills. Even, multi-skilling has become a necessity.

Workers who cannot adapt themselves to these new demands have to be given the option of going home through voluntary retirement schemes. Accordingly, the conciliation machinery is not compelling the employers to retain the existing work force under all circumstances. Interest disputes resolution through arbitration and wage boards are moving into the museum of history. The appropriate Governments are generally permitting lay off, retrenchments and closures even though, they were adamantly, declining the same in the 70s and 80s. Even the apex court has become very strict about indiscipline and lethargy of the workers in the industry. Instances have been quoted earlier in this study.

As regards the changes in the industrial relations machinery, it is felt that inspection of establishments cannot be done away with. However, the process of inspection can be used to create awareness and to educate the employers and workers with regard to benefits of timely and genuine compliance. Selective and purposeful inspections have to replace routine statistics oriented inspections.

Similarly, the conciliation officers need to be well aware of the new challenges posed by globalisation before the employers and employees and equip themselves with necessary knowledge, attitude and skills to handle industrial disputes whose nature and dimensions will be very different from industrial disputes hitherto handled.

To be successful, they have to avoid 5 'A's and promote 3 'H's:

A1 ..... Anger	H1 ..... Honesty
A2 ..... Anxiety	H2..... Health
A3 ..... Annoyance	H3 ..... Helpfulness
A4 ..... Arrogance	
A5 ..... Arguments	

The process of globalisation has forced trade unions to be defensive and maintain a low profile. Therefore, there is a need for the industrial relations machinery to be more proactive and vigilant so that undercurrents of discontentment and grievances are detected in time as unions may not report the grievance in changed environment.

Labour Market Flexibility

Even within the organised sector, an increasing number of jobs are approximating the character of these in the unorganised sector as a result of the increasing labour market flexibility in the wake of globalisation. A comprehensive survey of about 1300 firms scattered over 10 States and nine important manufacturing industry groups, shows that between 1991 and 1998, employment increased at the rate 2.84 per cent per annum. Nonmanual employment increased at 5 per cent per annum whereas manual employment increased at 2.29 per cent. This increase is in total employment was brought by increasing the share of non-permanent employees and increase in manual employment by increasing the share of women workers. Smaller firms grew faster than bigger firms. Employers who increased fixed capital per worker reduced manual employment. Employers increased employment but only of one or other category of nonregular flexible workers.

It was found that as a whole over the 7 years of liberalisation dualism in the labour market did increase. The share of permanent manual workers declined from close to 68 per cent in 1991 to 64 per cent in 1998. Not only did the share of non-permanent increase but the share of casual in non-permanent increased even faster. It is the big firms that resorted to the greater use of non-permanent workers. Also, firms employing 500 workers or more increased the share of temporary workers.

Casual employment did not show an association with size of employment. Women workers were mostly employed in large firms. Firms employing 1000 workers or more accounted for more than 75 per cent of all women workers. Firms, which employ a higher share of non-permanent, also employ a higher share of women. Firms employing 50-99 workers and 500 and over report an increase in the share of female workers.

From the above, one should not hasten to conclude that there is no rigidity in the Indian labour market. Irrespective of its impact on employment, a degree of excessive or unwarranted protection to labour may lead to inflexibility in labour adjustment required for restructuring of enterprises in the interest of competitive efficiency. In the wake of liberalisation, this problem has been brought center stage and there has been frequent demand by the industry and foreign investors to have some kind of 'exit' policy – the right of hiring and firing. In this respect the provisions of the I.D. Act which lay down conditions and procedures for retrenchment of workers have been widely criticised. This is because under the law prior permission of the government is required to retrench workers or effect closures in the case of enterprises employing more than 100 workers and such permissions in the past were generally not granted by the Central and the State Governments.

Of late, the scenario has changed in the wake of globalisation. The Labour Ministry of the Central Government and the Labour Departments of the State Governments are regularly conducting the hearing of applications for lay-off, retrenchment and closure by inviting representatives of the workers and employers. After following the principles of natural justice, orders are issued on the basis of merits of each case taking due note of the long-term viability and competitiveness of the enterprise.

In spite of these obstacles, many enterprises were able to adjust their workforce by rationalisation and technological changes, but the process has been tardy.

Several routes have been found out – illegal closures by not paying electricity bills, etc. All these have only added to the problem of labour – they are neither paid their wages nor their due compensation. Although, unions have generally resisted any legislative or executive move to make closure and retrenchment easier, in recent years unions at the enterprise level have generally been found to be accepting the inevitability of adjustments in the workforce in the face of globalisation and industrial restructuring.

Static Labour Policy

A remarkable feature of industrial relations in the wake of globalisation is the gradual withdrawal of the State in their traditional role of actively supporting the organised labour. Though, Labour law reforms will be explained later in greater detail are not taking place both the labour administration and adjudication machinery have been more willing than before to entertain the concerns of industry. Some State governments have taken the initiative to make small changes in labour laws and a major effort to drastically simplify the returns to be submitted by employers and ease the pressure of labour inspections.

Labour Law Reforms

In India we have a plethora of labour laws. There are certain overlapping provisions also. Hence, there is an urgent need for rationalisation, codification and simplification of labour laws. The National Labour Law Association (NLLA) had conducted a study in great detail and prepared a draft legislation in this context. However, the Labour Code prepared by the NLLA could not be utilised for various reasons. As it may not be possible to introduce major labour law reforms, it is envisaged that the government may go in for piecemeal reforms in particular by amending certain provisions of I.D. Act and C.L. (R&A) Act. It is well accepted that survival of workers depends upon survival of industry. Therefore, creation of conditions and environment conducive not only for survival but further growth of industry is the need of the hour.

Industrial Disputes Act: Mr. Yashwant Sinha, the then Finance Minister in his budget speech stated that the chapter VB would be amended to raise the existing limit from 100 workers to 1000 workers. The Chapter V-B of the I.D. Act regulates lay off, retrenchment and closure in an industrial establishment which engages more than 100 workmen, and which is not of a seasonal character. This resulted in criticism from several trade union quarters. The severest criticism emanated from the founder President of BMS.

The Task Force on Employment Opportunities recommended doing away completely with the permission clause in all establishments. The threshold limit of 100 was introduced by the 1976 amendment to the ID Act. Prior to that, the limit was 300 or more workers. The Second National Labour Commission has recognised the need for providing flexibility to the employers in handling labour to promote competitiveness and improve productivity in the context of globalisation. The Commission has taken care to provide a safety net cushion to the workers.

The Commission believes if the employer could decide the size of the employment at the start of the business, why should he not do so during the conduct of the business. Therefore, it has recommended the repeal of section 9A which relates to issue of notice of change in the conditions of work. The Commission has also favoured complete freedom to the employers to lay off or retrench workers. However, the Commission has suggested payment of all dues to the workers and higher compensation to the workers than provided in the I.D. Act.

Just as an industrialist has a right to establishing a factory or start a mining or plantation operation, equity demands that he should have freedom to close down the establishment. In the era of globalisation and severe competition in the manufacturing, mining and plantation sectors it is necessary to have an urgent re-look into the provisions of the Industrial Disputes Act relating to lay off, retrenchment and closure. Time has come to review the provisions in the I.D. Act relating to this subject. A simpler hire and fire policy can attract more FDI in the manufacturing, plantation and mining sector.

It is well neigh impossible to raise the existing limit from 100 to 1000 workers as announced by a former Finance Minister in his Budget speech. What is feasible is to initiate a continuous social dialogue to convince the trade unions to increase this figure initially to 200 though the Second National Labour Commission has given a clear-cut rationale to increase the figure to 300. As the UPA Government is supported by Left parties and Left trade unionists are opposed to any such move in view of the specific provision in the National Common Minimum Programme relating to protection of the rights of the workers, it is going to be a slow and arduous path leading to the desired goal.

The two clauses which are considered out of tune in a globalised scenario cover the following aspects:-

(a) Rationalisation, standardisation or improvement of plant or technique which is likely to lead to retrenchment of workmen;

(b) Any increase or reduction in the number of persons employed or to be employed in any occupation or process or department or shift.

As globalisation has resulted in increased competition, the manufacturing industry was adversely affected resulting in diminishing rate of growth in this sector. The sector could not face the competition given by the Chinese goods flooding the market at affordable prices. It is reported that the rate of growth of manufacturing sector of China is almost twice that of India. The time has come to deal with these two clauses of Fourth Schedule appended to the I.D. Act as rationalisation, technological upgradation and improved productivity are of an imminent necessity.

Contract Labour (Regulation & Abolition) Act, 1970: The Second Labour Commission has recommended the use of contract labour for conduct of non core activities and for sporadic and seasonal demands it should be permissible even for core activities.

However, the 2nd NCL has taken care to look after the welfare of the workers and accordingly, has recommended that the contract labour should be paid at the same rate as the regular worker, following the principle of 'equal pay for equal work'. While, the most trade unions are against relaxation of these provisions, the employers are not happy with equating the wages of the regular workers with the contract workers.

Recommendations of the Group of Ministers on amendments to section 10 of the Contract Labour (Regulation & Abolition) Act.

The National Democratic Alliance (NDA) Government had set up a Group of Ministers to look into the Labour Law reforms. This was headed by the then Deputy Chairman, Planning Commission. The Group had almost finalised the recommendations to amend Section 10 of the C.L.(R&A) Act to permit contract labour in the following operations or processes namely:

(a) sweeping, cleaning, dusting and gardening;
(b) collection and disposal of garbage and waste;
(c) security, watch and ward;
(d) maintenance and repair of plant, machinery and equipments;
(e) house-keeping, laundry, canteen and courier;
(f) loading and unloading;
(g) information technology;
(h) support services in respect of an establishment relating to hospital, educational and training institution, guest house, club and transport;
(i) export oriented units established in Special Economic Zones and units exporting more than seventy five per cent or more of their production; and
(j) construction and maintenance of buildings, roads and bridges.

Globalisation has led to liberalisation, contractualisation, casualisation and creation of a host of temporary jobs. The current structure of the C.L.(R&A) Act puts a severe constraint on the employers in creating temporary and casual jobs. In advanced countries, this is not the case. Section 10 of the C.L.(R&A) Act reads as follows:-

"*Prohibition of employment of contract labour:* (1) Notwithstanding anything contained in this Act, the appropriate Government may, after consultation with the Central Board or, as the case may be, a State Board, prohibit, by notification in the Official Gazette, employment of contract labour in any process, operation or other work in any establishment. (2) Before issuing any notification under sub-section (1) in relation to an establishment, the appropriate Government shall have regard to the conditions of work and benefits provided for the contract labour in that establishment and other relevant factors, such as –

(a) whether the process, operation or other work is incidental to, or necessary for the industry, trade, business, manufacture or occupation that is carried on in the establishment;

(b) whether it is of perennial nature, that is to say, it is of sufficient duration having regard to the nature of industry, trade, business, manufacture or occupation carried on in that establishment;

(c) whether it is done ordinarily through regular workmen in that establishment or an establishment similar thereto;

(d) whether it is sufficient to employ considerable number of wholetime workmen.

Explanation – If a question arises whether any process or operation or other work is of perennial nature, the decision of the appropriate Government thereon shall be final."

The Central Government and State Governments have set up tripartite Advisory Boards to advise the appropriate Government on these matters and during the last three decades, these boards have met at regular intervals and have recommended abolition of contract labour in several processes and operations in a large number of industrial establishments.

The current thinking is that this provision is not in tune with the requirement of the Indian industry facing severe competition in a globalised world. Most employers feel that Section 10 should be repealed, whereas most trade unions are opposed to such a move. The via media could be what has been recommended by the Group of

Ministers (GOM) constituted by the NDA Government. In the current scenario, trade unions apprehend loss of jobs. Section 10 of the Act could be amended to incorporate the provisions suggested by the GOM. It can facilitate more efficient functioning of the industries.

In the fast changing scenario, new types of industries are coming up, certain old industries are getting closed. There was bird flu which hit China and South East Asia and there was a sudden spurt of demand for the Indian goods. The industrialists cannot be expected to engage permanent workers to meet such contingencies. Security, gardening, housekeeping – these are all activities which can easily be outsourced without endangering the job security of core group of workers.

When the Western world is outsourcing several of its activities to India, why should there be a hindrance for the Indian industrialists to outsource some of their activities without burdening themselves with a permanent workforce for peripheral activities? Hence, there is an urgent need to amend Section 10 of the C.L.(R&A) Act to promote contract labour in 10 sets of activities enumerated above. A flexible contract based labour market framework for manufacturing would attract more domestic investment. It will also attract more FDI. The FDI would also bring with it access to cutting edge technology and it will also be critical for the next phase of globalisation.

The C.L.(R&A) Act, 1970 applies to (a) to every establishment in which 20 or more workmen are employed on any date of the preceding 12 months as contract labour and (b) to every contractor who employs or who employ on any date of the preceding 12 months 20 or more workmen. The Act does not ban temporary employment. In the era of globalisation, temporary jobs have become the new buzz word in the corporate world. Temporary employment is fast emerging as the first choice for many individuals and companies. World-wide temporary staffing is a $200 billion industry. While the multi national companies were the early converts, other corporates too are jumping on the bandwagon. Tata Consultancy Services (TCS) has emerged as the largest plaver with 44,000 temporary hands.

Labour Laws (Exemption from Furnishing Returns and Maintaining Registers by Certain Establishments) Act, 1988

In a globalised scenario, it is necessary to improve the competitiveness of small-scale industries and to simplify their functioning vis-à-vis, the requirement of various labour laws.

Small establishments will be required to maintain only three master registers and will be required to submit only one core return in lieu of the existing returns prescribed under the various labour laws. Similarly, very small establishments would be allowed to combine the three master registers into a single register. Further, they would be required to submit only one annual core return in lieu of the existing returns prescribed under the various labour laws. Formats of the registers and returns have been prescribed in the Act itself.

However, in view of the special requirements of social security legislation such as recovery of contribution from employers and employees their accountability, reimbursement etc. no exemption has been given in relation to social security legislation. The enactments from which exemption is sought to be given have been mentioned in the schedule to the Act.

Repeal of Chapter VB may not result in a panacea for all the ailments faced by Indian industry. Here a need has arisen to distinguish between labour reforms and labour law reforms. A lot of time is wasted by the workers by late coming, early going, extended lunch and tea intervals, sleeping during night shifts etc. This can be avoided. Similarly, workers need to accept retraining and redeployment with equanimity.

Managements need to view workers as human beings with a humane approach and improve facilities for the health, safety and well-being of workers on the shop floor. They should take up schemes to provide social safety net for those workers who have been rationalised, retrenched and displaced.

Impact on industrial relations including in newly emerging services

Most of the trade unions have opposed the policy of globalisation, economic reforms, privatisation and disinvestments. They attempted to demonstrate unity in such opposition and organised nation-wide strikes and bandhs. The marked feature of post globalisation is that the unions in the private sector hesitate to go on strike. The public sector undertakings viz. Coal India, Singareni Collieries Ltd., Indian

Airlines, Air India, ports and docks, banking and insurance sector, telecom, power sector continued to be plagued by industrial unrest.

After the great railway strike of 1974 which paralysed the railways functioning throughout India for nearly a month, it has been generally quiet on the railway front. The well established Permanent Negotiating Machinery is functioning more or less smoothly. Similarly, after the historic strike of textile workers in Maharashtra in 1982 which resulted in loss of employment of more than 75,000 workers, the textile workers are generally hesitant to go on strike, barring a few exceptions viz. the prolonged strike of Delhi textile workers in 1986.

Workers of Coal India Ltd. have participated in several agitational programmes even after the advent of globalisation. It appears there is no impact of globalisation on the trade unions operating in Singareni Collieries Company Ltd. The workmen of public sector airlines industry have gone on sporadic strikes from time to time even after the opening up of the economy. The trade unions operating on ports and docks have agitated on several occasions on the issue of Productivity Linked Bonus. They have demanded this bonus on all ports basis which is not a rational one. The staff had to concede for all-round computerisation and also flexible deployment policy. The insurance sector workers have been agitating for revision of their salary from time to time.

Power sector reforms have resulted in unbundling and privatisation of power sector companies resulting in acceleration of agitational programmes by the unions. The Indian telecom industry is moving forward in a revolutionary mode. The private sector has not been affected by any visible industrial relation problems.

Information Technology Sector

The profile of the professionals in the Indian Software Labour Market in terms of their social background, gender and marital status across the sampled firms is illustrative of the rather elitist nature of the industry. Though, the software industry creates a significant potential for employment, given the magnitude of unemployment in India amidst a shrinking public and private sector, the IT industry will not have the capacity to absorb the growing supply of labour force entering the labour market. The requirements of learning and adapting equally bring about a high degree of insecurity for the professionals.

Business process outsourcing

Nearly 75% of US and European multi-national companies now use outsourcing or shared services to support their financial functions. The findings are based on interviews with CFOs and MDs of 127 Europe-based and 151 USbased companies. The trend of MNCs wanting to increase their outsourcing offers tremendous opportunity for the service providers with facilities in India, as they are cost effective and bring value to clients. The BPO industry in India in 2004 had recorded a growth of 50% over 2003.

The BPO industry is booming and a lot of companies will try outsourcing to Indian firms. Some potential areas they would consider include low-end customer care business. Besides, financial services, insurance, airline, hospitality, IT, automobile and publishing would also attract attention of going forward. There is tremendous potential in the knowledge process outsourcing space. The workers have long working hours. Youngsters are burning both ends of the candle. It has become a virtual rat race. They face a lot of stress and even psychological problems.

BPO is an emerging IT enabled service sector which functions in unionless environment. The workers in BPOs are given fancy designations such as executives, officers etc. and are made to believe that they are not workers employed in other sectors. The workers in some BPOs are provided with some mechanism designed to create avenues to air their grievances but with least damage to the firm and through creation of empowering situations such as consultative committee, group etc.

Tourism and Retail Sector

The tourism sector is looking up with the launching of heritage-tourism, eco-tourism, health-tourism, adventure-tourism and Buddhist circuit-tourism in "Incredible India". There are indications that medical tourism is likely to make a headway in the days to come. In view of the existence of large number of hospitals in the private sector which can offer super specialty treatment at reasonable cost and with almost no waiting period, it is attracting an international spectrum of patients.

The retail sector is a fast emerging growth sector. This can be seen in the major metropolitan cities and its suburbs and also in the major cities with the establishment of huge malls which provide almost everything under one roof. In the retail sector, the employers are trying very hard to retain workers. Official estimates put the industry attrition level between 30% and 40%. There is also an element of poaching by rival outfits. Hence, many big retail stores are recruiting 10% more than required staff at the front-end level.

Wage Setting Mechanism

Less than 2% of the workforce in India is covered by collective bargaining agreements as compared to 15% in USA, 18% in Mexico, 80% in Australia, 15% in China, 20% in Japan, 3% in Malaysia and 27% in Thailand and 90% in France, Italy, Finland and Belgium. Despite this low percentage, collective bargaining is a preferred method of resolving interest disputes. This is especially so because arbitration and wage boards are losing importance. Industrial adjudication is time consuming and can be utilised only as a means of last resort.

Informal economy

The problems faced by the workers in the informal economy are multifarious. These can be resolved by a slew of measures:

(a) Organising the unorganised sector workers
(b) expansion of the central and State level welfare schemes
(c) drafting of a comprehensive Bill on unorganised sector workers' welfare
(d) resolution of the problems of informal sector enterprises
(e) skill development and
(f) employment generation.

The solution to the problem of the informal sector in rural areas lies in the extension of the two-fold strategy as suggested by Sheila Bhalla.

On the production side, the rate of growth of farm output must be pushed continuously, while on the labour supply side, the existing agricultural workers must be absorbed increasingly in non-farm jobs.

(a) *Organising the unorganised sector workers:* In Kerala and West Bengal, an appreciable degree of unionisation of workers in the informal sector has taken place. Despite several efforts in this direction, much headway could not be made so far in other States except in Gujarat where a large number of women workers have been organised by SEWA.

Self employed women workers are there all over India. But the need of the hour is an adequate number of selfless and courageous women leaders. With the empowerment of women in rural and urban areas through the constitutional amendment of Articles 73 and 74 providing for compulsory reservation of 33 1/3% seats in the local bodies.

(b) *Expansion of the Welfare Schemes:* At present, the hospitals and dispensaries run by the Employees State Insurance Corporation (ESIC) are utilised to the extent of 50% to 60% of their capacity. Some of the hospitals and dispensaries run by the Welfare Organisation of the Central Government have become defunct. It is possible to extend the ESIC medical facilities available to the beedi, mica, iron ore, manganese ore, dolomite and cinema workers who are presently covered by the welfare schemes by transfer of funds by the Welfare Organisation to the ESIC to meet the pro-rata expenditure incurred. This will result in a synergy between these two organisations and the workers will be the ultimate beneficiaries.

As has been elucidated earlier, Kerala State has covered several categories of workers under the State level welfare schemes. Other States can also follow suit after studying the Kerala model.

(c) *Drafting of a comprehensive Bill on Unorganised Sector Workers 'Welfare:* Efforts made to draft a Bill on unorganised sector workers' has been mentioned. As this Bill did not find support from the trade unions and employers, the Government decided to introduce an Unorganised Sector Workers Welfare Scheme in 50 districts only on a pilot basis. The following steps are required to make the scheme acceptable to the social partners and beneficial to the workers concerned:

(1) Beneficiary oriented study based on a random sampling method has to be conducted in different parts of the country by an independent agency to give a proper feedback to the decision making authority to enable it to structure the scheme properly, and make it viable.

(2) The draft scheme has to be extensively discussed with the

(i) Trade union organisations

(ii) NGOs

(iii) Employers' Organisations

(iv)Academicians

(v) Political parties and also

(vi)State Governments and also

(vii)Actuaries

Based on the above, a comprehensive scheme has to be prepared and implemented. After gaining some experience, a comprehensive Bill should be introduced in the Parliament.

(4) *Resolution of the problems of informal sector enterprises:* The United Progressive Alliance Government had committed in its Common Minimum Programme to set up a National Commission on Enterprises in the Unorganised/Informal Sector.

The Commission will recommend measures considered necessary for bringing about improvement in the productivity of these enterprises, generating large scale employment opportunities on a sustainable basis, particularly in the rural areas, enhancing the competitiveness of the sector in the emerging global environment, linking of the sector with the institutional frame work in areas such as credit, raw materials, infrastructure, technology upgradation and the marketing and formulation of suitable arrangements for skill development.

Employment

Today there are 550 million people who work, but still live on less than US $1 a day. These "working poor" represent 20 per cent of total world employment. In spite of the record levels of global unemployment, the reality for most of the world's poor is that they must work – often for long hours, in poor working conditions and without basic rights and representation – in jobs that are not productive enough to enable them to lift themselves and their families out of poverty. While it is clear that employment is central to poverty reduction, it is "decent and productive" employment that matters, not employment alone.

This employment challenge has taken center stage in the global community, most recently in the Report of the World Commission on the Social Dimension of Globalisation, which drew attention to the need to make decent and productive employment a central objective of macro-economic and social policies as a key endeavour to promote fairer globalisation.

The World Employment Report shows that bridging the "global productivity divide", particularly in parts of the economy where the majority of people work is essential for fighting poverty and stimulating growth in both output and "decent and productive" employment. Decent work has many components; the fundamentally economic one of an income adequate enough to escape from poverty must ultimately come from growth – growth in output, growth in productivity, and growth in jobs.

Food for Work Programme

The Food Corporation of India (FCI) procures rice and wheat on a massive scale during the harvest season. Whatever quantity comes to the mandies is procured provided these grains conform to fair average quality at the support price fixed by the Government on an annual basis. Accordingly, the granaries of FCI are overflowing. Equitable distribution of food grains between different districts of the country does not take place due to lack of purchasing power, especially amongst the rural people in the poorest pockets. The programme covers 150 poor districts of the country wherein part of the wages for those workers who are engaged in asset creation would be paid in the form of food. Therefore, the Food For Work Programme is a boon to the unemployed as well as working poor in these districts. This is a first step towards the National Employment Guarantee Programme.

National Employment Guarantee Programme

The first pledge of the Common Minimum Programme (CMP) reads: "The UPA government will immediately enact a National Employment Guarantee Act. This will provide a legal guarantee for at least 100 days of employment to begin with on asset-creating public works programmes every year at minimum wages for at least one able-bodied person in every rural, urban poor and lower middleclass household".

ILO chief Backs Job Guarantee Programme

Endorsing the Common Minimum Programme's proposal for a National Employment Guarantee Programme, the Director-General of International Labour Organisation, Juan Somavia, said in an interview to 'The Hindu that India has the potential to achieve "a real breakthrough internationally" with its promise of "more inclusive" growth.

Calling for a change in the way the success of economic policy is measured, he said: "Today, growth is the main thing but growth is not sufficient because as the exampie of India and other parts of the world shows, you have jobless growth. So why not change the criterion of success to job creation and basic social protection?" Once this baseline is laid out, a country should organise its policies to serve this goal. "Of course you want growth, sound macro-management and low inflation for providing employment. But we need the policies to converge towards the goal of employment."

National Employment Guarantee Bill

The Finance Minister in his budget speech has also announced that the Government would introduce bring a National Employment Bill to provide for a legal guarantee for at least 100 days of employment in asset creating/works programmes every year at minimum wages for at least one able-bodied adult person in every rural/urban poor and lower middle class household who volunteers himself/herself to do any kind of unskilled manual work in rural/urban areas in the country. This Bill titled "The National Rural Employment Guarantee Bill, 2004" has since been introduced in the Lok Sabha by the Minister for Rural

Development on 21.12.2004. It has been referred to the Standing Committee of the Parliament.

As the Bill suffers from severe lacunae, it has to be transformed to meet the desired objective of generation of adequate employment opportunities and also to lift the workers above the poverty line by providing them decent work. Accordingly –

(a) the workers have to be paid as per the Minimum Wages Act for doing four categories of work – unskilled, skilled, semi-skilled and highly skilled. There is no escape from this because the Supreme Court has held that any industry which does not pay minimum wages has no right to exist.

(b) Artificial restriction on the number of workers from a family has to be done away with as only those who are in dire need would come for work.

(c) At least 100 days of work per year has to be provided.

(d) No distinction should be made between able bodied persons and others as has been rightly advised by the National Human Rights Commission

(e) Advance plan of action is to be prepared to identify and list out productive asset creating works by involving institutions of local self-government

(f) A synergy has to be built in between government departments, NGOs and local Panchayats and lastly

(g) Urban areas have to be included.

References

Bamber, G.J. & Lansbury, R.D. 1993. *International and Comparative Industrial Relations,* Routledge, London.

Fergusson, J. 1997. 'Casual Employment Contracts: Continuing Confusion when Protection and Free Market Clash', *New Zealand Journal of Industrial Relations,* 22/1, pp. 123-142.

Sharma, B. 1996. *Industrial Relations in ASEAN: A Comparative Study,* International Book Services, Kuala Lumpur.

Verma, A., Kocahn, T. & Lansbury, R. 1995. *Employment Relations in the Growing Asian Economies,* Routledge, London.

3

Employment Relations in Asia-Pacific Region

Before reviewing the changing employment relations in the Asia-Pacific region, we discuss the possible links between industrialisation, democratisation and employment relations in the Asia Pacific region. First, some clarification of the use of these terms is in order. Thus it includes the institutions of industrial relations: employees and their organisations, employers and their associations, and the state and its departments with labour portfolios as well as the objective phenomena of human resource management (HRM).

Both *transformation* and *democratisation* have been used indiscriminately in the literature. Transformation can mean a change in appearance or a complete change in character, i.e. a fundamental change. The latter can be seen in some countries. However, it is necessary to keep in mind the continuities in employment relations arrangements, and the exaggerations which, for political or commercial motives, may be made of the extent of change. *Democratisation* is the movement towards 'government by the people' which may involve 'direct' or more usually 'indirect' representation or 'government where control and power rests [sic] in the majority of the people [but implying] that the rights of the minority will be respected'. However, with micro-economic reform on political agendas over the past two decades the study of the micro-level has assumed increased importance.

When attempts were made to install democracy in Japan after 1945, particular attention was paid to employment relations, especially to trade unionism, which American New Dealers in the occupying powers' administration saw as a countervailing force to totalitarianism. Elsewhere in the Asia-Pacific region, notably in South Korea, before the Cold War set in there were US-led moves to democratise, but a subsequent roll back of militant trade unionism and leftist political parties helped to transform employment relations in a different direction. The South Korean union organisation, Chun Pyung, which had been banned in 1947 was superseded by Daehan Dogrib Chockseong Nodong, the precursor of South Korea's Daehan Nochong or Federation of Korean Trade Unions (FKTU) which, until 1997, remained the only officially recognised peak body.

Since the ending of the Cold War we can discern the growing autonomy of unions in various countries in the region as they have countered their governments' attempts to control them. Since the mid-1990s, Minju Nochong or the Korean Confederation of Trade Unions (KCTU) has challenged the legitimacy of the government-approved FKTU, and campaigned for the recognition of the teachers' union, Chonkyojo.

The re-emergence of independent labour movements in parts of the Asia-Pacific was tested by the 'Asian crisis' of the late 1990s. During periods of recession and rising unemployment, unions generally face a difficult task in gaining concessions from employers and governments. In Indonesia, the enforcement of labour standards continues to be weak, but the government did release the leader of the independent trade unions from detention and ratified the International Labour Organisation (ILO) Convention 87 on freedom of association. However, in spite of vigorous protests by South Korean unions the large Korean business conglomerates or chaebol were enabled by labour law amendments, to retrench substantial numbers of workers in the late 1990s. External pressures to improve human and trade union rights in the Asia-Pacific region have paralleled the promotion of democratisation. For example, in 1998, the ILO adopted a 'Declaration on Fundamental Principles and Rights to Work' which reaffirmed ILO members' obligations to promote and respect, among other standards, freedom of association, the right to organise and bargain collectively and non-discrimination in employment. Such pressures tend to be viewed with suspicion by governments in the region, at best as meddling in internal affairs, at worst as opportunistically forcing them to open up previously protected areas of their economies.

Industrialisation, Democratisation and Convergence

A long debated argument states that 'there is a global tendency for technological and market forces associated with industrialisation to push national employment relations systems towards uniformity or convergence'. We use this argument to help us compare employment relations in Asia-Pacific countries. Our first hypothesis is that as economies move towards becoming industrialised market economies (IMEs), their employment relations institutions and behaviour tend to converge on those that prevail in existing IMEs.

The rules, attitudes and behaviour of the parties in employment relations are also shaped by their political context. Against the background of assumptions about the consequences of democratisation, our second hypothesis is that major political changes, such as moves towards democratisation, will induce radical transformations in an economy's employment relations arrangements.

Industrialisation

Do the experiences of the Asia-Pacific region support these hypotheses, and if they appear to, which are the key explanatory factors? There has been a proliferation of commentaries, reports and academic writing which identifies the rapid industrialisation of the Asia-Pacific region and its emergence as a major geo-political entity. While the regional economic crisis of the late 1990s highlighted the problems associated with entrenched relationship economies, which in some cases tended to overshadow earlier economic successes, the second half of the 20th century has been a period of rapid economic growth for many countries in the region.

While regional and supranational trading alliances, including the Association of Southeast Asian Nations (ASEAN) and the Asia-Pacific Economic Cooperation (APEC) forum, have emerged, the member countries are more heterogeneous and loosely grouped than EU countries. During the 1990s ASEAN countries attempted to introduce policies aimed at greater economic co-operation; however, economic problems and political differences have tended to hamper such moves. Explanations for the rapid industrialisation of many of the Asia-Pacific countries have variously drawn on socio-economic approaches, political 'strong state' explanations, neo-Confucian ethics and cultural 'collectivist' models. Classifications may be somewhat arbitrary and there are many differences between the countries in each of the following categories, but a pattern is discernible and may facilitate discussion.

The first group includes the IMEs of Japan, New Zealand and Australia. Current reforms or structural adjustment programs in these countries are in part a response to the spread of industrialisation to other countries of the Asia-Pacific region. The second group, known as the 'Asian Tigers', includes the newly industrialised economies (NIEs) of South Korea and Taiwan. The 'Tigers' are clearly distinctive as post-Japan industrialisers and some of them moved towards the development of democratic institutions during the 1990s. The third group comprises the next generation of industrialisers and includes the People's Republic of China (PRC) and Indonesia. However, economic development in the PRC has been uneven, with growth rates in the special export zones (SEZs) greatly outstripping those of more isolated regions. Indonesia also achieved relatively high growth rates during the early to mid-1990s and had been expected to reach a higher level of industrial development by the early 21century.

Restructuring in Japan, Australia and New Zealand

Many explanations for the extraordinary growth of several Asia-Pacific economies since the early 1960s, beginning with Japan, suggest that employment relations may make a significant contribution to economic growth. This raises questions of universality and cultural or national uniqueness, either prescriptively, as with *Japan as No. 1: Lessons for America*, or analytically, as a justification for the development of a field of comparative HRM.

Japan: A Post-1945 Model

Since the early 1980s, there has been substantial interest in Japanese management and in the transferability of Japanese management styles to North America and Europe. Many studies have tended to oversimplify the Japanese model, focusing on the 'three pillars' typology of enterprise unionism, lifetime employment and seniority promotion. There is little exploration of the legal environment and the impact this has had on shaping Japan's industrial relations practices.

Problems in the Japanese economy during the 1990s, and a subsequent rise in its unemployment rate, led to suggestions that the Japanese employment relations model was under severe strain and required substantial adjustment.

The Japanese 'model' of employment relations has been linked to Japan's high economic growth rates in the post-1945 era. The evidence suggests that changes during the 1990s tended to be cyclical rather than structural in nature. However, some factors, such as an ageing population, deregulation and moves towards a service dominated economy, suggested the model would need to adapt to exist more easily within the constraints of lower economic growth. Japan was becoming a mature IME.

Australia: Towards Decentralised Bargaining

Many of the moves towards employment relations reform in Australia during the 1990s reflected a perceived need by governments to improve the competitiveness of the work force. Changes in employment relations legislation, therefore, were often linked to notions of microeconomic reform. From 1983 to 1996, the Australian polity was dominated by the Australian Labour Party (ALP). Its wage and prices 'Accord' with the Australian Council of Trade Unions (ACTU) was an important contributor to the ALP's electoral success at the federal level. The Accord broadly consisted of a trade-off whereby the ACTU agreed to moderate union pay claims and industrial action in exchange for a say in the determination of political, economic and industry policies. In 1983, the Accord was intended to enable Australia to pull out of economic recession without inflationary increases in labour costs. After periodic revision, it came to form part of a broad framework of economic and social restructuring which emphasised microeconomic reform.

Legislation in 1988 simplified and standardised dispute settlement and required federal tribunal jurisdiction to take greater cognisance of the interests of the parties and the wider community. Further legislation in 1993 extended the challenged to the traditional

Australian employment relations system by allowing for the ratification of non-union agreements.

Australia's post-1996 conservative coalition government claimed a mandate to further deregulate and reform employment relations in Australia and discontinue the previous (Labor) government's Accord with the unions. The *Workplace Relations Act* 1996 aimed to further decentralise the Australian employment relations system.. It included limiting the jurisdiction of centralised awards to twenty 'allowable matters' and promoting decentralised enterprise bargaining. Under the *Act* employees could negotiate collective (enterprise) agreements or individual contracts. However, at the time of writing, the coalition government is proposing a second-wave of reforms. If it succeeds in implementing most of its proposals, it will move Australia's federal industrial relations system closer to the current deregulated New Zealand model.

New Zealand: From Welfare State to Radical Reform

Until the mid-1980s, New Zealand was regarded as a welfare state with a regulated labour market surrounded by tariff protection. Since then it has dismantled much of the welfare state and deregulated its labour market. After relatively rapid economic growth in the mid-1990s, the economic downturn brought on by the Asian financial crisis in the late 1990s has prompted further restructuring and public sector reforms. As in Australia, the change process was initiated by a perceived need in the New Zealand polity to improve the competitiveness of the economy. However, the implementation of such policies was more thoroughgoing and less constrained in New Zealand than in the UK, the US or, for that matter, Australia due to New Zealand's relatively small population — less than four million —and its unicameral, unitary and centralised legislative assembly.

A particularly significant event in this radical program was the deregulation of employment relations by the Employment Contracts Act 1991 which union critics have described as 'an employers' charter'. It abolished the Arbitration Court and the award system, de-emphasised collective bargaining and withdrew exclusive jurisdiction rights from unions. The size and scope of unions have been severely curtailed so that many employers are no longer confronted by any effective countervailing power from unions and are more or less in a 'union-free' environment.

Comparison of Japan, Australia and New Zealand

In the post-1945 era Japan generally achieved higher economic growth rates than either Australia or New Zealand, with some claiming that Japanese employment relations practices were a contributing factor. Japan was governed for most of this period by a single party, the Liberal Democratic Party (LDP) With the LDP closely aligned to big business, unions generally made little contribution to economic and social policy.

In Australia, and even more so in New Zealand, there appears to have been a large-scale transformation in terms of employment relations since the early 1980s. These changes have not been driven by moves towards democratisation at the macro level. Rather, such changes have been induced by explicit political action by governments that were not significantly more or less democratic than their predecessors. In the 1990s there was little evidence that it was converging on a Western model, although some practices were being modified. For instance, in 1999, after the car manufacturer Renault bought a stake in Nissan, a former icon for Japanese employment relations, practices moved towards adopting Westernstyle employment relations, including the use of extensive redundancies. Subsequent changes to labour markets were shaped by product market considerations and policies of so-called economic-rationalism.

South Korea and Taiwan

Industrialisation in the NIEs generally begins with the development of labour intensive industries, such as clothing, textile and footwear manufacturing, which allow such them to exploit their comparative low wage advantage. The next stage of economic development may be to follow move to heavy industries, such as steel making, shipbuilding and motor vehicle manufacturing, often facilitated by government 'soft' loans. The next move is towards high-tech 'knowledge intensive' industries, requiring a highly educated work force. One of the consequences for employment relations is the need for increasingly sophisticated HRM practices as countries attempt to move their economies along the value-added path.

South Korea: Chaebol-led Development

South Korea's rapid industrialisation saw its per capita GDP rise from US$87 in 1962 to more than US$10 000 in 1987. During most of this period Korea was governed by a succession of strong authoritarian governments. There was a great deal of direct state intervention in the economy with economic development guided through the chaebol — large family run conglomerates. Such a concentration of economic power and government influence was blamed for much of the corruption exposed in the late 1990s, resulting in the collapse of the Hanbo group. This alliance of an authoritarian government and big business meant that union jurisdiction was limited; until 1997 the FKTU was the only recognised official union confederation.

Following student-led large-scale protests, the 29 June Democratisation Declaration in 1987 began moves towards more liberal political institutions. In this environment union membership grew rapidly, along with strikes and increased wage demands. While not officially recognised, there was an associated rapid growth in new independent trade unions. In 1995, a group of these merged to form the KCTU as a more radical alternative to the FKTU. These independent unions co-ordinated some notable large-scale industrial protests that attracted international media interest. Despite such public protests, union membership began to decline during the 1990s. This has been variously attributed to industrial restructuring and the growth of the services sector. Nevertheless, trade unions have become a more significant part of the South Korean polity.

Among the responses of the chaebol to increased worker demands has been that of seeking increased workforce flexibility. To assist in employment relations reform along these lines and to facilitate shifting the Korean economy towards more 'knowledge intensive' industries the government set up the multipartite Industrial Relations Reform Commission (IRRC) in 1996.

Along with the above developments a major impetus for industrial restructuring and reform of employment relations came from the Asian economic crisis during the late 1990s. Following the regional economic turmoil, the South Korean currency devalued sharply, causing severe problems for firms exposed to offshore loans. Following its call on the International Monetary Fund (IMF) for assistance, the government initiated an austerity drive to implement the IMF conditions. It also set up a Tripartite Commission with representatives from both the FKTU and the officially not recognised KCTU to oversee the process of structural and employment relations reform.

While the crisis exposed problems associated with high debt servicing ratios in the chaebol, some observers saw the government's willingness to embrace the IMF recommendations as being partially politically motivated. President Kim Dae-Jung — elected in 1998 — had long campaigned against the concentrated of power of the chaebol and their downsizing and/or restructuring might result in a diminution of their economic and political power. The lessening of chaebol influence could have major implications for South Korean employment relations. Company towns such as Woosan and, in the public sector, Pohang (POSCO), house and service large numbers of employees. Moves towards the creation of more small- to medium-sized enterprises could see a significant change in employment relations strategies.

Taiwan: Decentralised Industrialisation

During the 1980s and 1990s, Taiwan's political and economic landscape changed considerably. The legacy of a strong authoritarian government by the Kuomintang that had ruled Taiwan since the defeat of the mainland Chinese nationalists in 1949 gave way to a democratic and liberal approach. A maturing economy saw the growth of the service sector and moves towards the production of higher value-added, knowledge intensive goods. Many such firms had their origins as 'family-run' businesses governed by paternalistic employment relations practices.

Changes in the Taiwan economy required a better educated work force and created an awareness of a need for more sophisticated HRM. Government regulations, such as the Fair Labour Standards Law 1984, introduced wide-ranging and enforceable labour standards; however, the government attempted to promote a more voluntarist approach to employment relations in the 1990s. At the same time, the internationalisation of the economy has included largescale Taiwanese investment in the PRC, with many Taiwan's managers having to learn new skills to manage mainland Chinese employees.

Democratisation has in part led to the introduction of new social welfare legislation, such as unemployment insurance; however, its effect on the unions has been less clear. The growth of unionism in the services sector, traditionally difficult to organise, has been accompanied by a reduction in union membership in more traditional industries, and restrictions apply to organisation teachers and public sector employees. Unions, however, are more independent than under previous authoritarian governments and now more actively promote the welfare of their members. In 1997, recognition was not granted to a National Federation of Industrial Labor Unions (NFILU) formed by a breakaway from the officially recognised Chinese Federation of Labor (CFL). Although illegal as a federation, affiliates of a National Federation of of Independent Trade Unionists (NFITU) function legally as independent unions.

Employer responses to improved social welfare legislation include non-compliance and the substitution of subcontractors for employees. Employers have also put a greater focus on HRM to improve worker productivity, including improved training and incentive programs. Higher education requirements have resulted in many workers entering the workforce at a later age than previously. Thus, political changes in Taiwan appear to have led to increases in social welfare legislation that in turn have affected employment relations. While unions have achieved some independence, the growth of the service sector has been eroding their traditional base among industrial workers.

South Korea and Taiwan Compared

These two NIEs exhibit some similarities. Both underwent rapid industrialisation under strong authoritarian governments after 1945, particularly from the 1960s. In the 1980s and 1990s both countries moved towards more democratic institutions and open economies. Changes also occurred due to employers reacting to changing product markets. In both countries restrictions remain on organising in the public sector.

A major difference between the two IMEs is the industrial concentration of their economies. While Korea's economy is dominated by the chaebol, Taiwan's rapid industrialisation has been largely achieved through the growth of small- to medium-sized firms. Thus, employment relations in South Korea were developed by the policies and practices of a relatively small number of large conglomerates. In Taiwan Enforcement of the law was often ignored, especially before the onset of democratisation in the 1990s and remains limited due to a weak inspection authority.

China and Indonesia

The HRM practices and labour management policies of a third level of Asian industrialisers, including the PRC, have been attracting increased attention from scholars. Echoing the experiences of the NIEs, the third level of countries can get caught in a 'sandwich trap' of cheap labour competition from below and exclusion from higher value-added markets from above. It is arguable that these market influences have outweighed trends towards democratisation in influencing the transformation of employment relations in these countries. Political developments in Indonesia since the fall of the Suharto government, however, have been accompanied by more militant worker demonstrations.

China

The economic reforms instituted by Deng Xiaoping in the late 1970s moved the direction of the Chinese economy away from its former Maoist doctrines. Foreign owned and domestic private enterprises appeared and in 1992 the goal of a 'socialist market economy' was announced. In China the central planning priorities determined the state level employment relations policies which shaped enterprise level employment relations practices. Subsequent reforms meant that 'the employment relations policies of Chinese enterprises are driven by product market considerations and by state-level employment relations policies which are being adjusted to a market-driven economy'. As employees have shifted from state-owned to privately-operated firms this has had profound effects on employment relations.

Disputes arising from the rapid transfer of workers from 'lifetime' to contract employment appeared to provide the trigger for about 50 per cent of all labour disputes in the late 1980s and early 1990s. Structural reforms have been accompanied by large-scale lay-offs ¾ about 17 million by the end of 1998, and workers still employed were not getting paid. Worker grievances are not without protest and labour unrest is reported to be substantial but not mobilised.

While economic growth throughout the 1990s was relatively high, it was concentrated in the cities and special economic zones (SEZs) and Hong Kong. Attracted by the promise of jobs, many former rural workers migrated to the SEZs, but were paid substantially lower rates than local workers in similar industries; the practice of hiring workers from other regions was widespread. Thus, the PRC provided some of the cheapest labour in the world to the factories being developed by entrepreneurs in the SEZs.

There are between 60 and 70 million workers employed in the PRC's five SEZs and 14 'open cities'. Approximately 80 per cent of SEZ workers are young, unmarried women who are housed in dormitories where working conditions are said to be poor, especially health and safety. Few workers are unionised and attempts to organise unions independently of the All China Federation of Trade Unions (ACFTU) are suppressed.

During the early 1990s a tripartite employment relations system was developed consisting of the Labour Ministry, the Chinese Enterprise Directors' Association (CEDA) and the ACFTU.

China's transition towards a 'socialist market economy' with its associated employment relations changes has been relatively gradual. This has allowed state owned enterprises to soak up and/or retain workers who would otherwise become unemployed if a rapid transition to free market forces occurred. China's challenge, therefore, is to retrain such workers as the economy comes to be dominated by private firms.

Indonesia

Following the destruction of the Indonesian Communist Party (PKI) by the New Order government of Suharto in the mid-1960s, Indonesian employment relations were strictly controlled by a strong authoritarian government, supported by the military. Cheap labour and compliant workforce was seen by the government as necessary for economic growth, and the failure by employers to pay minimum wages was routinely ignored. The only union organisation recognised by the state —the SPSI—received much of its funding from the government, with military personnel appointed to many of its official positions. This includes notions of mutuality of interests, and of mutual respect and consultation between workers, employers and government. In practice these notions appear rarely to have been *achieved. While* economic growth throughout the 1980s and early 1990s remained relatively high, working conditions, particularly for women, appeared to be harsh.

Partly in response to the SPSI's perceived lack of effectiveness in representing worker interests, the 1990s witnessed the growth of independent unions that were not recognised by the state. The largest of these was the SBSI.

The ending of the Suharto government amid the economic turmoil of 1998 left Indonesian employment relations at a crossroads. Moves towards the establishment of more democratic processes and institutions could help create greater government recognition for workers' groups and rights. However, continuing political uncertainty, widespread economic problems and a legacy of vested interests make such a prospect difficult to predict with confidence.

PRC and Indonesia compared

The PRC and Indonesia share some similarities. Both countries have large populations and strong authoritarian governments, although the New Order government in Indonesia has been fiercely anticommunist. In both countries the influence of the government on employment relations has overshadowed that of employer or worker groups and industrialisation has been achieved through the production of labour intensive goods.

Industrialisation in the PRC has not been accompanied by any significant moves towards democratisation. It remains a one party state with little government tolerance for political dissent. The greatest effect on employment relations in the PRC has been the rapid increase in privately-owned firms that require a highly committed, more productive work force.

Likewise, at least until the late 1990s, industrialisation in Indonesia was not accompanied by any significant moves towards more democratic institutions and processes. The Suharto government maintained a tight control over the labour movement, with little tolerance for labour dissidents. While Suharto's fall in 1998 was accompanied by calis for greater recognition for workers' organisations, political instability has made for an uncertain future. It remains to be seen how the post-1999 government will change employment relations arrangements in Indonesia.

References

Atkinson, J. 1985. 'The Changing Corporation' in D. Clutterbuck (ed.), *New Patterns of Work,* Gower, Aldershot.

Bailey, E. K. 1995. 'International Compensation', in O. Shenkar (ed.), *Global Perspectives of Human Resource Management,* Prentice Hall, New Jersey.

International Labour Organisation 1997. 'Perspectives: Part-time work: Solution or Trap?', *International Labour Review*, Vol. 136, No. 4.

Vause, G.W. 1992. 'Labour Relations in Thailand', *East Asian Executive Reports,* 14(11) November 15, pp. 14-17.

4

Transformation in Employment Relations

Judging from the attention paid by researchers, it would seem that the 1980s and 1990s was a period of change, turmoil, and even transformation in industrial relations systems all over the world. Much of this literature has been based on evidence from the advanced industrial nations.

An industrial relations system should be treated as a single rational actor, but rather that particularly urgent external influences will spur action by various different actors. For example, it is possible that only one group of actors might respond "strategically" to an external influence, leaving the other actors to react to these actions. Or, that intended actions often have unintended consequences, but that the actors will continue to attempt to address a salient constraint in some manner until it is adequately accommodated or otherwise becomes less salient. A crucial aspect of the argument is that the most salient constraints facing industrial relations systems throughout the world have shifted over time. However, it is also necessary to note that historically, industrial relations systems have not changed all that much.

Yet, the last decade has been a period of upheaval in industrial relations systems in the West as well as in Asia, suggesting the possibility that urgent pressure for change has come from the same source. We argue here that there has been change recently in both the most salient constraints and in the overall systems.

In these first decades after the war, most governments and large companies gave priority to maintaining labor peace. For example, note that in the United States the Wagner Act was promulgated so as to provide a constructive structure for unions to organise in the wake of the sit-down strikes and other incidents of labor unrest during the depression, while the Taft-Hartley Act was designed as a counter to the powerful unions and the wave of strikes after World War II. And, this phenomenon was not limited to the U.S. In the Japanese case, for example, there seems to be support for the argument that the basis for the postwar Japanese industrial relations system was the need for the development of strong internal labor markets in Japan in the 1950s, given the problems of strikes and high labor turnover rates.

There is evidence that the introduction of formal IR rules and regulations in many other Asian nations focused initially on the control of conflict. Iindustrial peace or stability was seen as a pre-requisite for economic development in many of the countries. In effect, what we are highlighting is the tendency of industrial relations rules and regulations to focus heavily on addressing or reducing conflict at the time of their inception, though we also note that more highly developed nations such as Japan and the United States also emphasised industrial peace in the immediate post-war era.

However, we also want to stress that there have been many differences in the ways the different Asian nations sought to attain this goal of industrial peace; i.e., they used differing institutional mechanisms. And, it is also true that the goal of maintaining labor peace was influenced strongly by political considerations in some countries. For instance, several authors have suggested that labor suppression in East Asia was motivated not solely by the need for economic development, but as a means of political control to ensure the stability of the ruling regime. We argue that, in Asia as in the West, as product markets became more open to foreign trade, communism weakened, and radical unions and parties declined, labor peace became less of a priority. At the same time, increased product market competition from overseas made cost reduction on the shopfloor increasingly important. Such cost reductions often involved increased use of layoffs, temporary workers, and subcontractors. In some nations, cost reductions involved increased skills and labor reallocation within the firm.

This, of course, did not happen overnight. In the West, the relative importance of maintaining economic competitiveness at the firm level as the most salient constraint gradually grew over the last three decades. The oil shocks, accompanying developments in consumer markets, and the increasing integration of all manner of markets led to the disappearance of rents and thus an increased emphasis on firm-level competitiveness. Some systems adapted smoothly to these changes. But, for others, it took the pressures of the 1980s and 1990s, the increasing internationalisation and the integration of product and factor markets, along with the predictions and perceptions generated by these developments, to force the actors to begin seriously addressing the newly salient constraint of reducing unit labor costs and enhancing productivity.

We argue that Asian IR systems in the 1990s face, to some extent, the same pressures. Many Asian nations have experienced continuous and unparalleled economic growth during the last 30 years, fueled by low cost export-oriented industrialisation strategies; but, in the 1990s, given greater internationalisation of product and factor markets, some of them are faced with the need to upgrade to higher value-added exports, implying a greater need for functional flexibility such as in Korea and Malaysia. In other cases, Asian nations have responded to the pressures of competition by articulating industrialisation strategies that have opened their economies to a greater extent to both foreign direct investment and international trade, and are confronted with the need for both more functional and numerical flexibility in industrial relations as a part of this transition. For example, in China and India, nations which have only recently liberalised their economies, the pressures to compete in the international marketplace are driving changes in IR to emphasize firm-level competitiveness. Thus, the primary manifestation of the tightening of the "firm-level competitiveness" constraint can be seen in the search for more functional and numerical flexibility in industrial relations. This is not to say that flexibility was not a concern earlier, but more to say that it has become the central concern of IR actors in the 1990s in Asia.

Concepts of Stability and Flexibility

It is important to clarify a central part of our argument: the use of the terms "stability" and "flexibility," and their inter-relationship. Stability is used here in its broadest sense, and stabilityenhancing actions are interpreted to include the processes of eliminating the causes of industrial conflict, steering conflict away from the modality of strikes to the modality of compulsory third party dispute resolution, centralised control of wage increases, and, in some cases, clearly, asserting control over unions and strikes for political purposes. For some actors, stability at the time of institutionalisation of the IR system focused on the control of conflict.

Similarly, the ability of employers to layoff employees was restricted, by legislation, to eliminate one potential source of conflict. For the government of Singapore stability was seen as necessary for foreign investment, and implied the control of strikes through similar mechanisms found in India, but it also implied control over wage bargaining, through the institutional apparatus of the tripartite National Wages Council. Further, to reduce conflict, transfers, promotions, job assignments and layoffs were declared not bargainable subjects in Singapore.

In Singapore and Malaysia, giving the industrial arbitration court the authority to modify collective bargaining agreements on the grounds that it did not meet the national interest was another form of ensuring some degree of stability. In Malaysia, IR stability was linked with political stability, and union federations were not permitted to engage in political action. Our point is that stability, broadly defined, was a central concern of the dominant actors during the inception of most IR systems in Asia.

Although stability was the most pressing constraint addressed at that time by the actors, we do not argue that these systems were not flexible. In fact, in some of the countries, the institutions that were designed to create stability also provided a high degree of functional flexibility in particular. For example, the Singapore case suggests that while the restrictions on bargaining subjects (transfers, promotions, layoffs and job assignments) were designed to reduce industrial disputes, they also provided employers with considerable degree of flexibility in allocating workers. An even more powerful example is that of Japan, where the institutions that provided labor peace in the post-war era also allowed for a great deal of functional flexibility. But, in Singapore and Japan, the facilitation of flexibility was not the central imperative driving the development of their IR systems at mid-century; rather, the initial achievement of labor stability provided an environment in which employers were later able to seek functional flexibility.

Flexibility is also a multidimensional concept. As Grenier, Giles, and Belanger suggest, it is important to distinguish the institutional level at which flexibility is examined, and the different types of flexibility. Thus, flexibility can be examined at the level of the labor market, or at the level of the firm, or the establishment. Flexibility at the level of the labor market refers to those economy- or industry-wide institutions that have undergone change to make the labor market function more effectively. Decentralisation in wage bargaining from the industry level to the firm level would be one example of a movement toward this form of flexibility.

In this chapter we highlight flexibility at the level of the firm or establishment, which focuses heavily on the manner in which internal labor markets are configured to meet organisational needs. There are two primary strategies for achieving this form of flexibility, functional and numerical. They refer to "how" and "how much" labor is used. Functional flexibility strategies refer to those actions that modify existing internal labor markets. Numerical flexibility strategies typically involve increased use of casual and temporary labor, subcontracting, layoffs, retrenchments, and other actions which reduce employment security and the number of workers, and externalise parts of the production system. Other terms for the two types of flexibility include static and dynamic flexibility.

Because numerical and functional flexibility have different goals many have argued that they are incompatible. Yet, Streeck suggests that some numerical flexibility operations such as the creative use of overtime and work sharing can coexist with functional flexibility. Grenier et al. suggest that functional and numerical flexibility can coexist in a firm, if the workforce is divided into a core group that is the target of functional flexibility strategies and a peripheral group that is the target of numerical flexibility strategies.

Having defined numerical and functional flexibility, we will use these definitions in our characterisations of how industrial relations systems are changing in the countries in this study. In sum, our hypothesis is that industrial relations actors in the 1980s and 1990s have taken a number of actions to pursue numerical and/or functional flexibility in employment, IR, and HR practices and policies, as they try to adjust from older sets of salient constraints to the newer constraints. We will attempt to characterise what types of flexibility strategies that predominated during the period of change in a given system.

Note further that we are not arguing that industrial relations systems hinder or enhance the different types of flexibility. Instead, the argument is that the actors are now emphasising numerical and/or functional flexibility as goals and are trying out various methods by which to gain this flexibility.

One method is to change some of the institutions, rules, and practices to achieve this. These are the major themes we shall investigate in the case studies that follow. It is important to note that there have been two years of severe economic crisis in East and Southeast Asia.

Country Cases

Japan

There is general agreement that the central features of the Japanese industrial relations system have included workplace focused enterprise unions, lifetime employment systems, broad based training, and seniority based wages. There is also agreement that one of the key outcomes of the Japanese IR system, when examined in conjunction with related Japanese institutions such as the keiretsu system and the system of production organisation is the simultaneous achievement of stability in labor market terms and considerable functional flexibility in workplace level industrial relations through the development of internal labor markets.

IR Policy and Practice prior to 1990s

There is disagreement on the date of institutionalisation of the Japanese industrial relations system. Taira suggests that the lifetime employment practice developed in the late 1800s in the silk industry where employers, forced to compete for scarce labor, instituted lifetime employment to create stable employment conditions. The key practices were encouraged by the government, which institutionalised several of them during the inter-war period in its Factories Act of 1938. Enterprise unionism emerged post war based on the structure of the firms. Jacoby and Gordon also suggest that precursors to the current system could be seen in the company unions of the 1920s, with institutionalisation occurring during the inter-war period. Cusumano argues that it was the early labor-management crises in the post-war period, coupled with the revolution in production management that account for the creation of the more advanced aspects of the internal labor market in Japanese industry, while Okayama also credits the industrial strife of the 1950s as the most important variable in the development of the Japanese IR system.

Clearly, these authors suggest that the most salient constraint in Japan during this period was the need for labor peace. However, the institutional structures that provided stable internal labor markets also provided Japanese employers a high degree of functional flexibility in the use of human resources, as lifetime employment, firm specific training, and enterprise based unionism became widespread. And the interconnections among corporations given the keiretsu structure further enhanced flexibility, as workers could be transferred from one company to another when needed, within the keiretsu. These connections also made it more possible for firms to sustain their promise of lifetime employment.

The development of internal labor markets had an impact on the wider labor market and education systems as well, as Nakamura and Nitta suggest. Nakamura and Nitta note that the development of internal labor markets and lifetime employment systems created a highly segmented labor force, with little inter-segment mobility. Thus, those with lifetime employment were invariably those who graduated out of the best schools, and those at lesser schools were forced to enter a different segment of the labor market, from which upward mobility was not possible. This system also made education very competitive, as families strove to ensure that their children did well enough to get into the best schools and thus into lifetime jobs. Thus, the picture that emerges is one characterised by highly functionally flexible IR systems within firms, in a context of a fair degree of rigidity in the labor market more generally.

It is also true that there were several changes in the Japanese system over the 1970s and 1980s. Notably, there was an erosion in the seniority based wage concept, as wages began to be tied increasingly to skills acquisition and productivity, while employers had started the practice of mid career hires in white collar and technical occupations. The practice of "shukko" had gained in prominence over the last two decades.

Recent Changes

Our argument is that in the 1990s there has been acceleration in change already underway, as well as changes in other practices that constitute the core of the Japanese system. This has been due in large part to the effect of the recession of the 1990s, as Berggeren argues, which has been the deepest one since the war. Thus, in the 1990s, there has been a significant questioning of the lifetime employment concept, with severe declines in job security on an unprecedented scale,, changes in hiring practices from schools and universities, a dramatic increase in outsourcing strategies, the introduction of limited term employment contracts for some occupations, increased wage flexibility, and some degree of union restructuring, along with evidence of breaking up of some keiretsus. By themselves, any one of these changes might suggest a gradual adaptation to new economic circumstances, but all of this happening together in the 1990s suggests the critical importance of the 1990s recession in forcing employers to question the existing practices and act to change them.

One facet of change is the decline in job security and lifetime employment, as well as changes in hiring practices. Berggerren reported the massive declines in capacity utilisation, particularly in the auto and electronics sectors, as Japanese manufacturers located more and more production in Southeast Asia in response to cost pressures. Shimokawa and Toyonaga report similar excess capacity problems in the auto and electrical industries. In the electrical industry, Toyonaga argues that increased outsourcing of production from Japan to other Asian countries has resulted in a net decrease of employment. In these industries, both layoffs and plant closures have occurred apart from large job losses for casual/temporary workers and women. In general, there has been an increase in layoffs as a function of downsizing and the average tenure in large firms decreased in the 1990-1994 period. In 1995, 4.2 jobs were lost per 100 workers, compared to 2.1 jobs in 1991.

The 1990s have witnessed a sudden and dramatic increase in outsourcing within Japan as well, termed "work commissioning." A Ministry of Labor survey finds that 45 per cent of 4500 firms surveyed had increased outsourcing due to the need for increased numerical flexibility. The survey shows two mechanisms of outsourcing. Either the work itself is subcontracted outside the company, or the job is kept within the firm's premises, but is done by "dispatched workers". In the latter case, regular female employees have been the first to lose their jobs to "dispatched" workers.

Apart from the clear evidence of job loss, suggestive of a declining commitment to lifetime employment, there are chinks in the hiring system, which is an integral part of lifetime employment. First, there has been a reduction in hiring, and second, there have been changes in the hiring practices of large firms. A recent Ministry of Labor survey reports that the percentage of graduates hired by large companies fell 17 per cent among men, but 41 per cent among women. The ratio of job openings to job applicants fell to.47. The placement rate for 4-year university graduates was 65.6 per cent, the lowest figure since 1951. Only 62 per cent of high school graduates obtained jobs in 1996, the lowest rate since 1978. Changes in hiring practices by trendsetting firms provide better clues as to whether hiring practices are being transformed.

Siegel reports that the number of mid career hires have increased substantially over the last decade while many companies have started five year employment contracts for some occupations, such as software engineers. Berggerren and Lincoln and Nakata document several other companies that stopped the practice of recruiting graduates from the elite universities, in favor of second tier schools. And, last fall Nissan hired contingent workers for the first time. Two reasons are driving such changes in hiring, suggest Lincoln and Nakata: the cost savings induced by hiring less elite graduates, and the fact that fast changing technologies are undermining the traditional system of taking novices and providing firm specific skills. Thus, larger chinks are appearing in the lifetime employment and recruitment system. In what has been seen as an effort to "legitimise" contractual employment, the Japanese Diet passed a new law providing legal backing for limited duration employment contracts in March of 1998, thus providing a legal basis for the breakup of the lifetime employment norm..

These changes in the employment relationship are set against a wider picture of change in IR and HR in Japan. For instance, there are changes in organisational structure towards flatter organisations, eliminating the dual hierarchy system that has existed for decades. Yamakawa points out changes in corporate governance to make decisions much quicker: "the competitive and global market has driven Japanese companies to change their management style to make speedy decisions and cut operations costs, including that of human resources".

Lincoln and Nakata document several cases where the determinants of pay have shifted from seniority to performance. While wage increases have been getting smaller, there is ample evidence that the variation in wage increases and bonus payments are increasing, and recently, the National Personnel Authority has recommended pay cuts for government servants to keep in step with the declines in compensation for the private sector. Benson's longitudinal surveys also suggest an increase in wage flexibility generally. These changes have reduced the power of trade unions. This is evidenced by the recent merger of Zenkin Rengo with Kinzoku Kikai, as well as the establishment of a new union federation in the commercial sector by July 2000, and further, the encouragement of industrial federations in land transportation to merge in 2003. These changes, we argue, are a consequence of the need for increased numerical flexibility. Observers have often painted the Japanese IR and HR system as being highly functionally flexible, particularly in terms of the ability of Japanese employers to adapt to market conditions. Key elements in this flexibility have been the patterns of subcontracting, the use of temporary labor that enabled the lifetime employment system, highly sophisticated internal labor markets and the keiretsu system. However, the experience of the 1990s indicates that there are now different types of flexibility being sought.

We view these changes as a movement towards industrial relations system transformation, given that the evidence suggests changes in most aspects of employment relations in Japan, such as job security, hiring, corporate governance, wages and wage flexibility and the role of seniority, as well as union structure, and would seemingly consist of a significant eroding of the "three pillars" and a move towards a more individual based system such as in the United States.

There is also some evidence that the keiretsu system is breaking down after the crisis, possibly as a result of firms' capital requirements, and thus one major source of the "stickiness" seems to be weakening. Other observers, however, suggest that there is considerable "stickiness" still remaining in the Japanese system and are hard pressed to decide whether these changes are fundamental. Although the Japanese IR system witnessed some change in the 1970s and 1980s, the 1990s has seen a major acceleration of change in several different facets of the system, which, taken together, may well represent the beginnings of a radical change in Japanese industrial relations.

South Korea

IR policy and practice prior to 1987

Although there were several changes in Korean industrial relations regulation after the war, the 1953 legislation regarding trade unions and labor disputes formally established industrial relations in Korea. The rights granted to trade unions however was revoked during the 1960s period and thereafter. During the 1945-1960 period, workplace industrial relations in the major conglomerates known as the chaebol was closely modeled on the Japanese system, and has been described by various authors as "paternalistic" or "authoritarian".

Leggett, in reviewing the development of South Korean industrial relations during the 1945-1960 period, sums up its primary characteristics: "the subordination of workers and trade unions to the combined, institutionalised interests of a repressive state and monopolistic capitalism".The methods by which different regimes subordinated labor varied by regime. But, as Kim, Kim, and Park and Lee argue, these methods were clearly introduced to deal with industrial conflict that might threaten the prosperity of the chaebol and thus economic development generally. Apart from direct repression through the use of force, the state also mandated labor-management councils in every enterprise, introduced tripartite commissions at provincial levels to resolve disputes, and promulgated laws that restricted direct action by labor through mandated cooling-off periods before 1980. In early 1981 legal changes mandated the formation of Japanese-style enterprise unions, although the government ensured its system of political control by forcing all enterprise unions to be part of the FKTU. Further given the involvement of both students and church organisations, the government prohibited the involvement of "third parties" in unions. While these actions were clearly politically motivated, they also helped the chaebol contain or avoid industrial conflict, and continue their "authoritarian" management styles. Although there were some efforts to introduce some labor protection laws and regulate vocational and skills training, the primary focus was political control of IR activity.

Incidentally, the various restrictions on union activities also provided employers with substantial control over the workplace, to pursue the Japanese-style internal labor market arrangements at the workplace level that are characteristic of large Korean chaebol. The chaebol workplace human resource practices were similar to those of Japan, directed as Leggett argues, at achieving a "unified internal labor market", which included implicit employment guarantees, seniority based wages, formalised recruitment from good schools, but also cultural and ideological programs as part of a strategy to weaken independent trade unions and to promote company-loyal unionism, a point also made by Woo.Paternalism thrived under an authoritarian framework. But whatever the interpretation, power was clearly in favor of the employer during these periods.

Recent changes

With democratisation in 1987, industrial relations legislation and practice has changed substantially, with the Korean IR system entering what Leggett calls a transitional period. With liberalisation of labor law, the trade union movement mushroomed, with a sharp increase in union density and strikes during the 1987-1989 period. The hegemony of the FKTU was finally broken as new independent unions formed and some of them created the KCTU in opposition to the FKTU. Bargaining power thus appeared to be with the unions in the years immediately following democratisation.

Given the erosion of their competitive position, Korean chaebol have reacted to the militant union demands by following a mixture of suppressive policies, and progressive HR practices, although these practices were introduced by only some of the chaebol. On the other hand, in the early 1990s, employers were calling for the need to cut labor, given the increases in costs. The unions too have been divided during this period. One the one hand, some unions, notably those affiliated with the FKTU, advocated moderation given the needs of Korean competitiveness, but the independent unions that started forming around 1991 and finally grew into the KCTU in 1995 were not in agreement with the policies of the FKTU.

The erosion in competitive position also saw the increase in Korean investment abroad in low cost areas, particularly in Asia and Latin America. As Korean exports and profits started to decline during the 1994-1995 period, employers began to step up their demands for industrial relations restructuring, to make workplaces more flexible, and to get rid of the implicit lifetime employment contract that existed in the large chaebol. Although these efforts were met with some degree of resistance by unions, there was some progress in the movement toward functional flexibility and upskilling as well as restructuring.

The government of Kim Young-Sam responded to the growing union militancy in 1996 with a predawn clandestine reform of labor legislation, which on the one hand allowed union participation in politics and allowed multiple unions in the workplace by 2002, while on the other hand avoided recognition of other peak federations until 2000, and most importantly, increased the authority of employers to lay off employees. In general, the nine years following democratisation can be characterised as a period of experimentation and diversification in industrial relations practice and regulation.

The Asian economic crisis beginning in 1997 hastened the process of industrial relations restructuring. The IMF bailout of the South Korean economy, coupled with the accession of Kim Dae-Jung, paved the way for far-reaching changes in industrial relations in 1998. For the first time, labor was given participation in national decisions through the creation of the Tripartite commission. The Commission issued a social pact for dealing with the economic crisis, with several key decisions on industrial relations. These included the establishment of an unemployment insurance fund coupled with expansion in the amount and periods of unemployment benefits as part of a social safety net package, collective bargaining rights for the public sector from 1999, the freedom of labor unions to be active politically, a revision of labor laws to permit layoffs, the ability to use temporary labor for periods up to one year, advance notification of intended layoffs, and various obligations of the employer in the case of layoffs. In addition, the agreement introduced a change in the long-standing practice of employers paying the wages of full time union leaders. And, Park argues that the labor movement's willingness to accept layoffs could have happened only at this juncture, when the pressure of the economic crisis was great, and with the trust that labor has in President Kim Dae-Jung, although it is not clear that all workers supported the agreement.

The effects of the social pact are still being played out. On the one hand, the agreement has met several of labor's long-standing demands, such as recognition of the KCTU as a national federation, collective bargaining rights for teachers, and most important, a voice in national decision making through the peak level tripartite commission. However, the economic crisis and the IMF bailout, coupled with the law permitting layoffs, have weakened workplace unions considerably.

The KCTU, at best a sceptical participant in the tripartite commission, has thereafter shown unwillingness to cooperate in the tripartite commission, and efforts of the various chaebol to restructure and layoff have been met by a wave of strikes. Although a strike at Hyundai in response to layoffs in 1998 was settled through government intervention, local unions continue to resort to the strike in the face of restructuring efforts by corporations. One consequence is that several companies have since then attempted to guarantee some degree of job security. Companies and unions are also making attempts to increase labor-management cooperation. However, it is difficult to determine whether these examples are part of a sustainable trend.

Since the Korean economy has begun its recovery from the financial crisis in 1999, our talks with various Korean scholars suggest that the tripartite commission has not lived up to its promise of creating a social dialogue at the national level. By January 1999, the agreement between the government, employers and unions via the tripartite commission has broken down, primarily over the job security and employment flexibility issues.

The workers of the KCTU struck work in a campaign to limit employment cuts and replace them with work sharing. By April 24,

2000 automobile workers of Daewoo were on strike protesting the restructuring efforts and potential closure of Daewoo's automotive business, to which the government responded with arrests of striking workers and union leaders. Thus, there is considerable turmoil, and the new IR system forged in the midst of the economic crisis would appear to be another step in experimentation in South Korean industrial relations in its long run search for increased flexibility, both functional and numerical.In summary then, Korean industrial relations continues to be in a period of transition, with a lot of experimentation with institutions, and a high degree of diversity in practices. Employers have attempted to restructure their businesses and industrial relations, and the financial crisis has hastened the need for such restructuring. The IMF bailout and the accession of Kim Dae Jung has facilitated to some degree employers' push for increased flexibility. Despite a peak level agreement that permitted layoffs, however, the efforts of employers to enhance workplace level functional and numerical flexibility has been met with resistance by a labor movement that is stronger and more vocal. Clearly however, numerical flexibility has become a key aim for Korean employers, while job security has become a key goal of Korean unions, during the decade of the 1990s.

Singapore

IR policy and practice

Singapore's industrial relations system is well known for its distinctive tripartite features, and in the view of many observers, one of the most stable and functionally flexible IR systems in Asia. Upon adoption of its export oriented industrialisation program, based on foreign investment in the 1960s, the focus of industrial relations policy in Singapore was to provide foreign investors with a "stable, cheap, and flexible industrial relations system".

Stability was promoted through the creation of a tripartite industrial relations structure with joint decisionmaking on all aspects of economic and social development. To create "responsible" unionism, the state provided funding and training to union leaders on economic development issues. To ensure that disputes did not result in strikes, the legislation provided for secret ballots on strikes, a notice period, and withdrawal of strikes once the dispute was under mediation or conciliation proceedings. An industrial arbitration court was established to deal with disputes not settled through mediation, and to take cognisance of all agreements, with the power to refuse to cognise agreements against the national interest. Strikes were prohibited in industries deemed "essential to the economic development process."

To create stability in wage negotiations, the tripartite National Wages Council recommended standard wage increases throughout the economy. At the workplace level, to prevent industrial disputes from arising over certain issues, bargaining was not allowed on transfers, promotions, job assignments, terminations, and hiring. While these laws certainly reduced disputes, it also created the preconditions for all types of flexibility as it gave the employer substantial control over the workplace. While the tripartite system clearly provides labor with a high degree of voice over national decisionmaking, it is important to point out, as Leggett does, that it is hard to see the Singapore labor movement as being truly independent of the ruling People's Action Party - PAP.

Recent changes

Since the 1960s, there have been changes in industrial relations and human resource regulations at regular intervals, in 1968, 1972, 1982, and 1984, yet these changes were minor, and did not depart from the basic framework. Each change has introduced a little more functional flexibility in industrial relations. In the early 1980s, for example, the need to upgrade its low-cost based export oriented industrialisation program to higher value-added export oriented industrialisation required more capital-intensive investors, highly skilled labor, and flexible arrangements between the two. The labor movement was restructured, and the establishment of enterprise unions in the future was encouraged. This was done to make individual collective bargaining agreements more sensitive to the economic environments facing individual firms. In support, the National Wages Council desisted from its practice of recommending uniform wage increases, and advocated differential increases based on the conditions of industries and firms. Over the subsequent years, the National Wages Council further decentralised its wage recommendations, promoting flexible compensation linked to productivity and the use of lump sum bonuses. Thus, over the years, the Singapore industrial relations system has moved in the direction of greater workplace flexibility, under a tripartite framework that guarantees some degree of IR stability.

What has this evolutionary process done to bargaining power? Although the structure is tripartite, Deyo, Leggett and Wilkinson suggest that the PAP has incorporated the labor movement through a combination of strategies over the years, notably, through some degree of repression, legislation and political incorporation. By the1970s, it became impossible to distinguish between party and labor elites. This has clearly continued in the 1990s, for instance, when the Head of the Economic Development Board, moved to become the head of the NTUC. Clearly, then, labor is the "junior partner" in a corporatist framework where government and employers are dominant. On the other hand, this status does provide labor with a degree of voice in all forms of national decisionmaking to an extent unmatched in Asia. The degree of voice clearly is influenced heavily the extent to which the party's and labor's interests are similar; for example, in dealing with the Asian economic crisis, avoiding retrenchment was a key issue for both labor and the party. The pursuit of functional flexibility under this framework has not made, to our knowledge, labor any weaker, given the existing institutional structure, and despite the gradual decline in trade union membership as a function of structural changes in the economy.

Much of the focus of government policy and institutions in recent years has been on increasing skills development and training in Singapore, through various legislative and institutional mechanisms. In response to the economic crisis, although no formal rules have changed, the tripartite partners have chosen to emphasize retraining, reskilling, and HRD more generally in an effort to improve the employment prospects for displaced workers.

Malaysia

IR policy and practice prior to 1985

The industrial relations institutions of the colonial period played a critical role in developing Malaysia's post-independence industrial relations system. The primary focus of colonial labor policy in

Malaysia was the elimination of communist unions, and the establishment of compliant and "responsible" unions. These objectives were met through the office of the Registrar of Trade Unions, which had wide powers to accord or not accord registration to unions, and through mandating occupational based unions. Post-independence industrial relations policy built on this foundation of control over union formation, but put in additional elements to meet the goal of stability in industrial relations for economic development and regime maintenance. Hiers and Arudsothy argue that these policies were designed to ensure that unions would not present a threat to the ruling coalition government.

On the bargaining front as well, industrial relations policy was geared to ensure both continued investment and to contain strikes for economic development. For example, employees had the right to strike, but that right was circumscribed by a series of administrative rules. At the level of the workplace, bargaining on job assignments, promotions, transfers, and layoff and retrenchment decisions were not allowed by the legislation, thus ensuring that disputes regarding these subjects would not result in conflict. Several authors highlight the importance of industrial relations stability via effective conflict management as the key basis for these workplace industrial relations regulations and legislation.

The principle of supremacy of economic development goals over unfettered trade union rights continued through Malaysia's phase of import substitution industrialisation until the middle 1970s, and deepened with the adoption of low cost labor intensive export oriented industrialisation predicated on foreign investment, primarily in the electronics sector. Kuruvilla documents an increase in government oversight and intervention in industrial relations, in terms of union formation, dispute settlement and various initiatives to keep labor costs low.

IR and HR practices of employers and firms also reflected this low cost focus. Foreign employers often refused to recognise unions, intimidated union activists, or inserted antiunion clauses in individual employment contracts. The growth of contract work as employers searched for increased numerical flexibility, and the employment of guest workers further reduced union power and influence.

Recent changes

By the late 1980s, further changes in industrial relations became apparent. Competition from other low cost producers forced Malaysia to adopt a more technology-intensive export strategy. And, in order to attract more technology-intensive investment, the focus of the state's industrial relations policy turned to one of skills development, rather than cost containment and union suppression. Government policies now focus on providing employers with incentives to invest in training, with the introduction of the Skills Development System, and reforming the education sector to ensure the continuous supply of skilled workers for industrial needs.

Foreign multinationals that dominate employment in the export sector have introduced new forms of work organisation and progressive human resource practices, many of which require greater worker involvement, but in a nonunion setting. Therefore, the gradual evolution to a high skill and "positive" human resource policy system is underway, in a non-union environment. There has been great interest in performance-based pay in Malaysia, given the concern that productivity growth is slower than wage growth. Recent legislative changes to the definition of the "wage" were designed to increase incentives among employers to adopt performance-based pay schemes.

In general the move towards highly flexible industrial relations and human resource practices can be discerned in Malaysia, similar to the path taken by Singapore. The Asian economic crisis has further intensified the drive to restructure IR/HR practices to enhance both functional and numerical flexibility. During the economic crisis, firms have restructured their business to a considerable extent, and have focused on pruning the labor force, introducing labor saving technology, and preparing for a more skill-intensive workforce. However, unlike in Singapore, Malaysian unions do not have any institutional bulwarks against major membership losses. Union density has been low in Malaysia and the labor movement has not had a significant voice at either national or local levels. Peetz and Todd note that union membership declined by 1 per cent during the economic crisis. Curiously, one consequence of the economic crisis has been the introduction of tripartism for the first time, although it is a limited form of tripartism. It is not clear whether this form of tripartism will remain once the crisis is over; Peetz and Todd argue that this as an important question for future research on Malaysia.

Philippines

IR policy and practice prior to 1980s

There is evidence to suggest that industrial peace was the driving focus of Philippines industrial relations policy at its inception. The Court of Industrial Relations (CIR) established in 1936 was created primarily to handle labor disputes, and Ramos argues that the CIR's primary function was "to contain the growth and militancy of the labor movement". The immediate post-war era saw a rise in industrial disputes during a period of reconstruction under an import-substitution industrialisation program. The ISI program lasted until the 1960s, and during this phase the Philippines witnessed its fastest growth.

To deal with the rising number of industrial disputes, the state initially put in place a system of bilateral collective bargaining, based largely on the Wagner Act in the U.S. The act itself was called the Industrial Peace Act of 1953, clearly signifying the underlying logic of the IR system: to promote industrial peace. In fact, the preamble to the law clearly states its aim "to eliminate the causes of industrial unrest". Thus, a U.S.-style system of collective bargaining was introduced, and this lasted until the declaration of martial law in 1972. From less than 50 collective bargaining contracts in 1953, the number increased to 852 contracts in 1972. This was accompanied by various pieces of labor and social welfare legislation, in particular minimum wage legislation.

Martial law in 1972 changed the nature of industrial relations drastically. The intensification of the country's export-oriented industrialisation program in the 1970s brought with it several changes in industrial relations policy. This was achieved by banning strikes and introducing compulsory arbitration to guarantee foreign investors industrial peace.

Various provisions, including the power of the Secretary of Labor to issue injunctions against strikes, weakened the ability of labor to push through their demands in several industries. Second, to maintain stability, the highly fragmented and decentralised unions were restructured along industrial union lines, and all trade unions were required to be affiliated to the government controlled Trade Union Congress of the Philippines. Third, various labor laws and standards were revised downward to continue to attract foreign investors, to capitalise on the Philippines competitive advantage of low labor costs. Although the more restrictive aspects of the Marcos regime were lifted with the ascendancy of Corazon Aquino in 1986, Philippine industrial relations policy continued its low cost 26 focus, with several restrictions on the ability of unions to strike.

Recent changes

When we examine firm level policies during the 1990s, it is clear that the firms are focusing heavily on flexibilising industrial relations further, given the competition from China and Vietnam in low cost assembly operations that were the mainstay of the Philippines' export oriented industrialisation program. Numerical flexibility appears to be the key term here. In a wide-ranging paper on globalisation's impact, Barranco-Fernando documents the trends in practices. Two of the most pervasive forms of employment flexibility include subcontracting and labor-only subcontracting. While Barranco-Fernando documents the large increases in outsourcing and labor-only contracting, a recent survey by the Bureau of Employment and Labor Statistics suggest that in manufacturing roughly 25% of the jobs are done by labor service contractors.

The "casualisation" of what were permanent jobs is also accompanied by an increasing anti-union stance taken by employers. This movement has clearly weakened trade unionism, at both national and workplace levels. Collective bargaining coverage declined from 621,000 in 1993 to 540,000 in 1998. And there is anecdotal evidence that the large scale retrenchments and subcontracting have resulted in losses of trade union members.

The Asian economic crisis has clearly accelerated these trends. In a more recent investigation of the effects of the crisis on industrial relations, case studies of 16 firms in diverse industries suggest dramatic efforts to reduce headcount, increase subcontracting, and restructure industrial relations in view of increasing low-cost competition from China and Vietnam. Clearly, there is a focus on the workplace that is driving change in Philippines industrial relations.

It is against the weakness of the trade union movement that the efforts at tripartism during the economic crisis must be evaluated. The aims of tripartism are to help alleviate the effects of the crisis, but to also promote numerical flexibility at the same time. The tripartite social accord signed in February 1998 eased restrictions on layoffs to promote economic restructuring, while improving social protection through the expansion of social security. The social accord also encouraged firms to use layoffs as a last resort and to explore alternatives to layoffs. The Philippines has also seen the increased use of labor-management councils, introduced by employers with government encouragement but with limited union acceptance. While it is too early to evaluate the effect of these councils on labor-management cooperation, this remains an interesting question for future research.

India

IR policy and practice prior to 1991

In his wide-ranging examination of the colonial origins of Indian industrial relations policy, Desousa highlights how the Indian government built on colonial labor institutions and regulations to fashion an industrial relations system that sought to control industrial conflict through a plethora of protective labor legislation.

Under this regime, many aspects of workplace IR and HR were regulated, including detailed laws on safety and health, leave, dismissal and layoffs so as to avoid sources of conflict. The industrial disputes act mandated that employers could layoff workers only temporarily and provided that employers must seek, government permission for retrenchment and even closure of factories. The method of dispute settlement also reflects the underlying purpose of this act: ensuring that conflict did not undermine economic development. Thus, although the right to strike existed, it could be exercised only after due notice, and the strike had to be stopped when either party requested third party intervention through government conciliation officers. If conciliation failed, the government had the power to refer the dispute to compulsory arbitration, or to a labor court or industrial tribunal for final decision. Thus, laws regarding labor standards, protection of employees against unfair dismissal, and retrenchment and closure would, in theory, reduce the potential sources of conflict, and should conflict arise, the dispute settlement mechanism would be able to contain and resolve it.

This worker-centered industrial relations policy was sustained to a large extent by the country's country's import substitution industrialisation strategy which emphasized the growth and long term development of heavy capital goods industries with largely indigenous technology, coupled with a policy of industrial licensing, import controls and restrictions on foreign ownership that protected both public and private sector firms from international competition.

The protectionism afforded to manufacturers also resulted in the growth of inefficient firms. In industrial relations terms, these inefficiencies were reflected in excess employment in public sector industries such as power, and in the private sector, in an inability to negotiate the introduction of labor-saving new technology or rationalisation and labor cost control strategies that involved workforce reduction, along with a high incidence of strikes. Further, the absence of a sole bargaining agent legislation created a multiplicity of unions at each workplace; unions competed with each other for membership in a given workplace, resulting in highly conflictual industrial relations, as the conditions for a stable partnership between employers and unions did not exist.

Thus, although the initial goal of labor policy was to provide workers with a high degree of protection, and ensure some degree of stability in terms of both employment for workers as well as conflict avoidance, collaborative labor-management relations did not emerge. It should be noted however, that there was more diversity in industrial relations regulation than the picture painted above....largely because the different states in India enact their own industrial relations laws, and also because of differing institutional histories in different states.

Recent changes

In 1991, Indian economic policy witnessed a dramatic turn with the dismantling of the 40 year old Import substitution industrialisation program and the adoption of a liberalised open economy. The effects of such a major change in economic policy after 45 years of ISI have been dramatic. Overnight, Indian businesses have been threatened by international competition that they are not prepared to face. These pressures have resulted in major debates regarding industrial relations policy and have brought about a shift in the relative power of business and labor. Industrial relations legislation reform is on the agenda. A tripartite committee formed for this purpose has recommended the creation of a safety net for retraining of retrenched workers and for retrenchment compensation, although the legislation has not been changed to date.

Industrial relations practices are also undergoing change. One significant outcome of structural adjustment and liberalisation has been the employer push for workforce reduction. Given the inability to retrench, employers have introduced voluntary retirement schemes (VRS) to shed excess labor. Although precise estimates of the number of people on VRS are not available, Venkataratnam projected a total of 5 million jobs will be lost through VRS in the public sector. The number of lockouts has increased dramatically, even as strikes have declined.

In addition, in order to avoid unionisation, employers are promoting workers into administrative and supervisory ranks to take them outside the purview of the Industrial Disputes Act. There are also increased efforts of employers to invest in joint consultation for productivity improvement. Venkataratnam suggests that for the first time, employers feel that the government is on their side, and this has brought about what many call "employer militancy," with collective bargaining contracts showing an ascendancy of management rights.

The beginnings of a government-business coalition is increasingly apparent. The traditional link between unions and political parties provided the labor movement with considerable voice despite their low density figures. The government-labor coalition has weakened considerably, given the state's enthusiastic support for economic liberalisation and labor's opposition to it.

Clearly, the IR system is exhibiting tensions as it attempts to break with the rigid existing policies and practices. The need to compete both domestically and globally with the best in the world has forced the Indian employer to strive for increased numerical flexibility, and this has been manifested in the need to reduce headcount, restructure industrial relations, attempt labormanagement collaboration, and in some cases to avoid unions. Hiers and Kuruvilla, in a wide ranging survey of Indian industry in 1997 provide numerous examples of the movement towards numerical flexibility and a clear increase in greenfield nonunion plants. Another recent study covering 300 collective bargaining agreements in the Indian private sector found that one out of two included provisions for greater numerical flexibility and closer cooperation in the labor-management relationship.

In essence, these practices have accentuated the diversity existing in Indian industrial relations considerably. Bhattacherjee suggests that there is so much more variation in the Indian industrial relations scenario that it is no longer appropriate to think of one "national" Indian IR system. Overall, the evidence clearly suggests a shift away from "maintaining labor peace" as a key underlying imperative of the industrial relations system, and towards "the enhancement of firmlevel competitiveness through increases in numerical flexibility" as India becomes more integrated into the world economy.

China

IR policy and practice prior to 1980s

China's industrial relations system must be understood in terms of its economic and political organisation. Although the All-China Federation of Trade Unions was set up as early as 1925, its incorporation into the Chinese communist party defined the labor movement's role within a state-dominated, import substitution industrialisation policy in a centrally planned closed economy. The trade union constitution's preamble states the role of the union rather clearly: "The Trade Unions of China are the mass organisation of the working class led by the party and are the transmission belts between the party and the masses". Therefore, although the unions played a variety of economic and political roles, the role of transmission belt was the most central.

The transmission belt ostensibly contributed to the development of the state's industrial, employment, and welfare goals. The main characteristics of the system included state ownership of industrial enterprises, the implicit guarantee of employment for workers, an administrated allocation of labor irrespective of the price mechanism.

Although the emphasis varied over time, the broad industrial policy followed was a mixture of heavy industrialisation in the core sectors of the economy, coupled with both import substitution industries and small scale industrialisation to promote economic growth in the rural sector. The administrative bureaucracy at central and regional levels governed industry, while the party and the trade unions developed parallel bureaucracies. In industrial relations terms, however, the workplace was most important. Thus, the enterprise shouldered many of the responsibilities that are the province of national social security in other nations.

Warner suggests that the Danwei provided a sense of identity for the industrial worker based on cradle-tograve welfare benefits. The term "iron rice bowl" is used to describe this inclusive IR system. Note also the often heard quotation that the Chinese industrial enterprise was not organised to make profits, but to fulfill the economic and social policy of the state. Within this system, industrial relations consisted of a dualistic structure of codetermination. Warner provides an analysis of IR in the Chinese factory, which we summarise here. The trade union focused on day-to-day shop floor problems, but walked a fine line between its responsibilities of educating the workers, ensuring the success of the enterprise, and ensuring that the management of the enterprise did not exploit workers. Workers congresses met about four times a year and had responsibility for strategic issues, such as the scrutiny of plans and budgets, decisions on enterprise funds for welfare activities, changes in organisational structure and payment systems, and election of the enterprise director and other key management personnel. Thus, the workers congresses made key decisions that trade unions carried out on a regular basis.

The glue that held this together was the presence of party members in each enterprise, who were often responsible, through their presence in trade unions, workers congresses, and management, for all important decisions. The combination of administrative labor allocation and the iron rice bowl produced a rigid and inflexible system within the enterprise, and outside as well. The absence of numerical flexibility was further reinforced by the absence of labor mobility given the household registration system. This has been cited as the "greatest institutional barrier to free labor mobility".

Thus, the objectives of industrial relations policy was in some sense to support the economic and social structure that communism built, in other words, mobilisation of the mass of workers behind economic policies. Note, however, that there were numerous differences under different regimes and across different industries in how workers congresses and trade unions operated.

Recent changes

The Chinese industrial relations system has been in considerable ferment since the opening up of the Chinese economy post-1978, and in particular post-1983. There is a lot of research on the change in economic development strategy, and we will not revisit that research here. But the change in economic policy brought about a greater decentralisation in the SOE's, which were allowed to manage themselves more independently, and an increase in the number of FIE's, foreign-owned joint venture firms in export and special economic zones all over the country. Decentralisation in the state sector implied changes in industrial relations and human resource practices, with new practices that are increasingly focused on getting a higher degree of numerical and functional flexibility. Jackson for instance documents the early progress in instituting numerical flexibility by introducing the contract system to replace the lifetime employment system, and the flexibilisation of wages. Further, as part of these reforms, the Chinese government enacted a new labor law in 1994 that essentially sought to create a new industrial relations system within the socialist market economy, but the implementation of this law has not been uniform.

In terms of industrial relations legislation, the government's focus in the foreign-investment sector is to keep basic labor protection and welfare laws as similar as possible to the state-owned sector. Thus, in joint venture firms there are detailed rules regarding industrial relations and human resource practices. There is a ceiling regarding wage payment and in effect a legislated system regarding employee benefits that parallels the state-provided benefits at the Danwei. Every enterprise must have a union, which can attend the board meetings of the companies, and which get a company supported office, 2 per cent of the wage bill, and the salaries of union reps paid by the company. The purposes of unions here are the same, to ensure the success of the enterprise, while there is also a strong emphasis on ensuring that workers do not get exploited and that their basic rights are protected. Thus, Western multinationals have a very different reputation as employers than Korean and Taiwanese companies.

Variation is facilitated by weak and haphazard enforcement of labor legislation. Wage setting is determined by the enterprise. On average, in 1995 wages in the FIE sector were about 1.45 times the wages in the state-owned sector. Other employment practices are completely within the discretion of the employer, subject to the basic standards legislation. Despite the ACFTU directive to organise every workplace, only 36 per cent of workplaces have been organised so far, with the labor movement showing little ability, or interest, in speeding up the organisation rate, and as several observers have noted, have little resources with which to do so. Employment contracts are short term, highly specific, impose restrictions on their employees, can be unilaterally changed by the employer, and in several cases, no contracts are signed at all.

There is increased variation in industrial relations within the state-owned sector as well. There has been pressure to restructure industrial relations and human resource practices in this sector to increase productivity, upgrade skills, restructure work practices and increase numerical flexibility. Despite regulations to limit management autonomy to lay-off workers, there have been widespread violations leading to increasing unemployment and worker protests.

There is a much more variance in earnings, especially within-industry, based on the different economic circumstances of firms. In other smaller state owned enterprises that have been recently bought by foreign concerns, notably in the low cost labor intensive manufacturing sector dominated by investors from Hong Kong and Taiwan, industrial relations and human resource management is characterised by low wages, refusal to follow minimum wage laws, blatant violation of labor law provisions, high rates of wildcat strikes and labor disputes, and very little job security. Lee documents that in these sectors, changes in IR and HR emphasizing numerical flexibility have taken a heavy toll on the workers.Chan suggests that the employment system in the state sector is clearly in transition, and has already shifted away from the stateoriented system, but the key challenge is in the method of adjustment to the market economy and the considerable variation in the ability of different SOE managements to adapt. The labor movement in China has been slow to adapt to these changes. In addition, decentralisation of decisionmaking down to the enterprise level has not been matched by adequate autonomy for unions or the right to strike.

Chan notes that the labor movement has limited funds, limited organisers, and tends to view new organisation as a bureaucratic exercise. In the FIE sector many labor regulations are not enforced given that provincial governments believe that enforcing such laws may drive off foreign investment. Thus, the power of the labor movement has been weakened by the changes.

The net effect of the changes in economic policy and the changes in labor law have been an increase in the diversity of industrial relations and human resource practices in China, diversity within state enterprises and between state enterprises and FIE's. In effect, there is a clear transition from centralised IR and a highly welfarist and rigid system to a more profit-driven, flexibility-oriented IR and HR system.

What is less well known is the nature of HR/IR in the rapidly expanding non-foreign, private sector of the Chinese economy, especially in large firms. Zhao and Nichols convey the degree of experimentation rather well in their textile industry study: "The managements' labor control strategies owe something to long established cultural forms; they owe something a more recent socialist practice and ideology; and they owe something to a mixture of practices in the capitalist world". But, all of the evidence taken together indicates that the most salient constraint facing industrial relations in China has shifted to the need to enhance enterprise competitiveness.

5

Employment Relations in India

In order to understand the issues and problems associated with industrial relations, it is desirable to study its various evolutionary phases. Practically speaking, the growth of industrial relations in India is in no way different from that of other parts of the globe. The various stages of industrial relations progressed from primitive stage to factory or industrial capitalism stage. The emergence of tripartite consultative system and voluntary and statutory approach to industrial relations, immensely contributed to the growth of a particular system of industrial relations in our country. Also the fast changing technological development, industrial production techniques, and ideological values have brought forth in the industrial world a unique type of employer-employee relationship.

India was greatly advanced in the field of industry and commerce in the past, as evidenced from its ancient literature. In ancient times, the highest occupation in our country was agriculture followed by trading. Manual services formed the third rung of occupation. Small manufacturers in their cottages, mostly on hereditary basis, carried on a large number of occupations. From the very early days, craftsmen and workers felt the necessity of being united. The utility of unions has been stated in *Sukla Yajurveda Samhita*, "if men are united, nothing can deter them." Kautilyas's *Arthashastra* gives a comprehensive picture of the organisation and functions of the social and political institutions of India and a good description of unions of employees, craftsmen or artisans. There were well-organised guilds, which worked according to their own byelaws for the management of the unions. However, there were no organisations of workers during the Mughal rule. The labourers were entirely dependent on their masters and forced work was taken from them. The working relations, however, in those days were more or less of a personal character and are very much distinguishable from the present-day industrial relations as have gradually developed with the growth of largescale industries.

Study of Modern Industrial Relations in India

A study of modern industrial relations in India can be made in three distinct phases. The first phase can be considered to have commenced from the middle of the nineteenth century and ended by the end of the First World War. The second phase comprises the period thereafter till the attainment of independence in 1947, and the third phase represents the post-independence era.

First Phase

During the first phase, the British Government in India was largely interested in enforcing penalties for breach of contract and in regulating the conditions of work with a view to minimising the competitive advantages of indigenous employers against the British employers. A series of legislative measures were adopted during the latter half of the nineteenth century, which can be considered as the beginning of industrial relations in India.

The close of the First World War gave a new twist to the labour policy, as it created certain social, economic and political conditions that raised new hopes among the people for a new social order. There was intense labour unrest because workers' earnings did not keep pace with the rise in prices and with their aspirations. The establishment of International Labour Organisation (ILO) in 1919 greatly influenced the labour legislation and industrial relations policy in India. The emergence of trade unions in India, particularly the formation of All India Trade Union Congress (AITUC) in 1920 was another significant event in the history of industrial relations in our country.

Second Phase

The policy after the First World War related to improvement in the working conditions and provision of social security benefits. During the two decades following the war, a number of laws were enacted for the implementation of the above policy. The Trade Disputes Act, 1929 sought to provide a conciliation machinery to bring about peaceful settlement of disputes.

The Second World War gave a new spurt in the labour field. The exigencies of the war made it essential for the government to maintain an adequately contented labour force for maximising production. The Government of India had, therefore, to step in and assume wide powers of controlling and regulating the conditions of work and welfare of industrial workers. It embarked upon a two-fold action in this regard, namely, (i) statutory regulation of industrial relations through the Defence of India rules and the orders made thereunder; and (ii) bringing all the interests together at a common forum for shaping labour policy.

Tripartite consultative system was one of the most important developments in the sphere of industrial relations in our country. Tripartite consultation epitomises the faith of India in the ILO's philosophy and objectives. The Royal Commission on Labour recommended the need for tripartite labour machinery on the pattern of ILO as early as 1931. The conference consisted of two organisations, namely, the Indian Labour Conference (ILC) and the Standing Labour Committee (SLC). In the state sphere, State Labour Advisory Boards were also set up for consultation on labour matters. Gradually, tripartism developed into a full-fledged system, a kind of parliament for labour and management. The objectives set before the two tripartite bodies at the time of their inception in 1942 were: (a) promotion of uniformity in labour legislation; (b) laying down of a procedure for the settlement of industrial disputes; and (c) discussion of all matters of All-India importance as between employers and employees. They facilitated enactment of central legislation and enabled discussion on all labour matters of national importance. Different social, economic and administrative matters concerning labour policies and programmes were discussed in the various meetings of ILC/SLC.

Third Phase

After independence, an Industrial Truce Resolution was adopted in

1947 at a tripartite conference. The conference emphasised the need for respecting the mutuality of interests between labour and capital. It recommended to the parties the method of mutual discussion of all problems common to both, and settle all disputes without recourse to interruption in or slowing down of production. The post-independence period of industrial relations policy aimed at the establishment of peace in industry, and grant of a fair deal to workers. The government sought to achieve these aims through appropriate labour legislation, labour administration, and industrial adjudication. State intervention in industrial relations was justified on the ground that it helped to check the growth of industrial unrest. Since 1958 a new approach was introduced to counteract the unhealthy trends of litigation and delays in adjudication. Its emphasis was based on the principles of industrial democracy, on prevention of unrest by timely action at the appropriate stages, and giving of adequate attention to root causes of industrial unrest.

While the groundwork of labour policy was prepared during the forties, a superstructure on this groundwork was built in the fifties. It is the Constitution of India and the five-year plans, which largely helped in raising the superstructure. The Preamble to the Constitution and the chapter on Directive Principles of State Policy enunciate the elements of labour policy. The successive five-year plans since 1951 clearly enunciated the directions of industrial relations policy.

A brief account of the industrial relations policy during five-year plans is given below: The approach to labour problems in the First Five-Year Plan (1951-56) was based on considerations which were related, on the one hand, "to the requirements of the wellbeing of the working class", and on the other, "to its vital contribution to the economic stability and progress of the country." It considered the worker as "the principal instrument in the fulfilment of the targets of the Plan and in the achievement of economic progress. Further, the Plan stated that harmonious relations between capital and labour are essential for the realisation of the Plan in the industrial sector.

Much of what had been said in regard to industrial relations in the First Plan was reiterated in the Second Five-Year Plan (1956-61). The Second Plan considered a strong trade union movement to be necessary both for safeguarding the interests of labour and for realising the targets of production. Multiplicity of trade unions, political rivalries, lack of resources, and disunity in the ranks of workers were, according to the Plan document, some of the major weaknesses in a number of existing unions. It also emphasised on the increased association of labour with management.

The Third Five-Year Plan (1961-66) expressed great hopes in the voluntary approach initiated during the Second Plan period to give a more positive orientation to industrial relations, based on moral rather than legal sanctions. The Plan highlighted the need for increasing application of the principle of voluntary arbitration in resolving differences between workers and employers and reccmmended that the government should take the initiative in drawing up panels of arbitrators on a regional and industry-wise basis. Further, the Plan recommended that the works committees should be strengthened and made an active agency for the democratic administration of labour matters. The Fourth Five-Year Plan (1969-74) suggested no changes in the system of regulating labour relations by legislative and voluntary arrangements started from earlier plans. It also laid stress on strengthening labour administration for better enforcement of labour laws, research in labour laws, and expansion of training programmes for labour officers.

The Fifth Five-Year Plan (1974-79) laid great emphasis on employment, both in rural and urban sectors. After the promulgation of emergency in June 1975, the government devised a new pattern of bipartite consultative process in an attempt to create a climate of healthy industrial relations, leading to increased production, by eschewing lay-offs, retrenchments, closures, strikes and lockouts. The new machinery sought to formulate policies at the national, state, and industry levels for the speedy resolution of industrial conflicts and for promoting industrial harmony. During the emergency, the Government of India through a resolution adopted a scheme of workers' participation in industry at shop and plant levels on 30th October, 1975. According to the sixth Five-Year Plan (1980-85), strikes and lockouts should be resorted to only in the last stage. Effective arrangements should also be made for the settlement of inter-union disputes and to discourage unfair practices and irresponsible conduct. While suggesting the growth of trade unions on healthy lines, the Plan stressed on their social obligations and roles in many areas of nation building activities and in improving the quality of life of workers.

The thrust of the Seventh Five-Year Plan (1986-91) is on improvement in capacity utilisation, efficiency and productivity. The Plan states that a sound policy of tackling industrial sickness in future has to be evolved which while protecting the interests of labour would also take into account the fact that Government cannot bear the huge burden of losses. In the proper management of industrial relations the responsibility of unions and employees has to be identified and inter-union rivalry and intra-union divisions should be avoided.

According to the Eighth Five-Year Plan (1992-97), labour participation in management is a means of bringing about a state of industrial democracy. Ever since independence, the government has been stressing the need to introduce workers' participation in management and various schemes were notified from time to time. However, the results have fallen far short of expectations. The need to bring forward a suitable legislation for effective implementation of the scheme has been felt.

According to the Ninth Five-Year Plan (1997-2002), the planning process attempts to create conditions for improvement in labour productivity and for provision of social security to supplement the operations of the labour market. The resources have been directed through the plan programmes towards skill formation and development, exchange of information on job opportunities, monitoring of working conditions, creation of industrial harmony, and insurance against disease and unemployment for the workers and their families. The planning commission observed that the situation of surplus labour, coupled with the employment of most of the workers in the unorganised segments of the economy, has given rise to unhealthy social practices like bonded labour, child labour, and adverse working conditions faced by the migrant labour.

Government's Role

The main issue in regard to the government's role in industrial relations is the degree of state intervention. In India, particularly after independence, the government has been playing a comprehensive and dominant role in shaping the pattern of industrial relations. In the mixed economy of our country, the state has emerged as a big employer. It accepts the responsibility of ensuring conformity to these norms through the administrative and judicial mechanism. It enacts legislation on labour and implements both the substantive and procedural laws.

The industrial relations policy of the government forms part of the broader labour policy. The tenets of this policy, as stated by the National Commission on Labour, are:

(i) primacy to the maintenance of industrial peace;
(ii) encouragement for mutual settlement of disputes through collective bargaining and voluntary arbitration;
(iii) recognition of the workers' right to peaceful direct action, i.e., strike; and
(iv) tripartite consultation.

The state intervention primarily aims at preserving industrial peace and has, therefore, focused attention on: (a) the avoidance of industriai disputes; and (b) the expeditious settlement of industrial disputes when they do arise.

Current Developments

The current developments in the field of industrial relations are basically related to structural changes, acquisitions and mergers, globalisation, liberalisation, and technological changes.

Structural Changes

The main aspects of the structural changes having an impact on the industrial relations system in the country could be mentioned as:

i) Production reorganisation or decentralised production making a 'thin organised sector employment more thinner. The large-sized units shifted to flatter structures and opted for decentralised decision-making. These units reorganised their production by trimming their size and carrying out production in multiple units or by externalising their production. These measures of economic reforms have distinctly affected the industrial relations system in the country as it has limited its institutions and practices to the formal organised sector in the large-sized units.

ii) Globalisation and technological changes proved disruptive for the system in terms of displacement of labour, i.e., job losses, destabilising the wage structure, and a shift in skill/occupation composition of labour.

iii) Ascendancy in managerial rights and the weakening of trade unions gave greater flexibility to management in utilisation of labour and in handling industrial conflict.

Mergers and Acquisitions

In merger, two or more existing companies go into liquidation and a new company is formed to takeover their business. An acquisition arises when there is a purchase by one company of the whole or part of the shares, or the whole or part of the assets, of another company in consideration for payment in cash or by issue of shares or other securities in the acquiring company or partly in one form and partly in the other.

The concept of mergers and acquisitions is very much popular in the current economic scenario. More so, it is a significantly popular concept after 1990s in India on the birth of economic liberalisation and globalisation. The basic premises for mergers and acquisitions are the consolidation process for survival of existing undertakings, and large groups absorbing the small entities.

A series of personnel problems normally occur when one company acquires another. People aspect is very important in the process of acquisition. The communications framework is the most important factor for smooth integration in an acquisition. With effective communication, the acquiring company can develop a climate of confidence and, hopefully, eliminate much of the friction, which frequently occurs. The labour relations considerations when one company acquires another are union relations history, representation of employees in unions, history of work stoppages, strikes and lockouts, grievance settlement, collective bargaining and signing of agreements and settlements.

Globalisation

Globalisation can be conceptually explained as the process of economic or commercial integration of a company or a country with the rest of the world. The magnitude of such integration will determine the extent of globalisation accomplished by the company or the country as the case may be. It is important to note that globalisation is not an 'event' but a 'process.'

Some segments of the labour force have suffered from the direct and indirect effects of globalisation more than others. Increased trade and increased competition have led to job losses in the advanced economies, probably not too many in aggregate terms but concentrated in low-skilled labour intensive industries with high labour costs.

In the process of globalisation the power of trade unions, as measured by trade-union density, has declined almost everywhere around the world, in developed as well as in developing countries. Evidently, some other factors have contributed to the evolution of trade union membership such as the demise of state socialism in Central and Eastern Europe, the process of economic restructuring, and the shift from manufacturing to service employment. Only some developing countries have benefited from globalisation. In many countries, including the advanced economies, income inequality and poverty has grown considerably.

Technological Changes

The interrelationship between technological change and industrial relations time and again has been the focus of attention of groups in society. Technology has an impact on labour management issues such as manpower, job security, and training redundancy. All the three parties in industrial relations are closely concerned with the effects of technology. Technological change raises sensitive industrial relations issues, especially where it involves work intensification, rationalisation or reductions in employment. Industrial relations issues, especially relating to employment levels and work organisation, were seen as important in deciding upon new plant, machinery or equipment. The first category consists of redundancy, occupational adjustment, allocation of gains, and transfer and retraining problems. The second category includes psychological factors such as resistance to change, job satisfaction, and worker and union relations.

Privatisation

Privatisation is one of the major elements of structural adjustment process taking place in different parts of the world. It involves complex social and labour issues. Apprehensions about privatisation concern potential loss of present and future jobs. The trade unions are concerned about privatisation due to fears about job loss and potential adverse effects on the dynamics of trade unions and their rights.

Industrial Relations Scenario

The Second National Commission on Labour 2002 has made the following observations about the industrial relations scenario in India:

1) It is increasingly noticed that trade unions do not normally give a call for strike because they are afraid that a strike may lead to the closure of the unit.
2) Service sector workers feel they have become outsiders and are becoming increasingly disinterested in trade union activities.
3) There is a trend to resolve major disputes through negotiations at bipartite level.

   The nature of disputes or demands is changing. Instead of demanding higher wages, allowances or facilities, trade unions now demand job security and some are even willing to accept wage cuts or wage freezes in return for job protection.
4) The attitude of the Government, especially of the Central Government, towards workers and employers seems to have undergone a change. Now, permissions for closure or retrenchment are more easily granted.
5) The conciliation machinery is more eager to consider problems of employers and today consider issues like increase in productivity, cost reduction, financial difficulties of the employer, competition, market fluctuations, etc.
6) The industrial relations machinery is not pursuing seriously the recovery proceedings against employers who could not pay heavy dues of workers, if the financial position of the employer is very bad.

7) The labour adjudication machinery is more willing to entertain the concerns of industry.

Issues and Challenges

The foremost issue for the industrial relations system in India is that it has come under pressure to adapt to the new environment that has emerged after the introduction of structural changes envisaged under economic reforms. Under the impact of restructuring process, the large-sized firms are downsizing their activities and shifting their production to other smaller allied units. As such, the employment in the organised sector is shrinking and the major share of additional employment is being generated in the unorganised sector than in the organised sector. In a decentralised sector of small and medium sized units and the enterprises in the services sector and high-tech segment there is a wide differential in wage determination and benefits across the industries. Along with the wide dispersion of wages and other benefits, the other feature of this decentralised sector is the unemployment/job insecurity. The traditional industrial relations system and its institutions and practices were most suited to the tasks of protecting and promoting the interests of workers with secure permanent employment. The challenge for the industrial relations system lies in whether the new system can provide for any alternative to the traditional system.

REFERENCES

Government of India, 2002. *The Report of the Second National Commission on Labour*.

Mamoria, C.B., and Ganakar, S.B., 2000. *Dynamics of Industrial Relations*, Himalaya Publishing House, Mumbai.

Margerison, C.J., 1969. "What do we mean by industrial relations? A behavioural approach", *British Journal of Industrial Relations*, Vol. 7, No. 2,.

Salamon, Michael, 1998. *Industrial Relations Theory and Practice (3rd ed.)*, Prentice Hall.

6

Theories of Employment Relations

Employment relations constitute one of the most delicate and complex problems of the modern industrial society that is characterised by rapid change, industrial unrest and conflicting ideologies in the national and international spheres. It is a dynamic concept that depends upon the pattern of the society, economic system and political set-up of a country and changes with the changing economic and social order. It is an art of living together for the purposes of production, productive efficiency, human well-being and industrial progress. It comprises of a network of institutions, such as, trade unionism, collective bargaining, employers, the law, and the state, which are bound together by a set of common values and aspirations. These institutions are a social network of organisations, participants, processes and decisions: all of which interact and inter-relate together within the industrial relations environment and even beyond it.

There is no unanimity on the meaning and scope of industrial relations since different terms, such as labour-management relations, employer-employee relations, unionmanagement relations, personnel relations, human relations, are in use and are used synonymously. In its stricter sense, the term "industrial relations" means relationship between management and workmen in a unit or an industry. Dale Yoder defines it as a "whole field of relationship that exists because of the necessary collaboration of men and women in the employment process of an industry."

According to Allan Flanders, "the subject of industrial relations deals with certain regulated or institutionalised relationships in industry. Personal or in the language of sociology, "unstructured" relationships have their importance for management and workers, but they lie outside the scope of a system of industrial relations."

Professor Clegg defines industrial relations in the broadest terms as encompassing the rules governing employment together with the ways in which the rules are made and changed and their interpretation and administration."

To put it simply, industrial relations is that part of management which is concerned with the manpower of the enterprise. It is, thus, the relation created at different levels of the organisation by the diverse, complex and composite needs and aspirations and attitudes and approaches among the participants. In an organisation, these relationships may be personal and informal at one end, and may be highly institutional with legally prescribed structures and procedures, at the other end.

The four main parties who are actively associated with any industrial relations system are the workers, the managements, the organisations of workers and managements, and the State. Fundamentally, the term industrial relations refers to an organised relationship between two organised parties representing employers and employees regarding matters of collective interest. With the growth of professional management, the industrial relations scene is being represented by the representatives of both the employers and the employees. But the scope of industrial relations cannot merely be confined to common labour-management relations or employer-employee relations. It is a comprehensive and total concept embracing the sum total of relationships that exists at various levels of the organisational structure. More specifically, it connotes relations among workers themselves within the class of employees, relations among the managements within the managerial class, and relations between the two distinct classes of workers and management. It denotes all types of inter-group and intragroup relations within industry, both formal and informal. It consists of a complex network of relations that arise out of functional interdependence between workers and managements and between industrial organisations and society. The advances made in the field of science and technology also influence the state of industrial relations. There is greater divergence in industrial relations systems as a result of the divergent economic, social, political and cultural environments.

OBJECTIVES OF INDUSTRIAL RELATIONS

Apart from the primary objective of bringing about sound and healthy relations between employers and employees, industrial relations aim:

i) to facilitate production and productivity;

ii) to safeguard the rights and interests of both labour and management by enlisting their co-operation;

iii) to achieve a sound, harmonious, and mutually beneficial labour management relations;

iv) to avoid unhealthy atmosphere in the industry, especially work, stoppages, goslows, gheraos, strikes, lockouts; and

v) to establish and maintain industrial democracy.

The state endeavours to correct, through effective industrial relations, an imbalanced, disordered and maladjusted social and economic order with a view to reshaping the complex socio-economic relationships following technological and economic progress. It also controls and disciplines the parties concerned and adjusts their conflicting interests. In this process, it protects some and restrains others, depending upon the situation.

According to Kirkaldy, industrial relations in a country are intimately connected with the form of its political government; and the objectives of an industrial organisation may vary from purely economic to purely political ends. He divides the objectives of industrial relations into four categories:

i) improvement in the economic conditions of workers in the existing state of industrial management and political government;

ii) control exercised by the state over industrial undertakings with a view to regulating production and promoting harmonious industrial relations;

iii) socialisation or rationalisation of industries by making the state itself a major employer; and

iv) vesting of a proprietary interest of the workers in the industries in which they are employed.

The industrial relations objectives must follow the determination of business objectives which they should be intended to facilitate. In this context, the industrial relations policies and practices should not negate its intentions in other areas.

Approaches in Industrial Relations

The problems posed in the field of industrial relations cannot be solved within the limits of a single discipline, and hence it is bound to be inter-disciplinary in approach. It is an interdisciplinary field that includes inputs from sociology, psychology, law, history, politics, economics, accounting and other elements of management studies. Industrial relations, then, has a dual character, it is both an interdisciplinary field and a separate discipline in its own right. It is much more of an art than it is a science. Industrial relations is largely an applied field concerned with practice and the training of practitioners rather than with theory and measurement.

Any problem in industrial relations has to be approached on a multi-disciplinary basis, drawing from the contributions of the above disciplines. The causes of an industrial dispute may be, by nature, economic, social, psychological or political or a combination of any of them. Labour economics provides an economic interpretation of the problems growing out of employer-employee relationship. For instance, attitudes and morale surveys are powerful tools to discover causes of industrial strife and to evolve methods for their prevention. Labour laws and their interpretation by tribunals and courts contributes to the growth of industrial jurisprudence. Political aspects also assume importance in industrial relations, particularly in a developing economy dominated by centralised planning. In fact, the growth of industrial relations as a scientific discipline depends upon the extent to which it integrates the contribution of established disciplines in the social sciences.

There is no country where industrial relations is entirely a matter of tradition or custom nor is there a country where the employers, the workers or their organisations and the government do not at all interact to build up the country's industrial relations system. It has been a mixture of traditions, customs and a web of action, reaction and interaction between the parties. The concept of the system has been influential in establishing industrial relations as a discipline in its own right. The concepts of the system approach are operationally definable.

An industrial relations system may be defined as comprising the totality of power interactions of participants in a workplace, when these interactions involve industrial relations issues. An industrial relations system includes all the individuals and institutions that interact at the workplace. Regardless of the level at which the system exists, an industrial relations system can be viewed as having three components: (1) a set of individuals and institutions that interact; (2) a context within which the interaction takes place; and (3) an output that serves to govern the future relationship of the parties. The components of industrial relations system are:

i) *Participants:* The participants in the industrial relations sphere are composed of duly recognised representatives of the parties interacting in several roles within the system.
ii) *Issues:* The power interactions of the participants in a workplace create industrial relations issues.
iii) *Structure:* The structure consists of all forms of institutionalised behaviour in a system. The structure may include collective procedures, grievances, and settlement practices.
iv) *Boundaries:* In systems analysis, it is possible to find an issue which one participant is totally indifferent to resolving while, at the same time, the other participant is highly concerned about resolution of the same.

At least there are three marked features of the systems approach. They are:

i) *Inter-disciplinary Character:* Some theorists regard the systems approach to be universally applicable to all human relationships, in small or large units.
ii) *Suitability to Work Organisation and their Sub-systems:* The adaptability of the systems approach to organisation is also a frequently discussed trait.
iii) *Dynamic sspects:* A systems approach is oriented towards the study of interactions and changing relations.

Based on various components and features of industrial relations, a number of writers have attempted to produce various functional approaches to industrial relations, which are given below:

Dunlop's Approach

Among the contributions, the most outstanding has been that of Prof. John T. Dunlop of Harvard University. His systems treatment deserves special mention in view of its wider applicability. His book *Industrial Relations Systems* was a pioneering volume in which he presented an analytical framework of industrial relations.

An industrial relations system at any one time in its development is regarded as comprised of certain actors, certain contexts, an ideology, which binds the industrial relations system together, and a body of rules created to govern the actors at the workplace and work community. There are three sets of independent variables: the 'actors', the 'contexts' and the 'ideology' of the system. The principal groups identifiable in the system and which constitutes the structure of an industrial relations system are as follows:

The actors in a system: The actors are: (a) hierarchy of managers and their representatives in supervision, (b) a hierarchy of workers and any spokesmen, and (c) specialised governmental agencies concerned with workers, enterprises, and their relationships. These first two hierarchies are directly related to each other in that the managers have responsibilities at varying levels to issue instructions and the workers at each corresponding level have the duty to follow such instructions. The hierarchy of managers need have no relationship to the ownership of the capital assets of the workplace, the managers may be public or private or a mixture in varying proportions. The formal hierarchy of workers may be organised into several competing or complementary organisations, such as, works councils, unions, and parties. In other industrial relations systems, the role of the specialised governmental agencies, at least for many purposes, may be minor or constricted.

The contexts of a system: In an industrial relations system, the contexts or the determinants are of greater importance. The significant aspects of the environment in which the actors interact are the technological characteristics of the workplace and work community, the market or budgetary constraints that impinge on the actors, and the locus and distribution of power in the larger society.

The technological features of the workplace have a very far-reaching consequence for an industrial relations system influencing the form of management and employee organisation, the problems posed for supervision, many of the features of the required labour force and the potentialities of public regulation. For instance, the mining industry has a different technological context as compared to the manufacturing industry. Their place of work, the methods of work, and the mode of living, have profound influence on evolving a particular pattern of industrial relations system. Historically, this raises a range of questions concerning housing, community services and welfare activities which are frequently beyond the rules of workplace in many other sectors. Apart from the characteristics of the workplace, the development of technology also affects industrial relations by way of not only disturbing the existing employment patterns, but also by determining the size of the work force employed.

The market or budgetary constraints are a second feature of the environmental context, which is fundamental to an industrial relations system. These constraints often operate, in the first instance, directly upon the managerial hierarchy, but they necessarily condition all the actors in a particular system. The context may be a market for the output of the enterprise or a budgetary limitation or some combination of the two. The product market may vary in the degree and character of competition through the full spectrum from pure competition, monopolistic competition, to oligopoly and monopoly. The relevant market or budgetary constraints may be local, national, or international, depending on the industrial relations system. The locus and distribution of power in the larger society, of which the particular industrial relations complex is a sub-system, is a third analytical feature of the environmental context. At this juncture, the concern is not with the distribution of power within the industrial relations system, but also outside the system. The function of one of the actors in the industrial relations system, the specialised governmental agencies, is likely to be particularly influenced by the distribution of power in the larger society.

The ideology of an industrial relations system: The ideology is a philosophy or a systematised body of beliefs and sentiments held by the actors. An important element that completes the analytical system of industrial relations is the ideology or a set of ideas and beliefs commonly held by the actors that helps to bind or to integrate the system together as an entity. Each industrial relations system contains its ideology or shared understandings. The ideology defines the role and place of each actor and the ideas, which each actor holds towards the place and function of the others in the system. An industrial relations system requires that these ideologies be sufficiently compatible and consistent so as to permit a common set of ideas and an acceptable role for each actor.

The establishment of rules: The actors in a given context establish rules for the workplace and the work community, including those governing contracts among the actors in an industrial relations system. This network or web of rules consists of procedures for establishing rules, the substantive rules, and procedures for deciding their application to particular situations. Thus, the establishment and administration of these rules is the major concern or output of the industrial relations system. The actors who set the web of rules interact in the context of an industrial relations system taken as a whole. These rules are broadly grouped into three categories: (i) rules governing compensation in all its forms; (ii) the duties and performance expected from workers, including rules of discipline for failure to achieve these standards; and (iii) rules defining the rights and duties of workers. The rules change in response to change in the contexts and relative status of the actors.

Oxford Approach

According to this approach, the industrial relations system is a study of institutions of job regulations and the stress is on the substantive and procedural rules as in Dunlop's model. Flanders, the exponent of this approach, considers every business enterprise as a social system of production and distribution, which has a structured pattern of relationships. The "institution of job regulation" is categorised by him as internal and external – the former being an internal part of the industrial relations system such as code of work rules, wage structure, internal procedure of joint consultation, and grievance procedure. According to him, collective bargaining is central to the industrial relations system.

The "Oxford Approach" can be expressed in the form of an equation:

$$r = f(b) \text{ or } r = f(c)$$

where, r = the rules governing industrial relations

b = collective bargaining

c = conflict resolved through collective bargaining.

The "Oxford Approach" can be criticised on the ground that it is too narrow to provide a comprehensive framework for analysing industrial relations problems. It overemphasises the significance of the political process of collective bargaining and gives insufficient weight to the role of the deeper influences in the determination of rules.This narrowness of approach constitutes a severe limitation.

Industrial Sociology Approach

G. Margerison, an industrial sociologist, holds the view that the core of industrial relations is the nature and development of the conflict itself. Margerison argued that conflict is the basic concept that should form the basis of the study of industrial relations. The author criticised the prevalent approach to industrial relations, which was more concerned with studying the resolution of industrial conflict than its generation; with the consequences of industrial disputes than on their causes. According to this school of thought, there are two major conceptual levels of industrial relations. One is the intra-plant level where situational factors, such as job content, work task and technology, and interaction factors produce three types of conflict – distributive, structural, and human relations. The second level is outside the firm and, in the main, concerns with the conflict not resolved at the intraorganisational level. However, this approach rejects the special emphasis given to rule determination by the "systems and Oxford models".

The Action Theory Approach

Like the systems model, the action theory approach takes the collective regulation of industrial labour as its focal point. The actors operate within a framework, which can at best be described as a coalition relationship. The actors, it is claimed, agree in principle to cooperate in the resolution of the conflict, their cooperation taking the form of bargaining. Whereas the systems model of industrial relations constitutes a more or less comprehensive approach, it is hardly possible to speak of one uniform action theory concept.

Marxist Approach

The class conflict analysis of industrial relations derives its impetus from Marxist social thinking and interpretation. Marxism is essentially a method of social enquiry into the power relationships of society and a way of interpreting social reality. The application of Marxian theory as it relates to industrial relations derives indirectly from later Marxist scholars rather than directly from the works of Marx himself. Industrial relations, according to Marxists, are in the first instance, market-relations. To Marxists, industrial relations are essentially politicised and part of the class struggle. As Marx himself put it, "the mode of production in material life determines the general character of the social, political and spiritual process of life."

The Marxist approach is primarily oriented towards the historical development of the power relationship between capital and labour. It is also characterised by the struggle of these classes to consolidate and strengthen their respective positions with a view to exerting greater influence on each other. In this approach, industrial relations is equated with a power-struggle. The price payable for labour is determined by a confrontation between conflicting interests. The lower the price paid by the owner of the means of production for the labour he employs, the greater is his profit. The Marxist analysis of industrial relations, however, is not a comprehensive approach as it only takes into account the relations between capital and labour.

Pluralist Approach

Pluralism is a major theory in labour-management relations, which has many powerful advocates. The focus is on the resolution of conflict rather than its generation, or, in the words of the pluralist, on 'the institutions of job regulation.' Kerr is one of the important exponents of pluralism. According to him, the social environment is an important factor in industrial conflicts. The isolated masses of workers are more strike-prone as compared to dispersed groups. When industrial jobs become more pleasant and employees' get more integrated into the wider society, strikes will become less frequent. They claim that there has been a decline in strike activity all over the world in spite of an increase in union membership.

The theories on pluralism were evolved in the mid-sixties and early seventies when England witnessed a dramatic resurgence of industrial conflicts. However, the recent theories of pluralism emanate from British scholars, and in particular from Flanders and Fox. According to Flanders, conflict is inherent in the industrial system. He highlighted the need for a formal system of collective bargaining as a method of conflict resolution. Fox distinguishes between two distinct aspects of relationship between workers and management. The first is the market relationship, which concerns with the terms and conditions on which labour is hired. This relationship is essentially economic in character and based on contracts executed between the parties. The second aspect relates to the management's dealing with labour, the nature of their interaction, negotiations between the union and management, distribution of power in the organisation, and participation of the union in joint decision-making. The only difference is that in such a social structure, the worker will be deemed to be a better-paid wage slave.

Social action Approach

The social action approach of Weber has laid considerable importance to the question of control in the context of increasing rationalisation and bureaucratisation. Closely related to Weber's concern related to control in organisations was his concern with "power of control and dispersal". Thus a trade union in the Weber's scheme of things has both economic purposes as well as the goal of involvement in political and power struggles. Some of the major orientations in the Weberian approach have been to analyse the impact of techno-economic and politico-organisational changes on trade union structure and processes, to analyse the subjective interpretation of workers' approaches to trade unionism and finally to analyse the power of various components of the industrial relations environment – government, employers, trade unions and political parties.

Human Relations Approach

In the words of Keith Davies, human relations are "the integration of people into a work situation that motivates them to work together productively, cooperatively and with economic, psychological and social satisfactions." According to him, the goals of human relations are: (a) to get people to produce, (b) to cooperate through mutuality of interest, and (c) to gain satisfaction from their relationships. The human relations school founded by Elton Mayo and later propagated by Roethlisberger, Whitehead, W.F. Whyte, and Homans offers a coherent view of the nature of industrial conflict and harmony.

The human relations approach highlights certain policies and techniques to improve employee morale, efficiency and job satisfaction. It encourages the small work group to exercise considerable control over its environment and in the process helps to remove a major irritant in labour-management relations. However, Some of its views were criticised by Marxists, pluralists, and others on the ground that it encouraged dependency and discouraged individual development, and ignored the importance of technology and culture in industry. Taking a balanced view, however, it must be admitted that the human relations school has thrown a lot of light on certain aspects such as communication, management development, acceptance of workplace as a social system, group dynamics, and participation in management.

Gandhian Approach

Gandhiji can be called one of the greatest labour leaders of modern India. His approach to labour problems was completely new and refreshingly human. He held definite views regarding fixation and regulation of wages, organisation and functions of trade unions, necessity and desirability of collective bargaining, use and abuse of strikes, labour indiscipline, workers participation in management, conditions of work and living, and duties of workers.

Gandhiji had immense faith in the goodness of man and he believed that many of the evils of the modern world have been brought about by wrong systems and not by wrong individuals. He insisted on recognising each individual worker as a human being. He believed in non-violent communism, going so far as to say that "if communism comes without any violence, it would be welcome." Gandhiji laid down certain conditions for a successful strike. These are: (a) the cause of the strike must be just and there should be no strike without a grievance; (b) there should be no violence; and (c) non-strikers or "blacklegs" should never be molested. He was not against strikes but pleaded that they should be the last weapon in the armoury of industrial workers and hence should not be resorted to unless all peaceful and constitutional methods of negotiations, conciliation and arbitration are exhausted. His concept of trusteeship is a significant contribution in the sphere of industrial relations. They should regard themselves only as trustees, or co-owners. He also appealed to the workers to behave as trustees, not to regard the mill and machinery as belonging to the exploiting agents but to regard them as their own, protect them and put to the best use they can. In short, the theory of trusteeship is based on the view that all forms of property and human accomplishments are gifts of nature and as such, they belong not to any one individual but to society. It aimed at achieving economic equality and the material advancement of the "have-nots" in a capitalist society by non-violent means.

Gandhiji realised that relations between labour and management can either be a powerful stimulus to economic and social progress or an important factor in economic and social stagnation. According to him, industrial peace was an essential condition not only for the growth and development of the industry itself, but also in a great measure, for the improvement in the conditions of work and wages. At the same time, he not only endorsed the workers' right to adopt the method of collective bargaining but also actively supported it.

Human Resource Management Approach

The term, human resource management (HRM) has become increasingly used in the literature of personnel/industrial relations. The term has been applied to a diverse range of management strategies and, indeed, sometimes used simply as a more modern, and therefore more acceptable, term for personnel or industrial relations management. Some of the components of HRM are: (i) human resource organisation; (ii) human resource planning; (iii) human resource systems; (iv) human resource development; (v) human resource relationships; (vi) human resource utilisation; (vii) human resource accounting; and (viii) human resource audit. This approach emphasises individualism and the direct relationship between management and its employees.

MODELS AND THEORIES

The subject of industrial relations has undergone several changes because of vital contributions made by a number of disciplines. In developing theoretical models of industrial relations, it becomes necessary to appreciate the contributions made by various social scientists. Such models can be used for analysing concrete situations and to build a systematic and comprehensive theory of industrial relations. The different perspectives and theories enable us to understand industrial relations institutions, structures, processes and behaviour of individuals.

Basically, there are two main stands in theorising industrial relations. One group (externalists) lays emphasis on external factors like state of technology, methods of production, supply and demand in the product market and in the labour market, legalpolitical relationships, and so on. The environmental theorists have been primarily economists and to a smaller extent, lawyers, political scientists, and sociologists. The in-plant theories of internalists have their origin in the "human relations school" propounded by Elton Mayo and others. These theorists stress on employee motivation, attitude and morale, styles of supervision, and forms of management leadership.

A.W.J. Craig presented the input-output model of industrial relations system in the late 1960s. In his model, the actors and the context are similar to those of Dunlop's model. The main component of Craig's model are: (a) the inputs or the goals, and the values and power of the actors; (b) mechanism for the conversion of inputs into outputs; (c) the outputs of the system are the financial, psychological and social rewards for the workers.

One of the major objectives of theorising industrial relations is to help the practitioners to understand what is taking place and causes for the same. Industrial relations theory might be useful to practitioners if it could help them in three respects: first, to understand the present industrial relations situation; second, to forecast trends and to predict what will happen under specific given conditions; and third, to help the practitioners to bring about certain desired changes and to avoid certain other changes in the present or in the future state of industrial relations. One of the most difficult attempts in industrial relations is to build up a theory and to generalise on its activity, which is highly dynamic. The industrial relations system in an organisation works in the context of pressures, tensions and conflicts, and is mainly related to power politics, economic, cultural and other differences. An inter-mix of such dynamic factors, and key institutional variables, is necessary in theorising industrial relations.

References

Clegg H.A. 1960. *A New Approach to Industrial Democracy.* Blackwell, oxford..

Frenkel, S and Royal, C. 1996: *Globalization and Employment Relations*. Paper prepared for ILO/EASMAT, Bangkok; published under authorization as Centre for Corporate Change Paper No 63, University of New South Wales, Sydney.

Otto Kahn - Freund 1969. "Industrial Relations and the Law - Retrospect and Prospect". Vol. 7 *British Journal Of Industrial Relations*.

Roscoe Pound . 1921. "A Theory of Social Interests" in *Papers And Proceedings of the American Sociological Society*, May.

7

Labour Laws and Employment Relations

The Constitution of India has guaranteed some fundamental rights to the citisens and has also laid down certain directive principles of state policy for the achievement of a social order based on justice, liberty, equality and fraternity. The Constitution amply provides for the upliftment of labour by guaranteeing certain fundamental rights to all. Article 14 lays down that the State shall not deny to any person equality before the law or the equal protection of laws. The directive principles, though not enforceable by any court, are nevertheless fundamental in the governance of the country, and it shall be the duty of the State to apply those principles in making laws from time to time. The Government of India, therefore, enacted a series of legislations to protect the working class from exploitation and to bring about improvement in their working and living conditions. The goals set in our country by the Constitution have a bearing on industrial legislation and adjudication.

Constitutional Framework

Labour is in the concurrent list of the Constitution on which both the Centre as well as the States have the power to make laws. Article 254 has been enacted to clarify the position. Normally, as laid down in Clause (1), in case of any repugnancy between the Union and the State legislation, the legislation of the Union shall prevail. Articles 39, 41, 42 and 43 have a special relevance in the field of industrial legislation and adjudication. In fact, they are the substratum of industrial jurisprudence. Article 39 provides a motivation force to the directive principles by laying down that the State shall direct its policy towards equal pay for both men and women.

Article 41 lays down that the State shall, within the limits of its economic capacity and development, make effective provision for securing the right to work, to education and to public assistance in cases of unemployment, old age, sickness and disablement, and in other cases of undeserved want.

Article 42 enjoins the state government to make provision for securing just and humane conditions of work and for maternity relief.

Article 43 makes it obligatory for the State to secure by suitable legislation or economic organisation or in any other manner to all workers, agricultural, industrial, or otherwise, work, a living wage, conditions of work ensuring a decent standard of life and full enjoyment of leisure and social and cultural opportunities. Article 43-A makes it obligatory on the State to take steps by suitable legislation or otherwise to secure the participation of workers in the management of undertakings and industrial establishments. The Employees' State Insurance Act, 1948 is a pioneering piece of legislation in the field of social insurance. The Employees' State Insurance Scheme provides for benefits in cash except the medical benefit, which is in kind. The Employees' Provident Funds and Miscellaneous Provisions Act, 1952 and the Maternity Benefit Act, 1961 are also social security measures to help fulfill the objectives of directive principles of our Constitution. The Maternity Benefit Scheme is primarily designed to provide maternity leave with full wages and security of employment. The object of the Payment of Gratuity Act, 1972 is to provide a scheme for the payment of gratuity to employees employed in factories, mines, oil fields, plantations, ports, railways, shops and establishments. Besides social security benefits, efforts have also been made to provide ample opportunities for employment and for workers' education. The Apprentices Act, 1961 was enacted to supplement the programme of institutional training by on-the-job training and to regulate the training arrangements in industry. Employment exchanges play an important role for the job seekers. The Employment Exchanges Act, 1969 has made it obligatory on the employers to notify vacancies occurring in their establishments to the prescribed employment exchanges before they are filled.

Substantial steps have been taken to fulfill the object of Article 42 of the Constitution. The Factories Act, 1948 provides for health, safety, welfare, employment of young persons and women, hours of work for adults and children, holidays and leave with wages. Labour welfare funds have been set-up to provide welfare facilities to the workers employed in different mines such as coal, mica, iron ore and limestone. The Contract Labour Act of 1970, a piece of social legislation, provides for the abolition of contract labour wherever possible and to regulate the conditions of contract labour in establishments or employments where the abolition of contract labour system is not considered feasible for the time being. Article 43 of the Constitution provides for a living wage.It provides for the fixation of minimum rates of wages by the central or state governments within a specified period for workers employed in certain scheduled employments.

Impact of ILO on Industrial Relations

The International Labour Organisation (ILO) was set-up in 1919 by the Versailles Peace Conference as an autonomous body associated with the League of Nations. It became the first specialised agency of the United Nations in 1946. India has been a member of the ILO since its inception.

The aims and objectives of ILO are set out in the Preamble to its Constitution and in the Declaration of Philadelphia (1944), which was formally annexed to the Constitution in 1946. The Preamble affirms that universal and lasting peace can be established only if it is based upon social justice. The Philadelphia Charter is a reaffirmation of the principles on which the Organisation was originally based. In order to acheive its objective, the ILO has relied on its standard-setting function. The international labour standards take the form of Conventions and Recommendations.

The ILO adopted a series of Conventions and Recommendations covering hours of work, employment of women, children and young persons, weekly rest, holidays, leave with wages, night work, industrial safety, health, hygiene, labour inspection, social security, labour-management relations, freedom of association, wages and wage fixation, productivity, and employment.

The ILO has adopted 183 Conventions and 180 Recommendations so far. Out of 183 Conventions, India has ratified 39 Conventions. Conventions ratified by India have been incorporated in the existing legislation. Conventions not ratified by India have indirectly guided and shaped the Indian labour legislation in a far-reaching manner. The Conventions concerning basic human rights have considerable influence on Indian law and practice.

The Conventions have formed the sheet- anchor of Indian labour legislation, especially after 1946, when the Indian national government assumed office at the Centre. The ILO has also greatly influenced the trade union movement in our country. The AITUC owes its immediate origin to it. It is instrumental in improving the lot of the working class in our country. India's commitment to the ILO is reflected in its adherence to the institution of tripartism as a novel method for resolving labourmanagement conflicts. ILO and India have common aims, common goals and common destiny, as both of them are committed to world peace, freedom and social justice. Both are striving for the socio-economic betterment of the poverty stricken and underprivileged people.

Role of Law in Industrial Relations

All systems of industrial relations have a legal framework if they operate within a legal system. The legal framework may take the form of recognising the development of certain institutions and remove any impediments to their existence. The role of law in an industrial relations system may be perceived by the extent to which it attempts to regulate relationships, the extent to which it is obligatory rather than optional and the attitude of the parties to the legal system.

In India there has been a large degree of agreement on the need for reforms. Major disagreement, however, exists as to the part that law should play in any scheme of reforms.

The legal framework within which the industrial relations operates is in a constant state of flux. State and central legislation affecting industrial relations is a neverending phenomenon. The three central enactments which have a bearing on industrial relations in our country are: (a) the Trade Unions Act, 1926; (b) the Industrial Employment Act, 1946; and (c) the Industrial Disputes Act, 1947.

The Trade Unions Act 1926

The Central Government, after consulting Provincial Governments, drew up a Bill providing for the registration of trade unions, and introduced it in the Assembly on 31st August 1925. It was passed on 25th March 1926, and Indian Trade Unions Act, 1926 was brought into force on 1st June 1927. The Act extends to the whole country. It is divided into 33 Sections and contains 5 chapters. Certain acts do not apply to registered trade unions, namely:

i) The Societies Registration Act, 1860;

ii) The Co-operative Societies Act, 1912; and

iii) The Companies Act, 1956.

Object of the Act

The main object of the Act is to provide for the registration of trade unions and to give registered trade unions a legal and corporate status, and immunity to their officers and members from civil and criminal liability for legitimate trade union activities.

Appropriate Government: It means, in relation to trade unions whose objects are not confined to one State, the Central Government, and in relation to other trade unions, the State Government.

Executive: It means the body, by whatever name called; to which the management of the affairs of a trade union is entrusted.

Office-Bearer: It includes any member of the executive thereof, but does not include an auditor.

Trade Dispute: It means any dispute between employers and workmen, or workmen and workmen, or employers and employers, which is connected with the employment or non-employment or the terms of employment or the conditions of labour, of any person.

Workmen: It includes all persons employed in trade or industry whether or not in the employment of the employer with whom the trade dispute arises.

Trade Union: It means a combination, whether temporary or permanent, formed:

i) primarily for the purpose of regulating the relations between workmen and employers; or between workmen and workmen; or between employers and employers; or

ii) for imposing restrictive conditions on the conduct of any trade or business, and includes any federation of two or more trade unions.

The Act, however, does not affect

a) Any agreement between partners as to their own business;

b) Any agreement between an employer and those employed by him as to such employment; or

c) Any agreement in consideration of the sale of the goodwill of business or of instruction in any profession, trade or handicraft.

In common parlance, a trade union means an association of workers in a particular craft or industry. However, the expression "trade union" under the Act includes both employers' and workers' organisations. Employers' organisations can also be registered as trade unions.

Registration of a Trade Union

The Act provides that the appropriate government shall appoint a person as Registrar of Trade Unions for each state. It may also appoint as many Additional and Deputy Registrar of Trade Unions as it thinks fit.

Any seven or more members of a trade union may, by subscribing their names to the rules of the trade union and by otherwise complying with the provisions of this Act relating to registration, apply for its registration.

Provided that no trade union of workmen shall be registered unless at least ten percent or one hundred of the workmen, whichever is less engaged or employed in the establishment or industry with which it is connected are the members of such trade union on the date of making of application for registration.

Every application for the registration of a trade union shall be made to the Registrar, and shall be accompanied by a copy of the rules of the trade union and a statement of the following particulars, namely:

i) The names, occupations and addresses of the members making the application.

ii) The names, occupations and addresses of the place of work of the members of the trade unions making the application.

iii) The name of the trade union and the address of its head office; and

iv) The titles, names, ages, addresses and occupations of the office-bearers of the trade union.

Where a trade union has been in existence for more than one year before an application is made for its registration, there shall be delivered to the Registrar, together with the application, a general statement of the assets and liabilities of the trade union prepared in such form and containing such particulars as may be prescribed.

Rules of a trade union

A trade union is entitled to registration only if its executive is constituted in accordance with the provisions of the Act and its rules provide for the following matters:

a) The name of the trade union;

b) The objects for which the trade union has been established;

c) The purposes for which the general funds of the trade union shall be employed;

d) The maintenance of a list of the members of the trade union and adequate facilities for the inspection thereof by the office-bearers and members of the trade union;

e) The admission of ordinary members who shall be persons actually engaged or employed in an industry with which the trade union is connected, and also the admission of the number of honorary or temporary office-bearers to form the executive of the trade union;

f) The payment of a minimum subscription by members of the trade union which shall not be less than:

i) one rupee per annum for rural workers;

(ii) three rupees per annum for workers in other unorganised sectors; and

iii) twelve rupees per annum for workers in any other case.

g) The conditions under which any member shall be entitled to any benefit assured by the rules and under which any fine or forfeiture may be imposed on the members;

h) The manner in which the rules shall be amended, varied or rescinded;

i) The manner in which the members of the executive and other office-bearers of the trade union shall be appointed and removed;

j) The duration of period being not more than three years, for which the members of the executive and other office bearers of the trade union shall be elected;

k) The safe custody of the funds of the trade union, and annual audit of accounts thereof, and adequate facilities for the inspection of the account books by the office-bearers and members of the trade union; and

l) The manner in which the trade union may be dissolved.

Registrar of trade unions

The Registrar may call for information for the purpose of satisfying himself that an application complies with the above provisions or that the trade union is entitled to registration. He may refuse to register the trade union until such information is supplied.

If the name under which a trade union is proposed to be registered is identical with that by which any other existing trade union has been registered or, in the opinion of the Registrar, so nearly resembles that name as to be likely to deceive the public or the members of either trade union, the Registrar shall require the persons applying for registration to alter the name of the trade union stated in the application, and shall refuse to register the union until such alteration has been made. If all the terms of the Act are complied with, it is obligatory upon the Registrar to register a union. He has no discretion in the matter.

Cancellation of registration

A certificate of registration of a trade union may be withdrawn or cancelled by the Registrar in the following circumstances:

i) on the application of the trade union to be verified in such manner as may be prescribed; or

ii) if the Registrar is satisfied that -

   a) the certificate has been obtained by fraud or mistake; or

   b) the trade union has ceased to exist; or

   c) has wilfully and after notice from the Registrar contravened any provision of the Act; or

   d) allowed any rule to continue in force which is inconsistent with any such provision; or

   e) has rescinded any rule providing for any matter, provision for which is required in the rules of a trade union; or

   f) if the registered trade union of workmen ceases to have the requisite number of members.

If the cancellation is to be effected on account of clause (ii) above, the Registrar shall give to the trade union not less than two months' previous notice in writing, specifying the ground on which it is proposed to withdraw or cancel the certificate.

Appeal

If the registration of a trade union is refused or if a certificate of registration is withdrawn or cancelled, any person aggrieved or the trade union may appeal to the court. The appeal must be filed within sixty days of the date on which the Registrar passed the order against which the appeal is made.

Where the head office of a trade union is situated within the limits of a presidency town, the appeal lies to the High Court. This means there is only one right of appeal against the decision of the Registrar refusing registration of a trade union.

Where the head office is situated in any other area, the appeal lies to such court, not inferior to the court of an additional or assistant judge of a principal civil court of original jurisdiction, as the appropriate government may appoint in this behalf for that area. In the event of the dismissal of an appeal by any such court, the person aggrieved shall have a right of appeal to the High Court. This means that a trade union having its head office in areas other than presidency towns has two rights of appeal, i.e., first, to the local court exercising original jurisdiction and then to the High Court against the decision of the local court.

The appellate court may dismiss the appeal, or pass an order directing the Registrar to register the union and to issue a certificate of registration, or set aside the order for withdrawal or cancellation of the certificate, as the case may be. The Registrar shall comply with such order of the court.

For the purpose of an appeal, an appellate court shall follow the same procedure and have the same powers as it follows and has when trying a suit under the Code of Civil Procedure, 1908.

Notices

All communications and notices to a registered trade union may be addressed to its registered office. Notice of any change in the address of the head office shall be given within 14 days of such change to the Registrar in writing, and the changed address shall be recorded in the register.

Legal status of a registered union

A trade union, after registration, acquires the following characteristics:

(a) It becomes a body corporate by the name under which it is registered, and becomes a legal entity distinct from the members of which it is composed.

(b) It has perpetual succession and a common seal.

(c) It has the power to acquire and hold both movable and immovable property.

(d) It has the power to contract.

(e) It can by the name under which it is registered sue and be sued.

General fund

The general funds of a registered trade union shall not be spent on any objects other than the following:

a) The payment of salaries, allowances and expenses to the office-bearers of the trade union;

b) The payment of expenses for the administration of the trade union, including the audit of the accounts of the general funds of the trade union;

c) The prosecution or defence in any legal proceeding to which the trade union or any member thereof is a party, when such prosecution or defence is undertaken for the purpose of securing or protecting any rights of the trade union;

d) The conduct of trade disputes on behalf of the trade union or any member thereof;

e) The compensation of members for loss arising out of trade disputes;

f) The allowances to members or their dependents on account of death, old age, sickness, accident or unemployment of such members;

g) The issue of or the undertaking of liability under policies of assurance on the lives of members, or under policies insuring members against sickness, accident or unemployment;

h) The provision of educational, social or religious benefits for members or for the dependents of members;

i) The upkeep of a periodical published mainly for the purpose of discussing questions affecting employers or workmen as such;

j) The payment of contributions to any cause intended to benefit workmen in general.

k) Subject to any conditions; any other object notified by the appropriate government in the Official Gazette.

If the union funds are spent on any objects other than those specified, the expenditure will be unlawful and *ultra vires* the Act. The union can be restrained by injunction from applying its funds for any such object.

Political fund

A registered trade union may constitute a separate fund for political purposes from which payments may be made for the promotion of the civic and political interests of its members. This fund may be utilised only in furtherance of the following objects:

a) The payment of any expenses incurred by a candidate or prospective candidate for election as a member of any legislative body constituted under the constitution or under any local authority; or

b) The holding of any meeting or the distribution of any literature or documents in support of any such candidate or prospective candidate; or

c) The maintenance of any person who is a member of any legislative body constituted under the constitution or under any local authority; or

d) The registration of electors or the selection of a candidate for any legislative body constituted under the constitution or under any local authority;

(e) The holding of political meetings of any kind, or the distribution of political literature of any kind.

Expenditure for political purposes is in no case permitted out of the general funds. Not only this, even interest on investments of the political fund will have to be credited to the political fund.

The conditions for the creation of political fund are:

i) The fund can be created only from contributions separately levied for or made to that fund.

ii) Members must not be compelled to contribute to the fund.

iii) A member who does not contribute to the said fund must not be excluded from any benefits of the trade union, or placed under any disability or disadvantage, directly or indirectly, as compared with other members of the trade union, except in relation to the control or management of the political fund.

iv) Contribution to the political fund must not be made a condition for admission to the trade union.

Immunity from civil suit

A suit or other legal proceeding shall not be maintainable in any civil court against any registered trade union or any office-bearer or member thereof for any act done in contemplation or furtherance of a trade dispute to which a member of the trade union is a party. This protection is available only on the ground that such act induces some other person to break contract of employment, or that it is in interference with the trade, business or employment of some other person or with the right of some other person to dispose of his capital or of his labour as he wills.

An agreement between the members of a registered trade union shall not be void or voidable merely by reason of the fact that any of the objects of the agreement are in restraint of trade.

Executives and office bearers

The account books of a registered trade union and the list of members thereof shall be open to inspection by an officer-bearer or member of the trade union at such times as may be provided for in the rules of the trade union.

Subject to any rules of the trade union to the contrary, any person who has attained the age of fifteen years may be a member of a registered trade union and enjoy all the rights of a member.

A person shall be disqualified for being chosen as, and for being a member of the executive or any other office-bearer of a registered trade union, if

i) he has not attained the age of 18 years;
ii) he has been convicted by a court in India of an offence involving moral turpitude and sentenced to imprisonment, unless a period of 5 years has elapsed after his release.

Proportion of office bearers to be connected with industry are:

a) Not less than one-half of the total number of office-bearers of every registered trade union shall be persons actually engaged or employed in an industry with which the trade union is connected.
b) Not less than one-half of the total number of the office-bearers of every registered trade union in an unorganised sector shall be persons actually engaged or employed in an industry with which the trade union is connected.
c) All office-bearers of a registered trade union except not more than one-third of the total number of the office-bearers or five, whichever is less, shall be persons actually engaged or employed in the establishment or industry with which the trade union is connected.

d) No member of the Council of Ministers or a person holding an office of profit, in the Union of a State, shall be a member of the executive or other office-bearer of a registered trade union.

Rights of unions

Any registered trade union may, with the consent of not less than two-thirds of the total number and subject to certain conditions, change its name. Any two or more registered trade unions may amalgamate with or without the dissolution or division of the funds of such trade unions, or either or any of them, provided that –

i) The votes of at least half of the members of each or every such trade union entitled to vote are recorded; and
ii) At least 60 percent of the votes recorded are in favour of the proposal.

In the case of a change of name, the secretary and seven members of the union must give a notice in writing to the Registrar; in the case of an amalgamation, the secretary and seven members of each and every union which is a party to such amalgamation must give notice to the Registrar. If the Registrar is satisfied that the change of name is in order, and that the new name does not resemble that of any other existing trade union, he will register the change of name in his register. The change of name or the amalgamation has effect from the date of registration. It shall be registered by him if he is satisfied that the dissolution has been effected in accordance with the rules of the trade union. Dissolution shall have effect from the date of such registration.

Returns

There shall be sent annually to the registrar, on or before such date as may be prescribed, a general statement, audited in the prescribed manner, of all receipts and expenditure of every registered trade union during the year ending 31st December preceding such prescribed date, and of the assets and liabilities of the trade union existing on 31st December.

Together with the general statement, there shall be sent to the Registrar a statement showing all changes of office-bearers made by the trade union during the year to which the general statement refers, together also with a copy of the rules of the trade union corrected up to the date of the dispatch thereof to the Registrar.

INDUSTRIAL EMPLOYMENT (STANDING ORDERS) ACT

The matter pertaining to terms and conditions of industrial employment was first brought before the fifth Indian Labour Conference in 1943 and was subsequently deliberated in its sessions in 1944 and 1945. In order to fill the long-standing lacuna in Indian labour legislation, the legislature passed the Act on 23rd April 1946. The Act came into force on 1st April 1947.

Object of the Act

The object of the Act is "to require employers in industrial establishments to define with sufficient precision the conditions of employment under them and to make the said conditions known to workmen employed by them". The Act was enacted:

a) to bring about uniformity in terms and conditions of employment;
b) to minimise industrial conflicts;
c) to foster harmonious relations between employers and employees; and
d) to provide statutory sanctity and importance to the standing orders;
e) to provide for payment of subsistence allowance by the employer during suspension pending enquiry at the rate of 50 percent of the wages for the first 90 days of suspension and 75 percent for the remaining period if the delay in the completion of disciplinary proceedings is not directly attributable to the conduct of the workman concerned.

The Applicability

The Act extends to the whole of India. It applies to every industrial establishment wherein 100 or more workmen are employed, or were employed on any day of the preceding twelve months. Once the Act becomes applicable to an industrial establishment, it does not cease to apply by reason of a fall in the number of workmen in that establishment below 100. The appropriate government can also exempt any establishment or classes of establishments from all or any of the provisions of the Act.

The industrial establishments covered by the Act include railways, factories, mines, quarries, oilfields, tramways, motor omnibus services, docks, wharves, jetties, inland steam vessels, plantations, workshops and civil construction and maintenance works.

The amended Act of 1963 *inter alia* provides for the applicability of Model Standing Orders framed by the appropriate government to all industrial establishments covered by the Act until the standing orders framed by individual establishments are certified.

The Act is applicable to all workmen employed in any industrial establishment to do any skilled or unskilled, manual, supervisory, technical or clerical work.

Appropriate Government: "Appropriate Government" means in respect of industrial establishments under the control of the Central Government or a Railway Administration or in a major port, mine or oilfield, the Central Government, and in all other cases the State Government.

Certifying officer: "Certifying Officer" means a Labour Commissioner, or a Regional Labour Commissioner, and includes any other officer appointed by the appropriate government, by a notification in the Official Gazette, to perform all or any of the functions of a certifying officer under the Act.

Certification of Standing Orders

It is obligatory on the part of an employer or a group of employers to furnish five copies of the draft standing orders to the certifying officer within six months from the date on which the Act becomes applicable to his or their establishments. The draft shall be accompanied by a statement giving prescribed particulars of the workmen employed in the industrial establishment, including the name of the trade union, if any, to which they belong.

The draft standing orders have to provide for all matters set out in the Schedule to the Act and should conform, as far as practicable, to the model standing order prescribed by the government. The Schedule to the Act provides for the following matters:

i) Classification of workmen, e.g., whether permanent, temporary, apprentices, probationers, or *badlis*;

ii) Manner of intimating to workmen periods and hours of work, holidays, pay-days and wage rates;

iii) Shift working;

iv) Attendance and late-coming;

v) Conditions of, procedure in applying for, and the authority which may grant leave and holidays;

vi) Requirements to enter premises by certain gates, and liability to search;

vii) Closing and reopening of sections of the industrial establishment;

viii) Termination of employment, and the notice thereof to be given by employer and workmen;

ix) Suspension or dismissal for misconduct and acts or omissions which constitute misconduct;

x) Means of redress for workmen against unfair treatment or wrongful exactions by the employer or his agents or servants;

xi) Any other matter which may be prescribed.

On receipt of the draft standing orders, the certifying officer shall forward a copy thereof to the trade union of the workmen functioning in the establishment, and if no such union exists, to three representatives of the workmen in the establishment elected at a meeting called for the purpose. A notice in the prescribed form will be given inviting objections, if any, to the draft standing orders within fifteen days of the receipt of these orders. After giving to the parties an opportunity of being heard, the certifying officer shall decide whether or not any modification of the draft is necessary, and make an order in writing accordingly. The certifying officer shall thereupon certify the standing orders with or without modification, and forward the authenticated copies thereof to the employer and to the trade union or other prescribed representatives of the workmen within seven days from the date of his orders.

Model Standing Orders

When this Act becomes applicable to an industrial establishment for the first time, till the standing orders as finally certified under this Act come into operation in that establishment, the prescribed model standing orders shall be deemed to have been adopted in that establishment.

The Appeal

An aggrieved party may appeal to the appellate authority within thirty days from the date on which the copies of the standing orders were sent to the parties by the certifying officer. The order of the appellate authority shall be final. The Act empowers the appellate authority to do only two things, namely:

i) Confirm the standing orders in the form certified by the certifying officer, or

ii) Confirm the standing orders after amending them by making the necessary modifications or additions.

The certified standing orders become enforceable on the expiry of 30 days from the date on which the authenticated copies of the same are sent to the parties by the certifying officer.

Display of Standing Orders

A copy of all standing orders as finally certified under this Act shall be filed by the certifying officer in a register in the prescribed form maintained for the purpose. The certifying officer shall furnish a copy thereof to any person applying for it on payment of the prescribed fee.

Modification of Standing Orders

The standing orders finally certified under this Act shall not, except on agreement between the employer and the workmen, be liable to modification until the expiry of six months from the date on which the standing orders or the last modifications thereof came into operation.An employer or workman may apply to the certifying officer for modification of the standing orders. Such an application shall be accompanied by five copies of the proposed modifications made by an agreement between the employer and the workmen.

Study Powers of Certifying Officer

Every certifying officer and appellate authority shall have all the powers of a civil court for the purpose of:

i) receiving evidence,
ii) administering oaths,
iii) enforcing the attendance of witnesses, and
iv) compelling the discovery and production of documents.

This brings us to Acts of misconduct. The following acts or omissions on the part of a workman shall amount to misconduct:

i) wilful insubordination or disobedience, whether or not in combination with another, of any lawful and reasonable order of a superior;
ii) going on an illegal strike or abetting, inciting, instigating or acting in furtherance thereof;
iii) wilful slowing downing in performance of work, or abatement or instigation thereof;
iv) theft, fraud or dishonesty in connection with the employer's business or property or the theft of property of another workman within the premises of the establishment;
v) taking or giving bribes or any illegal gratification;
vi) habitual absence without leave, or absence without leave for more than ten consecutive days or overstaying the sanctioned leave without sufficient grounds or proper or satisfactory explanation;
vii) late attendance on less than four occasions within a month;
viii) habitual breach of any standing order or any law applicable to the establishment or any rules made there under;
ix) collection without the permission of the manager of any money within the premises of the establishment except as sanctioned by any law for the time being in force;
x) engaging in trade within the premises of the establishment;
xi) drunkenness, riotous, disorderly or indecent behaviour on the premises of the establishment;
xii) commission of any act subversive of discipline or good behaviour on the premises of the establishment;
xiii) habitual neglect of work, or gross or habitual negligence;
xiv) habitual breach of any rules or instructions for the maintenance and running of any department, or the maintenance of the cleanliness of any portion of the establishment;

xv) habitual commission of any act or omission for which a fine may be imposed under the Payment of Wages Act, 1936;

xvi) canvassing for union membership, or collection of union dues within the premises of the establishment, except in accordance with any law or with the permission of the manager;

xvii) wilful damage to work in process or to any property of the establishment;

xviii) holding meeting inside the premises of the establishment without the previous permission of the manager or except in accordance with the provisions of any law for the time being in force;

xix) disclosing to any unauthorised person any information in regard to the processes of the establishment which may come into the possession of the workman in the course of his works;

xx) gambling within the premises of the establishment;

xxi) smoking and spitting on the premises of the establishment where it is prohibited by the employer;

xxii) failure to observe safety instructions notified by the employer or interference with any safety device or equipment installed within the establishment;

xxiii) distribution or exhibiting within the premises of the establishment hand-bills, pamphlets, posters, and such other things or causing to be displayed by means of signs or writing or other visible representation on any matter without previous sanction of the manager;

xxiv) refusal to accept a chargesheet, order or other communication served in accordance with the standing orders;

xxv) unauthorised possession of any lethal weapon in the establishment.

Offences and {enalties

The Act provides for penalties and procedures in case where: (i) an employer fails to submit draft standing orders; (ii) who does any act in contravention of the standing orders finally certified under this Act for his industrial establishment. No prosecution for an offence shall be instituted except with the previous sanction of the appropriate government. No court inferior to that of a metropolitan magistrate or a judicial magistrate of the second class shall try any offence under the Act.

Obligations of Employers

i) Submit draft standing orders with the required information to the Certifying Officer for certification within the time limit mentioned in the Act.
ii) Act in conformity with the certified standing orders in the day-to-day dealings with the workmen.
iii) Modify certified standing orders only with the approval of the Certifying Officer.
iv) Post prominently the text of the certified standing orders near the entrance and also in all departments where workmen are employed.
v) Pay subsistence allowance to the charge-sheeted employee during suspension pending enquiry as per the Act and the Rules.

Obligations of Workmen

1) Work in conformity with the certified standing orders or model standing orders as the case may be.
2) Comply with the provisions of the Act in regard to modification and interpretation of standing orders.

INDUSTRIAL DISPUTES ACT 1947

The Industrial Disputes Bill was introduced in the Central Legislative Assembly on 8th October 1946. The Bill was passed by the Assembly in March 1947 and became law with effect from 1st April 1947. The Act contains 40 sections, which have been grouped in 9 chapters.

Object of the Act

The Preamble to the Act reads: "An Act to make provision for the investigation and settlement of industrial disputes and for certain other purposes." On the basis of various judgements given from time to time by the Supreme Court, the principal objectives of the Act may be stated as follows:

a) To ensure social justice to both employers and employees and advance the progress of industry by bringing about harmony and a cordial relationship between the parties.
b) To settle disputes arising between capital and labour by peaceful methods and through the machinery of conciliation, arbitration and, if necessary, by approaching the tribunals constituted under the Act.
c) To promote measures for securing and preserving amity and good relations between the employer and workmen.
d) To prevent illegal strikes and lockouts.
e) To provide compensation to workmen in cases of lay-off, retrenchment and closure.
f) To protect workmen against victimisation by the employer and to ensure termination of industrial disputes in a peaceful manner.
g) To promote collective bargaining.

The following are some of the important definitions:

Appropriate Government: It means:

a) in relation to any industrial dispute concerning any industry carried on by or under the authority of the Central Government or by a railway company, or any controlled industry as may be specified, or in relation to an industrial dispute concerning a banking or an insurance company, a mine, or an oil-field or a major port, the Central Government; and
b) in relation to any other industrial dispute, the State Government.

Award: It means an interim or a final determination of any industrial dispute or of any question relating thereto by any Labour Court, Industrial Tribunal, or National Industrial Tribunal and includes an arbitration award made under Section 10-A.

Public utility service: The phrase public utility service means:

i) Any railway service or any transport service for the carriage of passengers or goods by road, water or air;

ii) Any section of an industrial establishment on the working of which the safety of the establishment or the workmen employed therein depends;

iii) Any postal, telegraph or telephone service;

iv) Any industry which supplies power, light or water to the public;

v) Any system of public conservancy or sanitation;

vi) Any industry specified in the First Schedule which the appropriate government may, if satisfied that public emergency or public interest so requires, by notification in the Official Gazette, declare to be a public utility service for a specified period not exceeding six months in the first instance.

Industry: It means any business, trade, undertaking, manufacture or calling of employers and includes any calling, service, employment, handicraft or industrial occupation or avocation of workmen.

The definition is both exhaustive and inclusive and is very comprehensive in scope. It is in two parts.

The Supreme Court by a judgement of far reaching importance gave a wide implication to the meaning of industry. It laid down a triple test to decide the applicability of the I.D. Act to them. The triple test is: (i) systematic activity; (ii) cooperation between employers and employees; (iii) production and/or distribution of goods and services calculated to satisfy human wants and wishes. If these tests are satisfied *prima facie*, there is an "industry". As a consequence, schools, colleges, universities, hospitals, solicitor's offices, gymkhana, clubs, institutes, charitable projects were held to be industry.

Industrial dispute: Industrial dispute means any dispute or difference between employers and employers or between employers and workmen, or between workmen and workmen, which is connected with the employment or non-employment or the terms of employment or with the conditions of labour, of any person. The definition is in three parts. The first part refers to the factum of a real and substantial dispute, the second part to the parties to the dispute, and the third to the subject matter of the dispute.

It is a settled law that before any dispute between an employer and his workmen can be said to be industrial dispute under the Act, it must be sponsored by a substantial number of workmen. In other words, it is only a collective dispute that can constitute an industrial dispute. Where any employer discharges, dismisses, retrenches or otherwise terminates the services of an individual workman, any dispute or difference between that workman and his employer connected with, or arising out of, such discharge, dismissal, retrenchment or termination shall be deemed to be an industrial dispute notwithstanding that no other workman nor any union of workmen is a party to the dispute. The object is to give an individual dispute relating to discharge, dismissal, retrenchment or otherwise termination, the status of an industrial dispute.

Wages: 'Wages' means all remuneration capable of being expressed in terms of money, which would, if the terms of employment, expressed or implied, were fulfilled, be payable to a workman in respect of his employment, or of work done in such employment, and includes:

i) such allowances as the workman is for the time being entitled to;
ii) the value of any house accommodation, or of supply of light, water, medical attendance or other amenity or of any service or foodgrains or other articles;
iii) any travelling concession;
iv) any commission payable on the promotion of sales or business or both. but does not include:
    a) any bonus;
    b) any contribution paid or payable by the employer to any pension fund or provident fund or for the benefit of the workman under any law for the time being in force;
    c) any gratuity payable on the termination of his service.

Workman: "Workman" means any person, including an apprentice employed in any industry, to do any skilled or unskilled manual, supervisory, operational, technical or clerical work for hire or reward, whether the terms of employment be expressed or implied, and for the purposes of any proceeding under this Act in relation to an industrial dispute, includes any such person who has been dismissed, discharged or retrenched in connection with, or as a consequence of, that dispute or whose dismissal, discharge, or retrenchment has led to that dispute, but does not include any person:

i) **Who is subject to the Army Act, 1950, or the Air Force Act, 1950, or the Navy Act, 1934, or**

ii) **Who is employed in the police service or as an officer or other employee of prison; or**

iii) **Who is employed mainly in a managerial or administrative capacity; or**

iv) **Who being employed in a supervisory capacity, draws wages exceeding rupees 1,600 per mensem or exercises, either by the nature of the duties attached to the office or by reason of the powers vested in him, functions mainly of a managerial nature.**

Unless a person is employed in an industry, he will not be a workman within the meaning of the definition. Similarly, a person who performs supervisory work and draws wages exceeding rupees 1,600 per mensem is not a workman.

Authorities under the Act

Works committee: The Act empowers the appropriate government to require an employer of any industrial establishment where 100 or more workmen are employed or have been employed on any day in the preceding twelve months to constitute a works committee. This committee consists of representatives of the employer and of the workmen engaged in the establishment, provided that the number of representatives of the workmen is not less than the number of representatives of the employer. The duty of the works committee is to promote measures with a view to securing and preserving amity end, to comment upon matters of their common interest or concern and endeavour to compose any material difference of opinion in respect of such matters.

Conciliation officers: The appropriate government may appoint conciliation officers charged with the duty of mediating in, and promoting the settlement of, industrial disputes.

Board of conciliation: In a similar manner, a board of conciliation may also be constituted to promote the settlement of industrial disputes. A board shall consist of a chairman and two or four other members, as the appropriate government thinks fit.The chairman shall be an independent person and the other members shall be persons appointed in equal numbers to represent the parties to the dispute on the recommendation of the parties concerned.

Conciliation proceedings before a board are similar in nature to those before a conciliation officer. But members of the boards of conciliation enjoy more powers than those enjoyed by conciliation officers. However, unlike a conciliation officer, the board cannot admit a dispute in conciliation on its own; the board has no jurisdiction until the government makes a reference to it.

Courts of inquiry: The appropriate government may constitute a court of inquiry consisting of one or more independent persons to enquire into any matter connected with or relevant to an industrial dispute. Where a court consists of two or more members, one of them shall be appointed as chairman.

Labour courts: The appropriate government may constitute one or more labour courts to adjudicate industrial disputes relating to any of the following matters:

i) The propriety or legality of an order passed by an employer under the standing orders;
ii) The application and interpretation of standing orders;
iii) Discharge or dismissal of workmen, including retirement of, or grant of relief to, workmen wrongfully dismissed;
iv) Withdrawal of any customary concession or privilege;
v) Illegality or otherwise of a strike or lockout; and
vi) All matters other than those specified in the Third Schedule.

A labour court shall consist of one person only with necessary judicial qualifications, and will be appointed by the appropriate government.

Industrial tribunals: The appropriate government may, by a notification in the Official Gazette, constitute one or more industrial tribunals to adjudicate industrial disputes relating to any matter, whether specified in the Second Schedule or in the Third Schedule.

The Third Schedule provides for the adjudication of the following matters:

i) Wages, including the period and mode of payment;
ii) Compensation and other allowances;
iii) Hours of work and rest intervals;

iv) Leave with wages and holidays;

v) Bonus, profit-sharing, provident fund and gratuity;

vi) Shift working otherwise than in accordance with standing orders;

vii) Classification by grades;

viii) Rules of discipline;

ix) Rationalisation;

x) Retrenchment of workmen and closure of establishment; and

xi) Any other matter that may be prescribed.

National tribunals: The Central Government may, by a notification in the Official Gazette, constitute one or more national industrial tribunals for the adjudication of industrial disputes which, in the opinion of the Central Government, involve questions of national importance or are of such nature that industrial establishments situated in more than one State are likely to be interested in, or affected by, such disputes.

Notice of Change

Before effecting any change in the conditions of service relating to wages, contribution to provident fund, hours of work and rest intervals, compensatory and other allowances, leave with wages and holidays, introduction of new rules of discipline, withdrawal of any customary çoncession or privilege as given in the Fourth Schedule, the employer should give 21 days' notice to the workmen likely to be affected by the proposed changes. But the appropriate government may exempt certain industries from giving such notice, if it is of the opinion that such a change may affect the employers prejudicially or may cause serious repercussions on the industry concerned or that the public interest so requires.

Reference of Disputes

If an industrial dispute exists or is apprehended, the government may, by order in writing:

a) Refer the dispute to a board to promote a settlement of dispute;

b) Refer any matter connected with or relevant to the dispute to a court of inquiry;

c) Refer the dispute to labour court or tribunal for adjudication; and

d) The Central Government may refer the dispute to the national tribunal if it involves any question to national importance.

If a workman dies during the pendency of the proceedings, his legal heirs have the right to continue the proceedings.

Voluntary Reference of Disputes to Arbitration: Section 10-A provides for the voluntary arbitration of industrial disputes. Where any industrial dispute exists or is apprehended and the employer and the workmen agree to refer it to arbitration, they may, at any time before the dispute has been referred to a labour court or tribunal, by a written agreement, refer it for arbitration to such person or persons as may be specified in the arbitration agreement. If the arbitrators are equally divided in their opinion, the award of the umpire shall prevail and shall be deemed to be the arbitration award. A copy of the arbitration agreement shall be forwarded to the appropriate government and the conciliation officer. The essential features of voluntary arbitration are:

i) There should be an existing or apprehended industrial dispute;

ii) The reference should be made before the dispute has been referred under Section 10 to a labour court, an industrial tribunal or national tribunal; and

iii) The names of the person or persons to act as arbitrator or arbitrators must be specified in the arbitration agreement. Such persons may be presiding officers of labour courts, tribunals or national tribunals.

Procedure, Powers and Duties of Authorities

Conciliation officer: Every conciliation officer, member of a board, court or tribunal is deemed to be a public servant and may, for the purpose of inquiry into any existing or apprehended industrial dispute, enter the premises occupied by any establishment to which the dispute relates after giving a reasonable notice. They exercise, all the powers of a civil court while trying a suit. The conciliation officer has been vested with the power to enforce attendance of any person for the purpose of examination of such person. The duties of conciliation officer are:

1) He may hold conciliation proceedings where any industrial dispute exists or is apprehended.
2) He must investigate the dispute and all matters affecting the merits and the right settlement thereof, and try to induce the parties to come to a fair and amicable settlement.
3) Where a settlement of the dispute or any of the matters therein is arrived at, he must send a report to the government, together with a memorandum of settlement signed by the parties.
4) Where no settlement is reached, he must send to the government a full report in regard to the steps taken by him to ascertain the facts and circumstances of the dispute and a full statement of the facts and circumstances and the reasons why a settlement could not be reached.
5) He must send the report of the settlement or non-settlement of the dispute, as the case may be, within 14 days of the commencement of the conciliation proceedings or within such shorter period as may be fixed by the Government.

If, after considering the report where no settlement is reached, the appropriate government is satisfied that the case should be referred to a board or a tribunal, it may make such reference.

Duties of board of conciliation: The duties of the board of conciliation are similar to those of conciliation officers. The time limit for the submission of its report is two months.

Duties of court of inquiry: It is the duty of the court to inquire into the matters referred to it and report thereon to the appropriate government within six months from the commencement of its inquiry.

Duties of courts and tribunals: When an industrial dispute has been referred to a labour court, tribunal, or national tribunal for adjudication, it shall hold its proceedings expeditiously and submit its award to the appropriate government as soon as practicable on the conclusion of the adjudication.

Reports and Awards

The report of a board or court and the award of a tribunal must be in writing and must be signed by all its members. Of course, any member may record a minute of dissent. The award of a labour court, tribunal or national tribunal must be signed by its presiding officer. Where is any case, a Labour Court or Tribunal by its award directs reinstatement of any workman and the employer prefers any proceedings against such award in a High Court or Supreme Court, the employer is liable to pay such workman, during the period of pendency of such proceedings, full wages last drawn by him, inclusive of any maintenance allowance admissible to him under any rule. Money once paid cannot be recovered by the employer.

Powers of Labour Courts and Industrial Tribunals

Section 11-A reads as under:

> "Where an industrial dispute relating to the discharge or dismissal of a workman has been referred to a labour court, tribunal or national tribunal for adjudication and where, in the course of the adjudication proceedings the labour court, tribunal or national tribunal, as the case may be, is satisfied that the order of discharge or dismissal was not justified it may by its award set aside the order of discharge or dismissal and direct reinstatement of the workman on such terms and conditions, if any, as it thinks fit, or give such other relief to the workman, including the award of any lesser punishment in lieu of discharge or dismissal as the circumstances of the case may require: provided that in any proceeding under this Section, the labour court, tribunal or national tribunal, as the case may be, shall rely only on the materials or record and shall not take any fresh evidence in relation to the matter."

Under this Section, for the first time, power has been given to a tribunal to satisfy itself whether misconduct is proved. This is particularly so regarding even the findings arrived at by an employer in an enquiry properly held. The tribunal has also been given the power, for the first time, to interfere with the punishment imposed by an employer. Such restrictions are found in the proviso. The proviso only emphasises that the tribunal has to satisfy itself one way or the other regarding misconduct, punishment and relief to be granted to workmen only on the basis of the "materials on record" before it.

Settlements and Awards

"Settlement" as defined in Section 2(p) of the Industrial Disputes Act envisages two categories of settlement:

a) A settlement which is arrived at in the course of conciliation proceedings, i.e., which is arrived at with the assistance and concurrence of the conciliation officer, and;

b) An agreement between the employer and workmen arrived at otherwise than in the course of conciliation proceedings.

To be valid, an agreement under the second category should be in writing and signed by the parties thereto, and copies should be sent to an officer authorised for this purpose by the appropriate government and the conciliation officer. A settlement arrived at in the course of conciliation proceedings or as an award of a tribunal will be binding on:

i) All parties to the industrial dispute;

ii) All other parties summoned to appear in the proceedings as parties to the dispute unless they were so summoned without proper cause;

iii) Where a party is an employer, his heirs, successors or assignees in respect of the establishment to which the dispute relates

;iv) Where a party is composed of workmen, all persons who were employed in the establishment or part of the establishment, as the case may be, to which the disputes relates on the date of the dispute and all persons who subsequently become employed in that establishment or part of the establishment.

A settlement arrived at in the course of conciliation proceedings is binding for a period agreed upon by the parties. If no such period is agreed upon, the settlement will remain in force for a period of six months from the date on which the parties to the dispute sign the memorandum of settlement.

Strikes and Lockouts

Strike means a cessation of work by a body of persons employed in any industry acting in combination, or a concerted refusal, or a refusal under a common understanding, of any number of persons who are or have been so employed to continue to work or to accept employment.

Lockout means the closing of a place of employment, or the suspension of work, or the refusal by an employer to continue to employ any number of persons employed by him. The definition of strike postulates the following ingredients:

i) Plurality of workmen;

ii) Cessation of work or refusal to continue to work;

iii) Acting in combination or concerted action under a common understanding.

General prohibition of strikes: No group of workmen may strike in the following five situations:

i) When conciliation proceedings are going on before a board of conciliation and seven days thereafter;

ii) When adjudication is going on before a labour court or tribunal and two months thereafter;

iii) When and if an appropriate government in its reference prohibits the continuance of any strike;

iv) When arbitration is going on before an arbitrator and two months thereafter;

v) When a settlement or award is in operation. (Note that prohibition here is restricted to those matters only which are covered by the settlement or award)

Additional restrictions on strikes in public utility services:

i) A strike notice must be given to the employer and conciliation officer;

ii) The strike must not take place for 14 days after the notice has been given;

iii) The strike must not take place after six weeks following the notice;

iv) The strike must not take place before the day, if any, specified in the strike notice;

v) The strike must not take place during conciliation proceedings before a conciliation officer and seven days after the conclusion of such proceedings.

Some provisions are applicable only to public utility services while certain other provisions are general in character and are applicable to both public utility services as well as non-public utility services. In public utility services there can be no strike or lockout without notice or prescribed period. During the pendency of any conciliation proceedings before a conciliation officer, strike or lockout can be resorted to.

The employer's right to lockout is subjected to the same restrictions as the workmen's right to strike. The same rules apply with the same additional restrictions for public utilities. However, a strike is not illegal when it is declared because of an illegal lockout. Justifiability and legality are two different or distinct concepts. A strike may be legal but it may be unjustified or an unjustified strike may be legal. A strike may be both legal and justified. But a strike which is illegal cannot be justified. Both cannot co-exist in law.

Retrenchment and Closure (Chapter V-A)

Lay-off: Section 2 (kk) of the Act defines lay-off as "the failure, refusal or inability of an employer on account of shortage of coal and power or raw material or the accumulation of stocks or the breakdown of machinery or for any other reason to give employment to a workman whose name is borne on the muster rolls of his industrial establishment and who has not been retrenched."

Lay-off provisions of the Act are applicable to factories, mines and plantations where in 50 or more workmen on an average per working day have been employed in the preceding calendar month and who are not of seasonal character.

In industrial undertakings where lay-off provisions apply, only those workmen will be entitled to lay-off compensation whose names are borne on the muster rolls of the establishment and who are not *badli* or casual workers and who have completed one year of continuous service with the employer concerned.

A *"badli"* workman means a workman who is employed in an industrial establishment in the place of another workman whose name is borne on the muster rolls of the establishment but shall cease to be regarded as such for the purpose of this Section if he has completed one year's continuous service in the establishment for not less than 240 days.

Any single interruption in the employment not exceeding 10 days of unauthorised absence will not result in a break or discontinuity of employment.

Whenever a workman who is covered by the provisions mentioned in the above paragraphs is laid-off, he shall be entitled to lay-off compensation. He shall be paid by the employer for all days during which he is so laid-off except for weekly holidays that may intervene, compensation equal to fifty per cent of the total of the basic wages and dearness allowance that would have been payable if he had not been laid-off. Where a workman has been paid lay-off compensation for more than 45 days and is retrenched, the employer may deduct the amount so paid out of retrenchment compensation payable to him.

No compensation shall be paid to a workman:

i) If he refuses to accept any alternative employment in the same establishment or in any other establishment belonging to the same employer situated in the same town or village or situated within a radius of five miles from the establishment to which he belongs, provided that the wages in the alternative employment are the same as in the previous one;

ii) If he does not present himself for work at the establishment at the appointed time during working hours at least once a day;

iii) If such lay-off is due to a strike or slowing down of production on the part of the workmen in another part of the establishment.

Retrenchment: Section 2(oo) defines retrenchment as "the termination by the employer of the service of a workman for any reason whatsoever otherwise than as a punishment inflicted by way of disciplinary action."

All retrenchment will result in termination of service but all termination of service will not amount to retrenchment.

No workman who has been employed for one year can be retrenched until:

i) He has been given one month's notice in writing, indicating the reasons for retrenchment and the period of notice has expired, or the workman has been paid, in lieu of such notice, wages for the period of the notice;

ii) The workman has been paid compensation equivalent of fifteen days' average pay for every completed year of service or any part thereof in excess of six months; and

iii) Notice in the prescribed manner is served on the appropriate government.

Transfer of undertaking: Where the ownership or management of an undertaking is transferred to a new employer, every workman who has been in continuous service for one year in that undertaking before such transfer shall be entitled to notice and compensation as if the workman had been retrenched. The workman will not be entitled to such notice and compensation if:

i) The service of the workman has not been interrupted by such transfer;

ii) The terms and conditions of service after the transfer are not less favourable to the workman than those before the transfer.

iii) The new employer, under the terms of such transfer, is legally liable to pay retrenchment compensation to the workman on the basis that the service has been continuous and uninterrupted by the transfer.

Closure: Closure has been defined as the permanent closing down of a place of employment or part thereof. An employer intending to close down an undertaking shall be required to give sixty days' prior notice to the appropriate government stating clearly the reasons for the closure. But it shall not apply to:

i) An undertaking in which less than fifty workmen are employed or were employed on an average per working day in the preceding 12 months;

ii) An undertaking set up for the construction of buildings, bridges, roads, canals, dams or for other construction work or project.

If an undertaking is closed down, every workman, who has been in continuous service for not less than one year in that undertaking, shall be entitled to notice and compensation as if the workman had been retrenched.

The Act was amended in March 1976, imposing some restrictions on the employer's right of lay-off, entrenchment, and closure. These special provisions shall apply to all industrial establishments in which not less than 100 workmen were employed on an average per working day for the preceding 12 months.

Lay-off, Retrenchment and Closure (Chapter V-B)

Lay-off: No workman whose name is borne on the muster rolls of an industrial establishment is to be laid-off by his employer except with the previous permission of such authority as may be specified by the appropriate government by a notification in the Official Gazette, unless such lay-off is due to shortage of power or natural calamity. The authority to whom the application for permission has been made, may, after making such enquiry as he thinks fit, grant or refuse, for reasons to be recorded in writing, the permission applied for. If the authority does not communicate the permission or the refusal to grant the permission to the employer within a period of two months from the date on which the application is made, the permission applied for will be deemed to have been granted on the expiration of the said period of two months. In such circumstances, the workmen shall be entitled to all the benefits under any law for the time being in force as if they had not been laid-off.

Retrenchment: No workman employed in any industrial establishment, who has been in continuous service for not less than one year under an employer, shall be retrenched by that employer until:

i) The workman has been given three months' notice in writing, indicating the reasons for retrenchment and period of notice has expired, or the workman has been paid, in lieu of such notice, wages for the period of the notice: provided that no such notice shall be necessary if the retrenchment is under agreement, which specifies a date for the termination of service;
ii) The workman has been paid, at the time of retrenchment, compensation which shall be equivalent to 15 days' average pay for every completed year of continuous service or any part thereof in excess of six months; and
iii) Notice in the prescribed manner is served on the appropriate government or such authority as may be specified by the appropriate government by a notification in the Official Gazette, and the permission of such government or authority is obtained.

The appropriate government or authority may, after making such inquiry, grant or refuse, for reasons to be recorded in writing, the permission for the retrenchment. If the permission for the retrenchment is refused, such retrenchment shall be deemed to be illegal.

Closure: An employer who intends to close down an undertaking or an industrial establishment shall serve, for previous approval, at least ninety days before the date on which the intended closure is to become effective, a notice, in the prescribed manner, on the appropriate government, stating clearly the reasons for the intended closure of the undertaking.

If the appropriate government is satisfied that the reasons for the intended closure of the undertaking are not adequate and sufficient or that the closure is prejudicial to the public interest, it may direct the employer not to close down such undertaking. If the appropriate government does not communicate the permission or the refusal to grant the permission to the employer within a period of two months from the date on which the application is made, the permission applied for shall be deemed to have been granted on the expiration of the said period of two months. If the permission for closure is refused, the closure of the undertaking shall be deemed to be illegal. There is also a provision for restarting an undertaking closed down otherwise than for unavoidable circumstances beyond the control of the employer. In the case of such closure, every workman who has put up one year of continuous service shall be entitled to notice and compensation as if the said workman had been retrenched.

Penalties

The Act provides for penalties for illegal strikes and lockouts, for instigation to participate in an illegal strike, for giving financial aid for illegal strikes and lockouts, for breach of settlements and awards, for disclosing confidential information, and penalty for closure without notice.

Miscellaneous

Offence by companies: Where a person committing an offence under this Act is a company, or another body corporate, or an association of persons every director, manager, secretary, agent or other officer or person concerned with the management thereof shall, unless he proves that the offence was committed without his knowledge or consent, be deemed to be guilty of such offence.

Pendency of proceedings: During the pendency of any conciliation proceeding before a conciliation officer or a board or any proceeding before an arbitrator or a labour court or tribunal or national tribunal in respect of an industrial dispute, no employer shall:

a) In regard to any matter connected with the dispute, alter, to the prejudice of workmen concerned in such dispute, the conditions of service applicable to them immediately before the commencement of such proceeding; or
b) For any misconduct connected with the dispute, discharge or punish, whether by dismissal or otherwise, any workman concerned in such dispute, save with the express permission in writing of the authority before which the proceeding is pending.

During the pendency of any such proceeding in respect of an industrial dispute, the employer may, in accordance with the standing orders applicable to a workman concerned in such dispute:

a) Alter, in regard to any matter not connected with the dispute, discharge or punish, whether by dismissal or otherwise, that workman.
b) For any misconduct not connected with the dispute, discharge or punish, whether by dismissal or otherwise, that workman; provided that no such workman shall be discharged or dismissed unless he has been paid wages for one month and an application has been made by the employer to the authority before which the proceeding is pending for approval of the action taken by the employer. No employer shall, during the pendency of any such proceeding in respect of an industrial dispute, take any action against any protected workman concerned in such dispute:
    a) By altering, to the prejudice of such protected workman, the conditions of service applicable to him immediately before the commencement of such proceedings; or
    b) By discharging or punishing, whether by dismissal or otherwise, such protected workman, save with the express permission in writing of the authority before which the proceeding is pending.

A protected workman in an establishment means a workman who being a member of the executive or other office bearer of a registered trade union connected with the establishment, is recognised as such in accordance with rules made in this behalf.

In every establishment, the number of workman to be recognised as protected workman shall be one per cent of the total number of workmen employed therein, subject to a minimum number of 5 protected workman and a maximum number of 100 protected workmen, and for the aforesaid purpose, the appropriate government may make rules providing for the distribution of such protected workmen among various trade unions, if any, connected with the establishment and the manner in which the workmen may be chosen and recognised as protected workmen.

Power to transfer certain proceedings: The government may, by an order in writing withdraw any proceeding before any labour court or tribunal or national tribunal and transfer it to any other authority.

Recovery of money due from an employer: Where any money is due to a workman from an employer under a settlement or an award or otherwise, the workman may make an application to the government for recovery of the dues within a period not exceeding three months.

Representation of parties: A workman or an employer, who is a party to an industrial dispute, may be represented in any proceedings under the Act by an officer of a registered trade union or by an officer of the association of employers respectively. However, a party to a dispute may be represented by a legal practitioner in proceedings before a court or tribunal with the consent of the other party and with the permission of the adjudicator.

Power to exempt: The appropriate government is vested with the power to exempt any industrial establishment or undertaking, carried on by a department of that government, from all or any of the provisions of the Act.

Protection of action taken under the Act: No suit, prosecution or legal proceeding shall lie against any person for anything which is done, or intended to be done, in good faith in pursuance of this Act or any rules made there under.

Power to make rules: The appropriate government may, subject to the condition of previous publication, make rules for the purpose of giving effect to the provisions of this Act.

Obligations of Employers

1) Constitute Works Committees and provide all facilities for their proper working.
2) Implement all agreements, settlements and awards, and produce all documents and render other assistance for conciliating and adjudicating disputes.
3) Desist from declaring any illegal lockout.
4) Pay lay-off, retrenchment and closure compensation as required under the Act.
5) Avoid any change in service and employment conditions without giving 21 days notice.
6) Maintain *status quo* during pendency of disputes in conciliation and adjudication as laid down in the Act.
7) Avoid unfair labour practices.

Obligations of Workers

1) Abide by the agreements or settlements arrived at in conciliation, and awards given by the tribunals and arbitrators.
2) Desist from declaring or instigating any illegal strike.
3) Cooperate with all authorities set up under the Act in resolving disputes amicably and expeditiously.
4) Refrain from committing unfair labour practices specified under the Act.

References

Agarwal, S.L., 1978. *Labour Relations Law in India*, Macmillan Company of India Ltd.,New Delhi.

Briscoe, D.R. 1995, *International Human Resource Management*, Prentice Hall, New Jersey.

Indian Law Institute,1987. *Labour Law and Labour Relations Cases and Materials*, N.M. Tripathi Pvt. Ltd, Bombay.

Mallick, P.L., 1989. *Industrial Law*, Eastern Book Company, Lucknow.

8

Issues in Comparative Labour Relations

Labour relations should be seen as an essential part of management systems and techniques, and not as a discipline or activity apart from management. It then seeks to explain what sound industrial relations and labour relations policy formulation are, and thereafter to underline the importance and objectives of sound industrial relations in the current - and to some extent the future context. It next examines the role of various systems and mechanisms at different levels as well as their contribution to promoting sound industrial relations. It also attempts to identify some of the elements which may generally be regarded as features of a good industrial relations system.

Changes in labour relations within an organisation are often affected by management practices. Therefore attitudes towards industrial relations should be understood in the background of theories and practices relating to the management of enterprises and organisational behaviour. In this context it is useful to note two important - and diametrically opposite - theories about management. The first and earlier theory is to be found in the scientific management school, which viewed the worker as a mere cog in the organisational structure. Since, according to Taylor, the worker does not possess creative ability let alone intelligence and wisdom, the elements of a human-oriented management system which promotes sound industrial relations such as communication, consultation and participation, found no place in the theory. This concept of management can be seen as an ideal breeding ground for an industrial relations system based on conflict rather than on cooperation.

The opposite theory, appropriately styled the human relations school, had as one of its earliest and greatest exponents, Douglas McGregor. He gave an impetus to the development of a management theory which focused on the human being as part of an enterprise which, in turn, was viewed as a biological system, rather than as a machine. Human relations, trust, delegation of authority, etc. were some of the features of this theory.

Two basic realities of an organisation in McGregor's model is the dependence of every manager on people under him and the potential of people to be developed to match organisational goals. He therefore postulated that people are not by nature resistant to change in an organisation, and that people have the potential to be developed and to shoulder responsibility. As such, management's main task is to organise business in such a way as to match people's goals with organisational ones. McGregor believed that the dynamism for organisational growth is found in the employees of the organisation. It could be said that in McGregor's Theory Y is to be found the essence of human-oriented management and workplace industrial relations systems.

As explained by Bartlett and Ghoshal, in this concept of an enterprise top level managers see themselves as the designers of strategy, the architects of structure, and the managers of systems. The impact of the three S's was to create a management system which minimised the idiosyncrasies of human behaviour, emphasised discipline, focus and control, and led to the view that people were "replaceable parts".

The basic flaw - particularly in the context of today's globalised environment - of this concept is that it stifled the most scarce resource available to an enterprise: the knowledge, creativity and skills of people. Successful enterprises have now moved away from this corporate design, and their philosophy, which has transformed corporations enabling them to compete in the new competitive environment, consists of the following:

"First, they place less emphasis on following a clear strategic plan than on building a rich, engaging corporate purpose. Next, they focus less on formal structural design and more on effective management processes. Finally, they are less concerned with controlling employees' behaviour than with developing their capabilities and broadening their perspectives. In sum, they have moved beyond the old doctrine of strategy, structure, and systems to a softer, more organic model built on the development of purpose, process, and people."

Those enterprises which have effected a successful transformation to a more 'people focused' organisation recognise that the information necessary to formulate strategy is with their frontline people, who know what is actually going on, whether it be in the marketplace or on the shopfloor.

How do these developments relate to enterprise level labour relations? In essence, they heighten the importance of the basic concepts of information sharing, consultation and two-way communication. The effectiveness of the procedures and systems which are established for better information flow, understanding and, where possible, consensus building, is critical today to the successful management of enterprises and for achieving competitiveness. As such, the basic ingredients of sound enterprise level labour relations are inseparable from some of the essentials for managing an enterprise in today's globalised environment. They are reducing layers of management thus facilitating improved communication. Management today is more an activity rather than a badge of status or class within an organisation, and this change provides it with a wider professional base.

The present trend in labour relations and human resource management is to place greater emphasis on employee involvement, harmonious employer - employee relations and mechanisms, and on practices which promote them. One of the important consequences of globalisation and intense competition has been the pressure on firms to be flexible. Enterprises have sought to achieve this in two ways. First, through technology and a much wider worker skills base than before in order to enhance capacity to adapt to market changes. Second, by introducing a range of employee involvement schemes with a view to increasing labour-management cooperation at the shop floor level, necessary to achieve product and process innovation. Achieving flexibility does not depend on the absence of unions.

Manufacturers in Japan and Germany were more successful than those in Britain and France in achieving this flexibility. The former two countries after World War 11 institutionalised labour management consultation.Many organisations have successfully transformed themselves to promote the role of trust.In both strategies involving the use of technology and promotion of innovation, employees are a critical factor. The requirement of organisational flexibility and its industrial relations and human resource implications have had a major impact on the way organisations are structured how authority within the firm is exercised and on how decisions are arrived at and work organised.

Traditional assumptions that efficiency is achieved through managerial control, technology and allocation of resources have given way to the view that efficiency is the result of greater involvement of employees in their jobs, teams and the enterprise. Organisations which have made this shift tend to reflect the following characteristics: few hierarchical levels; wide spans of control; continuous staff development; self managing work teams; job rotation; commitment to quality; information sharing; pay systems which cater to performance rewards and not only payment for the job; generation of high performance expectations; a common corporate vision; and participative leadership styles. In Asia too there is a keen awareness in the business community that radical changes are necessary to sustain Asia's dynamic growth.

None of these shifts is feasible without a substantial change in traditional modes of dealing with people in an enterprise.

THEORIES AND ATTITUDES

At its inception, the labour market was dominated by the classical economics view which espoused free and unregulated labour markets. This laisses-faire capitalism led to social injustices and inequities since labour did not have the power to bargain with employers on terms which even approached a degree of equality in bargaining strength. Industrial relations, therefore, initially came to espouse a degree of labour market regulation to correct this unequal bargaining power. Consequently industrial relations developed in the context of the theory that problems in labour relations emanate largely from market imperfections which operate against the interests of labour and cause imbalances in the power relationships of employers and employees. These imperfections were external to the enterprise. These causes for labour problems - external and internal to the enterprise - needed to be addressed through a range of initiatives, both by the State through protective labour laws, conciliation and dispute settlement machinery, by voluntary action on the part of employees to protect themselves and further their interests through trade unionism and by redressing the balance of power.

The focus on relations external to the enterprise - especially through national and industry level collective bargaining - was initially welcomed even by employers in several industrialised countries because it reduced competitive advantage based on labour costs. Besides, collective bargaining in particular transferred one of the most conflictual aspects of the employment relationship - wages - out of the workplace, and made it the responsibility of the respective representatives of employers and employees. Unions naturally welcomed it as it gave them an influential base outside the workplace. When 'transferred' to developing countries, this concept sometimes had disastrous consequences because it facilitated the politicisation of unions.

However, regulation of the external labour market did not necessarily address all the causes of labour problems. A more pluralistic view recognised that labour problems or issues do not relate only to conflict between employers and employees. They include many other forms of problems such as low productivity, absenteeism, high labour turnover, lack of job security, unsatisfactory or unsafe working conditions, non recognition of performance in standardised wage systems, and lack of motivation. Many of these problems cannot be addressed through measures directed purely at the external labour market, and require measures to be taken within the enterprise. Corrective action should include the installation of human resource management policies and practices embodied in concepts such as recruitment and selection, leadership and motivation, employee development and retention, etc. The objective is to ensure a convergence of organisational and individual goals, and to balance individual and organisational needs. With the pressures on enterprises to adapt and change, it is not surprising that employers are pushing for greater concentration on issues at the enterprise level. In the final analysis the quality of an industrial relations system has to be judged by how it works in practice - and that means at the workplace level. This relative neglect provided the 'space' for the rise of human resource management.

Neither view is entirely correct or entirely incorrect, because industrial relations problems do flow from circumstances both external and internal to the enterprise. The problem is that there has been overemphasis on the environment external to the enterprise, so that inadequate attention has been paid to the policies and practices needed within the enterprise. The environment external to the enterprise should be facilitative, and at times "protective" in the sense that it needs to prescribe certain basic standards relating to such areas as social security, safety and health, freedom of association, weekly and other holidays and rest periods, etc.

In more recent times industrial relations has been influenced by other social sciences such as organisational psychology and behaviour. Traditionally economics and law were two main influences on industrial relations, which led to a concentration on macro level industrial relations, and therefore on unions, government and collective bargaining. Organisational behaviour has been influenced by psychology which centres on the individual, and by social psychology which focuses on relationships between people and on group behaviour. While labour problems are the result of imperfections in the employment relationship, industrial relations should be seen as the theories and methods which have been developed over time to address and correct these problems, in both the external and internal labour markets.

During the past decades labour relations was viewed by governments as a means of preventing or minimising conflict. In South and South East Asia this objective was achieved through dispute prevention and settlement mechanisms external to the enterprise. In South Asia the objective was also achieved through restrictions or prohibitions on the freedom of action of employers in matters such as termination of employment, closures and even transfers of employees.

On the other hand, several South East Asian countries resorted to measures to restrict trade union action and to control unions, as well as to avoid union multiplicity. While in South Asia the focus of industrial relations was on equity from the point of view of workers and unions, in South East Asia the emphasis was on economic efficiency and less on worker protection laws. Low unionisation in many Asian countries, strong governments in South East Asian countries and South Korea, and perceptions that unions could be potential obstacles to the direction of economic development led to a relative neglect of industrial relations. Moreover, hierarchical management systems and respect for authority, which have mirrored the external social system, have been inconsistent with consultation, two-way communication, and even with the concept of negotiating the employment relationship. Australia and New Zealand continued to focus on centralised industrial relations, though the emphasis has radically changed in New Zealand during this decade, and is changing in Australia.

But major changes are taking place in Asia. Employers as well as some governments are viewing labour relations from a more strategic perspective. It is increasingly appreciated that how people are managed impact on an enterprise's productivity and quality of goods and services, labour costs, quality of the workforce and its motivation, and on the prevention of disputes as well as on aligning employee aspirations with enterprise objectives.

Factors Affecting Labour Relations

The establishment of a sound or harmonious industrial relations system is a central theme for governments, employers, workers and their representatives, in their endeavours to achieve economic and social development.

The internationalisation of business, intense competition and rapid changes in technology, products and markets have increased the need for economies and enterprises to remain or become competitive. These trends have in turn necessitated a greater reliance than before on workers' skills, productivity and cooperation in achieving competitiveness.

The new information technology, the limits of which are not known in terms of its potential to effect change, is exerting a tremendous impact on the structure of organisations, the nature of work and the way it is organised, and even on the location where work is performed. In societies of the future information and knowledge will be - as in fact they already are - crucial to competitiveness. Technology is already facilitating changes in organisational structures so as to create flatter organisations. This has resulted in less management by command and supervision, in more emphasis on cooperation, information-sharing and communication, and in a more participative approach to managing people.

Many countries are undergoing a process of industrial restructuring which, in some cases, include privatisation of public sector undertakings and technology upgrading. This process has resulted in several social consequences such as redundancy, all of which have sometimes strained the relationships between employers and workers and between the latter and the government.

Another feature is the changes occurring in the workforces, to varying degrees, in both industrialised market economies and developing economies. Many countries have witnessed the emergence of workforces with higher levels of education and skills which need to be managed in a manner different from the way in which employees, especially blue collar employees, have hitherto been managed.

The skills of an employee are, therefore, an issue on which the interests of employers and employees converge, and the "development" of the employee is now of mutual advantage to both employers and employees. Consequently, there is a greater need than before for a cooperative and participative system of industrial relations. Further, the many emerging work arrangements do not fit into the traditional employment relationships. The tendency is to contract with outsiders to perform this work. Even manufacturing companies are becoming essentially assembly firms, and many service organisations now act as brokers, "connecting the customer with a supplier with some intervening advice".Another category of employees consists of the increasing number of temporary and part-time employees in the rapidly expanding service industries, some of which experience peak periods requiring a flexible labour force. Thus, instead of one workforce, we are moving towards these various groups, each with different contractual arrangements and requiring to be managed differently. The indications are that at the beginning of the next century less than half the workforce in industrialised countries will be in full-time employment as we know it.

The role of unions is changing. During the cold war, political considerations sometimes dominated or influenced union activities, attitudes and their role, especially in some of the developing countries. Unions are now gradually concentrating more on their traditional role in industrial relations, which is to improve the working conditions of their members and to protect their interests through negotiation.

OBJECTIVES OF SOUND INDUSTRIAL RELATIONS

A sound industrial relations system is not capable of precise definition. Every industrial relations system has to take into account, and reflect, cultural factors. Systems cannot change culture, but only behaviour within a cultural environment. As such, one can only describe some of the elements which have generally come to be recognised as contributing to a sound industrial relations system.

A sound industrial relations system is one in which relationships between management and employees (and their representatives) on the one hand, and between them and the State on the other, are more harmonious and cooperative than conflictual and creates an environment conducive to economic efficiency and the motivation, productivity and development of the employee and generates employee loyalty and mutual trust. Industrial relations itself may again be described as being concerned with the rules, processes and mechanisms through which the relationship between employers and employees and their respective representatives, as well as between them on the one hand and the State and its agencies on the other, is regulated.

The rules, processes and mechanisms of an industrial relations system are found in sources such as laws practices, customs, agreements and arrangements arrived at through a bipartite or tripartite process or through prescription by the State.

Industrial relations operates at different levels - at the national level, at the level of the industry and at the enterprise level. The elements which reflect a sound industrial relations system at all these levels are not necessarily the same. At the national level industrial relations operates so as to formulate labour relations policy. In market economies this is usually done through a tripartite process involving government, employers and workers and their representative organisations. This process may result in determining wages and other terms and conditions of employment for an industry or sector. It may also result in arrangements on issues which are of mutual concern such as training, ways of avoiding or settling disputes, etc.

At the enterprise level the relationship between employers and workers is more direct, but the interests of workers may be represented by unions. Employers' organisations, however, are not usually involved at the enterprise level in representing the employers' interests with workers or their union, but this does not mean that they do not have an important promotional role at this level. Sound relations at the enterprise level builds trust and confidence between workers and management, which is the point at which the system must ultimately be effective. Effectiveness at one level would naturally have some impact on the other.

A sound industrial relations system requires a labour management relations policy (LMRP). There are many specific objectives of such a policy, all of which go to make up the policy at the national level. The following are some of the objectives, the emphasis varying from country to country depending on the priorities and stage of development of each of them at any given point of time:

i. Employment and job security and increased employment opportunities.

ii. Raising living standards through improved terms and conditions of employment.

iii. Productivity improvement which enables employers to be more competitive and to increase their financial capacity to raise the living standards of the employees.

iv. Minimising conflict, achieving harmonious relations, resolving conflicts through peaceful means and establishing stable social relationships. In Western industrialised societies "harmony" and "harmonious relations" are not explicitly referred to either as an objective or as a means, though basically it represents an important objective in such societies. However, this concept is explicitly referred to in many Asian societies. Development has an economic and social dimension on the one hand and a cultural dimension on the other.

A sound industrial relations climate in an enterprise is essential to a number of issues which are critical to employers, employees and the community. The efficient production of goods and services depends to an extent on the existence of a harmonious industrial relations climate. Efficiency and quality depend on a motivated workforce, for which a sound industrial relations climate is necessary. Productivity - a key consideration of profitability, the ability of enterprises to grant better terms and conditions of employment and for economic and social development - needs a sound labour relations base. Therefore labour management relations should be geared to creating the climate appropriate to securing the cooperation necessary for productivity growth. Labour Management Relations (LMR) and Labour Management Cooperation (LMC) are also important to the creation of a culture which is oriented towards innovation, adaptable to and encourages change, where authority is decentralised and two-way communication, risk-taking and maximising opportunities are encouraged, and where the output rather than the process is what matters.

The experience of countries and regions which have good productivity records underlines the link between labour management relations and productivity. The Japan Productivity Centre, which was supported by the government, reached agreement with the national labour organisation and employers on the following matters:

a) In the long-term, productivity increases employment security. Therefore redundant workers should be relocated by the employer.
b) Concrete measures to enhance productivity should be decided through labour management consultation which will be promoted.
c) Productivity gains should be distributed fairly among management, employees and customers.

Similar principles were recognised by the productivity movement in Europe. The underlying theme here relevant to the present discussion is that all three principles mentioned above form a part of labour management relations and cooperation.

Another important link between labour management relations and productivity has arisen in the context of recent events in many societies and major changes in industrial relations such as the move towards labour market flexibility. These developments have partly resulted from intense competition, new technologies, shorter product life and so on, all of which require flexibility in the use of resources if an enterprise is to remain productive and competitive. These changes are more likely to achieve the objectives of increased productivity, if they are introduced through cooperation and consensus at the enterprise level.

A sound labour management relations system is important to the removal of one of the main objections of workers and unions to productivity drives by employers. Productivity increases have sometimes been opposed by workers and unions on the grounds that they do not result in equitable sharing of benefits to workers and that increased productivity may lead to redundancy. Developing understanding of basic productivity concepts and of the methods of increasing productivity, as, well as of the formulation of equitable productivity gain-sharing schemes help to dispel such suspicions. Labour management relations therefore play a crucial role in securing acceptance by workers and unions of the need for productivity improvement, and also in obtaining their commitment to achieving it.

Cooperation between management and workers or unions facilitates not only a settlement of disputes or disagreements but also the avoidance of disputes which may otherwise arise. At the industry level the relationship between employers' organisations and representatives of workers is a precondition to collective bargaining. Where collective bargaining takes place at the enterprise level, management workers/union relations determine to a great extent the success or otherwise of collective bargaining.

The importance of cooperation in industrial relations and the stability achieved through it to gain economic competitiveness are well illustrated by Germany and Japan.

This cooperation is reflected in Germany's system of collective bargaining in the system of co-determination, and in the vocational training system to which employers and unions have made a substantial contribution, thus ensuring a highly skilled workforce producing goods of the highest quality attractive to the global marketplace. The participative management system also explains the relatively easy acceptance by German workers of technological change.

In a broad sense, therefore, labour management relations policy formulation (LMRP) should aim at achieving social justice through a process of consensus by negotiation so as to avert adverse political, social and economic consequences. Labour relations reflects the power structure in society, and it emphasizes negotiation and reconciliation by peaceful means of the interests of government, workers and employers who are the main participants in the system. Consensus enables the policy formulated to be implemented with the minimum of conflict as it has the support of all three parties. Labour management relations policy also seeks to achieve an acceptable balance between labour and management, necessary for a negotiated development strategy and the establishment or preservation of a society which is essentially pluralist.

Labour-management relations policy formulation is one of the significant tasks at the national level, and its successful formulation and implementation can influence the labour relations climate at the industry and enterprise levels. Such policy formulation, however, can be formulated not only at the national level through a tripartite process, but also at the industry level on a bipartite basis as between employers' and workers' organisations. Whether bipartite policy formulation becomes a part of national policy depends largely on the respective strengths of employers' and workers' organisations. In Sweden, for instance, in the past, the agreements between the union and the employers' organisation tended to be translated into national policy instruments. The policies and methods of training of workers, for example, reflected what the two social partners had identified as appropriate for the industry. The pervasive influence of bipartite arrangements is felt only where there is a 'balance of power' between the social partners. There is less likelihood of bipartism impacting on national policy formulation in developing countries due to strong central governments in many cases, and their assumption of the role of identifying the direction of economic and social policies. The relative weakness of employers' and workers' organisations or of one of them, or the inability of such organisations to agree on the fundamentals of what the labour relations policy should be, often prevents bipartism from influencing national policy formulation.

Freedom of Association

The fundamental premise of a sound industrial relations system is the recognition and existence of the freedom of association accorded to both employers and workers. This freedom should include recognition of organisations of workers and employers as autonomous, independent bodies, subject neither to their domination by each other or by the government. Observance by states of the basic principles of the ILO Convention relating to Freedom of Association and Protection of the Right to Organise No. 87 is often regarded as the yardstick by which a country's recognition of this freedom is measured.

In essence, the Convention postulates that workers and employers, without distinction whatsoever, have the right to establish and to join organisations of their own choosing with a view to defending their respective interests, subject to national legislation which determines the extent to which the guarantees in the Convention will apply to the armed forces and the police. Such organisations have the right to draw up their own constitutions and rules, to elect their representatives in full freedom, to organise their administration and activities and to formulate their programmes. Public authorities are required to refrain from any interference which would restrict this right or impede the lawful exercise of this right. The acquisition of legal personality by these organisations shall not be subject to restrictive conditions. In exercising the rights provided for in the Convention, employers and workers and their respective organisations are required to respect the law of the land, which should not impair the guarantees in the Convention both in respect of its content and its application.

Tripartism and Labour Policy Formulation

Tripartism is the process through which the foundation for a sound industrial relations system can be laid at the national level. Ideally, tripartism is the process whereby the government, the most representative workers' and employers' organisations as independent and equal partners, consult with each other on labour market and related issues which are within their spheres of competence, and jointly formulate and implement national policies on such issues. However, this ideal situation is seldom reflected in practice, especially in developing countries or in societies with fairly authoritarian governments which believe that the direction of economic and social development is largely their responsibility.

There are many examples of tripartite mechanisms at the national level, as well as informal applications of tripartism. In many countries there are minimum wage fixing bodies which reflect the participation of all three parties, often leading to a consensus on minimum wages, and sometimes on other minimum terms of employment. In some countries agreements are reached at the national level among the three partners after a process of bargaining on important social policy issues. The principles agreed upon in the 1950s in Japan as a forerunner to its productivity movement did much towards assisting that country's productivity growth. In Japan, the Industry and Labour Conference has been a major form of cooperation at the national level, and consultative mechanisms exist at the industry level. In Singapore the National Productivity Board is a tripartite body, and is credited with much of the success in productivity improvement there.

At the national level the mechanisms and procedures could be either formal and institutionalised, or else informal and ad hoc. Where the labour administration system consults, on an ad hoc basis, workers' and employers' organisations on subjects falling within their purview, it represents a method of policy formulation on labour management relations. Sometimes these consultations may take place between the two social partners and other public authorities. For instance, a finance ministry may consult the social partners on an issue relating to wage policy.

National level policy formulation can take place through institutions which provide for periodic tripartite discussion and consultation. There are also examples of institutions with functions limited to a particular subject matter such as training, social security, minimum wages and safety and health. Such specialised bodies may even cover collective bargaining, as in the case of the Singapore National Wage Council created in 1972, which was empowered to issue annual guidelines to coordinate collective bargaining with overall economic policy so as to ensure that wages remain consistent with economic development.

Labour management relations policy formulation may take place and be reflected in basic agreements or codes or industrial relations charters in which all three parties in the labour relations system have participated. Some such agreements may be bipartite, and may cover a variety of subjects including principles and procedures of labour relations such as freedom of association, trade union recognition, collective bargaining, labour-management cooperation mechanisms, procedures for the prevention and settlement of disputes, etc. The 1983 Australian national consensus and the succeeding Accords on economic questions among the government, trade unions and employers contributed towards increased employment and profits, and a reduction in the days lost on account of strikes.Other examples include the agreements negotiated by the Tripartite Labour Conference in India the Code of Practice for Industrial Harmony the Code of Practice for the Promotion of Labour Relations the Pancasila Labour Relations and the labour policies resulting from tripartite consultations in Pakistan.

The desire to formulate and practice a tripartite approach to the solution of social policy issues depends very much on the existence of a value system in a society which underpins the whole system, and reflects an acceptance of the principles of cooperation, consultation and, most important, pluralism. In societies where a tradition of democracy is absent so is tripartism, or else it tends to be a 'cosmetic' exercise.

The contribution which tripartism can make to the establishment of a sound industrial relations system can hardly be over-emphasised. Tripartism's rationale is to be found in the principle of democracy, the essence of which is a sharing or diffusion of power flowing from the encouragement or recognition of various pressure groups in a society as an effective safeguard against the centralisation of power. Tripartism as a process is a part of a pluralistic outlook on society through which stability is maintained, freedom of association being the sine qua non, because without the right of association the interest groups in a society cannot function effectively.

Acceptance of the principle of sharing power entails recognition of the fact that capital and labour represent two important pressure groups in society, if for no other reason than that both of them taken together are the principal providers of goods and services and wealth-creators in a market economy.

Role of the Law

Industrial relations systems are founded on a framework of labour law which exerts an influence on the nature of the industrial relations system. However, recourse to the law and its potential to influence the resulting industrial relations system may sometimes be over-emphasised. It is useful, therefore, to examine, from three points of view, the role of the law in influencing an industrial relations system - what its objectives should be and the areas it should cover, as well as what the law cannot achieve.

In any working situation people need to cooperate with each other if there is to be maximum gain to themselves, to management and to society as a whole. Cooperation, however, is not easily obtained as people working together have conflicting interests.

The three main functions of the law in an industrial relations system have been describedas auxiliary, regulatory and restrictive. The first function is the support it gives to the autonomous system of collective bargaining, its operation and observance of agreements. The second function is one of providing a set of rules governing the terms and conditions of employment and supplementing those created by the parties themselves. The greater the coverage by collective bargaining, the less will be the regulatory function of the law. The third function prescribes what is permitted or forbidden in industrial conflict with a view to protecting the parties from each other, and the public from both of them.

One major objective of labour law is to create the legal framework which is necessary for employers, workers and their organisations to function effectively and as autonomous groups in the industrial relations system. Hence the law should protect the freedom of association so that the two parties are accorded the protections and guarantees found in the ILO Convention on the Freedom of Association and Protection of the Right to Organise No. 87. Since one of the major purposes of such association is to enable workers and employers to protect and further their interests, the law should also provide the legal framework needed to promote collective bargaining.

A second important function of labour law is to prescribe the minimum terms and conditions of employment which should be observed by employers in the course of conducting business. Therefore, the legal system often contains provisions stipulating the minimum conditions which must be observed in areas such as compensation for industrial accidents, social security, safety and health in enterprises, the minimum age of employment. The basic rules to be followed in terminating employment may be another area of the employment relationship which would need to be covered by minimum standards.

A third, and more general role for the law in industrial relations is as an instrument of social change. The law does not always merely or solely reflect contemporary thinking in society and does not necessarily lag behind social and other values. It sometimes anticipates them and can, on occasion, be employed to fashion new ideas and to effect changes in behaviour. It is not always possible to leave crucial and complex social issues to be solved through purely voluntary action such as collective bargaining. Sometimes, especially in developing countries, the absence of strong and independent trade unions reduces the effectiveness and role of voluntary action, and necessitates greater regulation through legal prescription. But intervention on this ground should not lead to the introduction of rigidities in the labour market through overregulation.

Legal prescription should be viewed as merely laying down minimum terms and defining the permissible boundaries of action within which the two parties (employers and workers) must operate. Over regulation through law could have adverse consequences on building a sound industrial relations system through voluntary action, and on the competitiveness of enterprises. This has been perceived to be so in countries such as India and Sri Lanka, where employers have for some time canvassed for greater flexibility and less legislative control over industrial relations. Over regulation is sometimes based on the misconception that sound industrial relations can be achieved through the law.

The creation of harmonious industrial relations needs to be achieved by other, nonlegal means; the law cannot 'compel' parties to establish good relations. By way of analogy, in a different field of human relations, the law can prescribe the rules to be followed if people wish to marry. But the law cannot create a happy relationship or marriage. Some countries, such as those in South Asia, which have a tradition of a plethora of labour laws, have tended to overlook the fact that if the energy expended by the State in enacting and enforcing a mass of labour laws had been spent in finding ways and means of encouraging mechanisms and systems geared to achieving sound labour relations, better results may have been achieved. In such countries parties tend to look to the law for the solution of what are essentially human relations problems, and creativity and innovation in industrial relations are consequently stifled.

Statute law is one of the specific means used by the State to condition industrial relations outcomes, and represents the most direct means of State intervention. Statutory regulation of minimum terms and conditions such as minimum wages, working conditions, safety and health, social security and protection become terms and conditions in contracts of employment which must conform to them; they cannot be 'bargained' away. Other statutory provisions may be of a more facilitating nature such as ones which establish the conditions and the environment for collective bargaining ; they are no less fundamental and important. Another - and more indirect - method through which the State influences industrial relations is the system of labour courts, tribunals or arbitration, which are a common feature in many countries. Through these institutions the State seeks to dispense equity in the employment relationship, and they may also protect collective interests as in the case of trade union rights. The pronouncements of these courts often constitute important limits to the freedom of action of the actors in industrial relations. Still another method of State intervention is through its 'administrative' role, for example, as conciliator or mediator.

LABOUR COURTS

The agents of change in industrial relations are usually trade unions, employers and their organisations, governments through legislation and administrative action, and the system of courts which may be a combination of the normal courts and special courts or tribunals set up to deal with matters pertaining to labour. These special courts vary in nature from country to country. They include labour courts and tribunals and arbitration systems - the latter sometimes the creation of collective bargaining agreements which provide for arbitration to settle disputes.

Courts and tribunals have generally not been a major factor in bringing about change in industrial relations in industrialised countries. The role of the 'courts would normally be limited to their powers of interpretation, which do not provide much scope to effect major changes in industrial relations. As in the case of legislation, the role of the courts can have little impact on the basic attitudes of management and workers towards each other at the enterprise level and can, therefore, do little to improve relations as such. The normal civil courts have not evinced an appreciation of labour issues, especially in Britain where, at the turn of the century, many decisions of the courts had to be reversed by legislation to enable trade unions to fulfil their role. However, there are some exceptions. In that country the courts have been responsible for formulating many of the rules relating to strikes. The use of the injunction in the USA during the early stages of its industrial relations evolution is another example. Australia is a good example of an industrialised country in which the courts system, as represented by the earlier Court of Conciliation and Arbitration and since 1988 the Australian Industrial Relations Commission, has had a fairly major influence on industrial relations. In those two countries thousands of court decisions have enunciated the rules regarding such issues as the grounds on which termination of employment may be considered fair or unfair; the principles of wage fixation; when trade union action may be considered legal or illegal, justified or unjustified; and even what forms of trade union action are permissible or not permissible.

In the final analysis the quality of relations between employers and employees in an enterprise depends on the policies, practices and procedures which exist at the enterprise level to deal with both individual and collective issues, and to promote labour-management cooperation. There are, therefore, numerous enterprise level mechanisms in different countries. The development of enterprise level industrial relations facilitates, as it did in Japan, adjustments to structural changes. Indeed, it is a way of reconciling the need for enhanced management flexibility with the need to ensure that employees' concerns are taken account of and their cooperation obtained without which successful change would hardly be possible.

The elements of a sound industrial relations system are closely linked to a progressive human resource management policy translated into practice. Harmonious industrial relations are more likely to exist in an enterprise where human resource management policies and practices are geared to proper recruitment and training, motivational systems, two-way communication, career development, a people-oriented leadership and management style, etc. Many of these human resource management activities have an impact on the overall industrial relations climate in an enterprise. Some of the best managed enterprises tend to integrate human resource management policies into their corporate culture and strategies.

Since the 1980s the emphasis in theory, and in the practice of some companies, has been on strategic human resource management. This transformation in the USA, for example, provided the following lessons:

i. Adversarial workplace relations are not in the interests of either employees or the enterprise.
ii. Competitive strategies based on low costs and low wages result in a high incidence of labourmanagement conflicts, a low level of trust, and are impediments to innovation and quality.
iii. Strategies based on technology and traditional industrial relations approaches only do not result in high levels of performance, which can be achieved by integrating innovations in human resource management with new technologies.
iv. Some forms of employee involvement such as Quality of Worklife and Quality Circle initiatives do not transform organisations or sustain themselves, without employee involvement at all levels of decision making, including strategic decision making.

The practice of human resource management did not match the theories expounded, though in the 1990s more progress has been made in narrowing the gap between theory and practice.

WORKER PARTICIPATION AND EMPLOYEE INVOLVEMENT

It is important at the outset to separate several issues relating to participation, communication and consultation: the principle of communication; the methods or means to give effect to this principle; and whether the principle and/or means should be enshrined in legislation, or should be the subject of bipartite negotiation, or should be at the employer's initiative.

There can hardly be any debate on the principle i.e. the value and need for consultation and communication in an age when it is accepted that information sharing and consultation are important to enterprise performance, productivity and employee motivation. Effective corporate strategies can no longer be developed by top management without information inputs from, and relying on the knowledge of, frontline employees. Consultation and communication mechanisms introduced voluntarily after consultation with employees is likely to be seen as part of an organisation's culture, rather than as ones imposed and reluctantly accepted.

There is no ideal model of communication and consultation because, to be effective, it must fit the purpose, the type of organisation, and cultural requirements if any. However, the value of models is that they underscore the need for such systems and provide useful guidelines which can be adapted to suit national and enterprise conditions.

The worker participation model that gives unions the most influence at enterprise level in the West is probably the co-determination and works council system in Germany. Co-determination takes the form of equal representation of management and workers on the supervisory boards of limited liability companies employing more than 2,000 employees. Though made more widely applicable by the Co-determination Acts of 1976, the system has been in vogue since 1951 in the steel and coal industries. Further, German law requires the establishment of a Works Council in undertakings employing a minimum of five persons. Co-determination represents a method of worker participation at a very high level in an enterprise. The powers of works councils are reflected in their rights of co-decision making on personnel matters such as welfare, accident prevention, leave arrangements and hours of work.

Few countries favour the German model of co-determination, even if it works well in Germany. It is perceived as providing scope for participation by unions rather than by employees. In any event, in countries with much lower union rates, participation on the German model will not necessarily mean that the employees are adequately represented.

With increasing acceptance of the fact that the crucial competitive weapon will be the skills and performance of the workforce, emphasis is being placed on greater involvement of employees in matters affecting their work and jobs, through consultation, information sharing and two-way communication procedures. This is all the more necessary in activities requiring the use of skills and knowledge. Greater worker involvement is likely to occur in the future for the following reasons:

i. Employees at all levels are acquiring higher educational qualifications and skills.

ii. Quality and productivity tend to increase when employees are more involved in arriving at decisions at the point of production.

iii. For effective decision making in modern enterprises there should be an information flow and analysis of data and information.

iv. Work today requires and involves more interpersonal skills, greater coordination among workers and sharing of information.

v. Enterprises which have moved beyond the stage of routine high volume production to more value added and knowledge-based activities need to promote increased innovation, creativity and better application of knowledge, all of which require worker involvement.

vi. Participation is a great motivational tool because it gives people a degree of control, recognises personal worth, and provides scope for personal growth.

Communication and consultation mechanisms, and quality of worklife programmes referred to below, are all aspects of employee involvement.

Communication

The starting point for any effective enterprise policy to install procedures and mechanisms to promote sound labour relations is communication, because it is relevant to a whole range of issues and other matters such as productivity, small group activities, joint consultation, performance appraisals, and motivation, as well as to organisational performance.

The performance of an organisation is affected by the manner in which that organisation communicates with its employees. This involves information exchange, and not merely one-way communication. The performance of employees in an organisation is conditioned by the performance of others in the organisation. Changes in an organisation can be brought about in an effective way where there is sufficient understanding between management and employees. For this purpose two-way communication tends to enhance understanding and cooperation and influence behaviour in a desired direction. Communication is essential not only in relation to existing employees but also in relation to new employees who must be made aware of what the job entails. Making available to employees the means of communicating their opinions and problems is also important to an effective performance appraisal system.

For effective communication in an enterprise it is necessary to develop communication channels not only at the macro level but also at the micro level. Effective leadership and decision-making are heavily dependent on communication and information flows. The way people respond to us is often influenced by how we project ourselves and how they perceive us. Projection of a feeling of inferiority or a lack of confidence tends to result in others not being receptive to what we wish to communicate, while an image of self-confidence tends to have the opposite effect. But,,speaking down to people and an image of arrogance create hostility and resentment and is an obstacle to communication. Being a sensitive communicator giving information and receiving feedback is an essential attribute of an effective manager.

Of all the resources available to an enterprise it is only people who are capable of being motivated. It is also a resource which is capable of being developed by management, and one over which the employer has a great degree of control. Effective two-way communication is an important source of motivation. Hence the link between productivity, motivation and effective two-way communication.

The link between productivity and communication is to be found in the fact that proper productivity management requires concerted or joint action between management and workers. For this purpose confidence between management and workers is essential, and the starting point of confidence-building is sharing information. This has prompted the view that productivity management is also information management - information helps to promote the commitment that is necessary to improve productivity.

In many organisations communication between people often occurs in the context of small group activities. Therefore two-way communication must reinforce productive small group activities and help to build and maintain an effective team. Effective communication would:

i. Create an atmosphere of trust, which is important to promoting increased productivity. If the environment generates mistrust, workers are likely to be suspicious as to whether they are receiving a fair share of the benefits of productivity gains.

ii. Promote an atmosphere of 'intimacy' and commitment to the group, which in turn would bind people together and prompt cooperation.

iii. Promote - especially where the elements of trust and intimacy are present integration of the worker in the activities of the group and a feeling of 'belonging' leading to greater motivation and productivity.

iv. Promote participation, which involves common goals, teamwork, discipline/commitment and cooperation.

v. Develop the skills and attitudes of the individual, engendering self-confidence and a sense of self worth. In a highly hierarchical and 'top-down' form of management there is little scope for development of the individual which is needed for innovation and creativity which, in turn, promote better productivity.

vi. Create a high degree of consensus in decision making. With consensus implementation of decisions will be quicker and easier because disputes or differences of opinion would be less likely compared to enterprises where decisions are taken unilaterally with little consultation and information-sharing.

It is worthwhile underlining some of the salient points in regard to the importance of two-way communication and small group activities:

i. Productivity improvement is primarily management's responsibility.

ii. Two-way communication and small group activities can promote cooperation, trust, intimacy, consensus-building, and generally improve the human relations climate within the enterprise.

iii. Productivity improvement - which is possible in the long term only in an environment which contains the elements referred to in (ii) above - enables enterprises to remain or become competitive.

There are several International Labour Standards of the ILO which seek to give effect to the elements of consultation, cooperation and communication. As regards consultation and cooperation, the Cooperation at the Level of the Undertaking Recommendation 1952 (No. 94) contemplates the promotion of consultation in the enterprise on matters of mutual concern not covered in collective bargaining or other machinery concerned with the prescription of terms and conditions of employment.

As regards communication, the Communications within the Undertaking Recommendation 1967 prescribes a communications policy for an enterprise. It underlines the importance, in the interests of both management and workers, of mutual trust and understanding which can be generated through an exchange of information. It contemplates the adoption by management of an effective communications policy, but only after consultation with representatives of workers. Among the main elements of a communications policy should be the following:

— Unions and employers have long been aware of the importance of information sharing in an industrial relations system after bitter and protracted strikes in the forties and early fifties, both management and labour made concerted efforts to restore industrial peace and to develop a stable industrial relations system these efforts led to the development of key aspects of the modern Japanese industrial relations system.

— Japanese joint consultation systems had their origins in the 1950s when it was promoted by the Japan Productivity Centre. It is estimated that by 1990 about 84 per cent of unionised enterprises had set up joint consultation schemes, and 44 per cent of non-unionised ones had joint consultation arrangements. These mechanisms, which are an aspect of two-way communication, deal with a variety of issues. In both union and non-union establishments the most common subjects which come within consultation are working conditions, working hours, leave, safety and health, welfare and cultural activities, bonus, pension and retirement payments, work scheduling, education and training, recruitment; transfers, lay off, job assignment.

— In Japan the frequency of joint consultation meetings vary. But on an average in unionised firms they may meet about 15 times and in non-unionised firms about 8 times a year. Research suggests that information-sharing through the joint consultation system has had a positive effect on profitability, labour productivity and on reducing labour costs, especially in the manufacturing sector.

— In Japan different views on the effectiveness of joint consultation exist in relation to unionised and non-unionised firms.

One of the important characteristics of Joint Consultation in Japan is that collective bargaining and joint consultation serve different objectives and are therefore not in conflict with each other. Bargainable issues are dealt with under collective bargaining and non-bargainable ones under joint consultation. Where during joint consultation some issues become bargainable, they will be transferred to the collective bargaining forum. It is also an important characteristic of the joint consultation system that it does not handle individual grievances, which are dealt with under grievance handling procedures.

Joint consultation has made a significant contribution to enterprise level labour relations by creating mutual understanding on a range of management issues which impinge on the lives of employees. In effect, therefore, collective bargaining takes place from a point which has achieved some degree of common objectives. Since information on wage criteria is also shared, differences in wage negotiations are narrowed, facilitating acceptable compromises and negotiations without disputes.

In essence, joint consultation has become the means through which information is shared; mutual understanding is promoted; participation in arriving at decisions is facilitated; and working conditions negotiated. As such, it is an essential part of Japanese enterprise level labour relations. The enterprise level union system significantly contributes to the workability and effectiveness of the joint consultation system.

In the Japanese industrial relations system at the enterprise level several other channels of communication exist such as small group activities grievance procedures; suggestion systems; shop floor meetings.

Quality circles, introduced in Japan in the early 1960s, had increased by the early 1990s to over three hundred thousand groups covering about 2 ½ million workers. A quality circle is a small group which performs quality control activities in the workshop to which it belongs. These groups, consisting of about 5-8 workers per group, are generally found in the larger enterprises.

The impact of quality circles is reflected in improved organisational performance, increased opportunities for employees to fulfil higher order needs which are not satisfied through normal routine work, and higher levels of motivation.

Quality of Working Life Programmes

Quality of Work Life (QWL) programmes aim at combating worker alienation, integrating workers and encouraging worker involvement in the enterprise. They also aim at increasing worker motivation and instilling a sense of responsibility as well as at changing work organisation so as to reduce costs and increase flexibility. The model QWL agreement was the one entered into between General Motors and the United Auto Workers' Union in 1973, and many other enterprises followed suit. "Empirical studies which have sought to determine the effectiveness of the quality of working life programmes have found positive effects of such programmes on reducing absenteeism, grievances, quits, and on increasing job satisfaction, and health and safety practices." Thomas A. Kochan and Kirsten R. Weverpoint out that studiesindicate that "unless worker participation programmes address the basic economic needs of employers as well as enhancing the economic security and job satisfaction of the employees, they are destined to occupy comparatively marginal status."

Training

The importance of human resources development in dispute prevention and settlement is often overlooked. Many workplace problems and issues are the result of unsatisfactory supervisory management and the lack of awareness on the part of employees about the workings of the enterprise.

Well managed enterprises see supervisors as critical to labour relations because it is they who interact most often with employees, are the first to identify problems, and it is their attitudes towards employees which condition the latter's views about the management. Supervisory development is therefore an important aspect of developing sound labour relations at the enterprise level.

Equally important in Japan is the investment in training and educating of employees. Career development opportunities afforded to employees usually commence with orientation and induction programmes for new recruits. Skills development through on-the-job and off-the-job training coupled with extensive job rotation, produce multi-skilled employees who are acquainted with how the company as a whole functions. Three important consequences flow from this. First, team work becomes the norm, and employees are able to support each other. Second, it is easier to find career development opportunities within the firm. Consequently employees tend to look to the "internal labour market" rather than to the external labour market for their advancement. Third, employees are more amenable than otherwise to look for long term gains rather than short term ones. When these practices are coupled with collective bargaining and consultation procedures, the result is a greater potential for cooperation, joint activity and mutual understanding. In fact, without human resources development it is doubtful whether establishing communication channels would be likely to have the desired result.

In each of these areas, there are implications for IR/HRM policies and practices and how they are resolved will be critical to achieving and maintaining enterprise competitiveness. On this basis, an employers' strategy in the area of employment relations must focus on achieving:

— appropriate attitudinal and behavioural changes, not only at enterprise, but at other, levels;
— a modern policy, legislative and institutional framework which ensures an effective industrial relations system;

- compensation systems linked to enterprise performance;
- a more literate, skilled and adaptable workforce, which is capable of experimentation and innovation;
- more flexible forms of work organisation and management; and
- culturally-sensitive management strategies, as firms invest within and beyond the region.

(a) Attitudinal and behavioural changes

IR is by nature adversarial. The task of minimising conflict in a time of change and producing mutually beneficial outcomes through negotiation is made harder by unnecessarily antagonistic attitudes. In addition, management practices involving close and rigid supervision and maintaining restrictive work practices are obstacles to the workplace changes now needed by employers. The need for change is likely to be accepted more readily where workers are well informed and are involved, to varying extents, in decision making. Such an approach needs to be supported by more effective recruitment, induction and training arrangements, career development strategies, appropriate motivational systems, and people-centred management approaches. Greater worker involvement in the enterprise should be reinforced by management making stronger efforts to improve relations with workers' representatives. In addition, collective bargaining remains an effective way to address issues of mutual concern.

All of these elements - both IR and HRM - have to be properly integrated into the corporate culture. Overall, this should enable much better use of the talents and abilities of the workforce, and the necessary enterprise changes to be progressed in a more timely and effective manner.

(b) Modern labour polices, legislation and institutions

Employers should be seeking "modern" labour policies, legislation and institutions which encourage industrial harmony. In particular, legislation should be proactive and facilitative in relation to the parties' needs, and avoid unnecessary complexity, while maintaining fair and reasonable minimum employment standards. The legislative framework should also give greater emphasis to the need for labour-management cooperation and settlement of grievances and disputes in the workplace.

(c) Compensation systems linked to enterprise performance

The trend towards decentralised collective bargaining and IR arrangements in the region has been based on the need to address efficiency and productivity issues at their source, the individual enterprise. It has been accompanied by employer demands to link wage increases to clearly identified performance criteria, both at the level of the individual manager and worker and overall enterprise performance. This view has been supported on the basis that productivity and/or profitability increases are the source of employers' capacity to pay, if business competitiveness is to be achieved or maintained.

Employers interested in developing performance-based compensation schemes should direct their attention to arrangements which seek to: achieve some measurable improvement in enterprise performance; attract and motivate competent staff, by providing a component of remuneration above what would otherwise be paid; reward sound performance without increasing labour costs; and achieve flexibility, through a variable component which can respond to changes in the market cycle or poor enterprise performance.

Employers have a number of possible approaches to choose from to develop a scheme to meet the circumstances of a particular enterprise.

(d) A skilled and adaptable workforce

The main sources of productivity growth are technological change, increases in capital intensity, economies of scale and improvements in labour efficiency. Education and training will play a vital role in promoting labour efficiency through the enhancement of workforce skills, and the World Bank has emphasised the significant link between skills development and a country's manufacturing export capacity.

Training of workers in narrow skills is no longer appropriate. Modern technology is increasingly demanding broader skills and new mixes of previously quite distinct skills.

To achieve the objective of a skilled and creative workforce, employers might examine a range of initiatives, in collaboration with government. These could include medium-sized and large companies pursuing particular initiatives in relation to the development of critical generic or industry-specific skills, and the possible implementation of payroll levy/subsidy schemes or other fund-based arrangements to finance training initiatives.

(e) Flexible forms of work organisation and management

Taking advantage of the scope for greater workplace flexibility through changes to work organisation is an important factor in the ability of firms to maintain and improve competitiveness.

Flexibility at the workplace requires workers to have several skills and a broader understanding of the production or work process to enable them to carry out a range of activities. To achieve this outcome, managers and supervisors need to be forward looking, inform and involve workers, and use approaches which enable people to develop and use properly their talents and abilities. This should lead to greater versatility for employers in how they organise and carry out work and a greater capacity to cope with fluctuations in production. The latter practices, in particular, inhibit flexibility and efficiency, and exist for reasons other than the safe and efficient performance of work tasks.

(f) Culturally-sensitive management strategies

Globalisation involves managers and workers moving from one country to another. In doing so, they enter into a new society and culture. Some aspects of these cultures are obvious and can with the necessary goodwill be adapted to. But there are other elements of culture which are not so visible. They include the assumptions made and premises relied on by the members of a certain society; values and unwritten codes of behaviour; and patterns of thinking and problem-solving. They are what the people in that society take for granted. These elements are the essence of a particular culture and are the most difficult to detect.

Managers assuming work responsibilities in a new country must acquaint themselves with both visible and invisible cultural traits, and adopt appropriate strategies to ensure that cultural mismanagement considerations do not become a source of reduced enterprise performance.

(f) Implementing a reform strategy

In implementing a reform agenda based on the above considerations, individual firms should be encouraged to experiment in relation to skills development, work organisation and other forms of improved IR/HRM practices and seek to use the outcomes as a basis for broader government or industry programmes to diffuse new practices on a wider basis. Such initiatives might be undertaken through informal contact with the wider group of firms with whom they conduct their business, and could include local benchmarking exercises. MNC's will continue to have an influential role in shaping local corporate cultures. MNC policies, practices and technologies influence domestic enterprises directly or indirectly.

ROLES OF EMPLOYERS' ORGANISATIONS

Employers' organisations, like trade unions, face a difficult situation in assisting their constituents in the face of the new demands being placed on them by globalisation. Not only do they face the need to become more representative and better able to provide services to their members like unions they confront very different situations from one country to another, and differ in their capacities to fulfil their functions effectively.

A key function of employers' organisations has always been to act as the mouthpiece for employers in seeking to influence the broad policy environment in a manner conducive to their constituents' interests. This representation role will remain significant. But "the ultimate credibility of employers' organisations will depend on the provision of quality services to enterprises and their capacity and skill in negotiating on behalf of employers". In this regard, considerable emphasis is now being given within the region to developing employers' organisations as strong professional organisations. Priority is being given to strategic planning; developing direct services to members across a range of issues and providing the necessary internal capacities to deliver these services.

More specifically, in the area of IR/HRM, employers' organisations need to have a role which is proactive and preventive ie, primarily concerned with promoting among their members the need for sound workplace relations which emphasise the importance of improved cooperation and consultation and effective negotiation to address workplace issues, thereby avoiding industrial disputes and providing a basis for achieving sustainable improvements in enterprise performance.

To achieve this objective, it is suggested that employers' organisations should organise their operations around two functional "poles", supported by a range of subsidiary services. The twin "poles" would consist of developing and/or maintaining an effective representational role and developing an sound information data base.

An active representational role to governments and trade unions in relation to national labour policies and legislation (as noted above), but also for securing public understanding and/or support on certain issues, remains a critical priority for employers' organisations. Many of the issues where influence is sought to be brought to bear are sensitive, have potential labour cost implications and/or are important to employers' day-to-day operations and therefore need careful handling. Employers' organisations need to be prepared to have a view on an increasingly broader range of issues.

A data base of the type proposed should enable easy access by the organisation itself and for its members. It should contain comprehensive information about such issues as: economic performance ; wage levels and trends; trends in and examples of performance-related pay and benefits "packages"; collective agreements; and decisions in court/tribunal cases on the interpretation of labour legislation and agreements and the handling of labour issues. So far as possible such a data base should also include information about "best practices" in relation to various issues both within the country concerned, and, particularly, among trading competitors.

These core functional activities should be supported by: advisory services of a legal nature or of a practical nature ; awareness-raising on issues related to the labour law and promoting sound approaches to IR/HRM issues more generally, training in relation to the handling of day-to-day employment relations issues and specific skills development;

undertaking a representational role with unions in relation to matters in dispute, in conciliation proceedings before a tribunal, and/or in legal proceedings before a court; and participating, on behalf of employer members, in a range of bipartite and tripartite fora, addressing a diverse range of issues.

ROLES OF GOVERNMENT AND TRADE UNIONS

Whatever policies or actions may be promoted or undertaken by one or more of the industrial relations parties will require a response from or have repercussions for other parties or interests.

Government

With its promises of greater FDI, higher export earnings and more employment, globalisation provides a powerful incentive for governments in Asia and the Pacific to liberalise and open their economies.

The essential challenge for governments in the region in the face of globalisation is to seek to encourage and regulate foreign participation in national economic development in a manner that promotes balanced growth with equity. Achieving such an objective is made difficult, however, because of increasing competition between governments for FDI.

In addition, globalisation means that governments have less control over economic planning, and will force policy changes by them, where there is a reluctance to respond. This does not necessarily mean, however, that the role of the State in IR becomes less important under globalisation, merely that its role is different in certain areas. Traditional interventions will still be required at policy and legislative levels, to establish and enforce minimum employment standards. There is a need to ensure that the economic reforms currently being implemented in various countries are accompanied by proper safety net programmes. In addition, new forms of institutional intervention may also be required, given the types of changes taking place in the organisation of production and work at enterprise level, and the fact that there is likely to be greater mobility between jobs and enterprises.

More specifically, export-led growth requires macro-economic measures aimed specifically at exports, industry development and labour markets. Governments need to decide which industries to stimulate and how they can integrate various macro- and micro-policies through a network of institutions that promote economic growth with equity.

But governments have to balance encouragement of investment on terms favourable to management with protecting workers' interests, both in the short and longer terms. Globalisation will impact on economic development in ways which lead to expansion and contraction in various sectors. Also, where there is competition between developing countries for investment protection of workers' interests may be difficult to secure. Workers have to have certain minimum conditions of employment to redress their relative inequality in bargaining power with employers. Governments have a responsibility to ensure that these standards are met by all employers, and, where those employers are foreign companies or MNC's, they must be encouraged to adopt socially responsible attitudes in relation to employment relationships and standards in their host country.

Governments also have to take measures to equip workers with the skills to take up new positions and to move from declining to new industries, possibly to new localities. Some form of income support has to be provided to those who lose jobs, but who are unable to find new positions. There is therefore a role for labour market policies to facilitate structural adjustment in an equitable manner. Such an approach will also require strengthening the capacity of Labour Ministries to provide increased employment services.

At a wider level, governments can encourage more broadly-based trade unionism that is productivityconscious and both promote and provide opportunities, formal and informal, for workers to be engaged in decision-making at a number of levels. Governments can also support trade union strategies to encourage democratic governance, awareness raising on key policy issues and training for union representatives on organisational and technical issues.

Government action in support of globalisation has to rely on policy planning and delivery services provided by the public sector. This sector has to be restructured to meet the demands of, or overcome problems arising from, globalisation. In this regard, Ministries of Labour often have a narrow and reactive role. Given the importance of industrial relations to economic development, they should be working more actively with planning and finance Ministries to generate development options, create more coherent and coordinated strategies and, generally, improve public sector efficiency.

Finally, governments should continue to promote bipartite and tripartitc institutions and processes to establish appropriate labour policy and standards. Inputs from all relevant parties should be considered. Not only will this limit potential conflict in the future, but it should establish a sound basis for investment and economic and employment growth.

Workers and their Organisations

There is no question that trade unions still have a role in Asia and the Pacific. But there is a need for more effective unionism. What do we mean by this? It has been described as a form of unionism which focuses on working with employers in implementing strategies to improve enterprise competitiveness and the quality of work through improvements in work organisation, labourmanagement relations and skills development, on the basis that an equitable share for workers in productivity gains will be achieved. This form of unionism is therefore proactive and strategic in approach, and is no longer concerned with union actions which are restrictive in nature. The development of effective unionism is contingent on the recognition and application of the rights of freedom of association, to organise and to bargain collectively. The needs of trade union organisations will vary from country to country in seeking to build effective unions. For example, awareness raising and training in relation to their role in a market oriented economy will have a much higher priority in the case of trade unions in countries in transition. But whatever individual country circumstances, key objectives of national trade union organisations must be to attract more workers into unions by improving recruitment, offering better services and communicating more effectively with and between members and officials.

In order to maintain support and influence at enterprise level, it will be necessary to build and maintain an active workplace union organisation. The availability of more skilled and technically capable union representatives in the workplace, supported by more professional and better resourced unions at higher levels will also be crucial in achieving these objectives. The extent to which trade unions can adopt and achieve advances through this more proactive role will depend on a number of considerations, including: government policy and attitudes at domestic and international levels; the response(s) of employers and their organisations; and union leadership, organisation and strategies.

References

Bhattacharya, B.B. and Mitra, A. 1993. .Employment and structural adjustment: A look at 1991 census data., in *Economic and Political Weekly*,(Mumbai, Sameeksha Trust, 18 Sep., pp.1989-95.

Chakravarty, S. 1974. *Reflections on the growth process in the Indian economy*, Mimeograph. Hyderabad, Hyderabad Administrative Staff College of India.

Datt, R. 1993. .New economic policy and its impact on industrial relations and employment in India., in *Indian Journal of Labour Economics.* Delhi, Indian Society of Labour Economics, 1, pp. 66-76.

Government of India. 1969. *Report of the Industrial Licensing Policy Enquiry Committee.* Delhi.

Joshi, V. and Little, I. 1996. *India's Economic Reforms: 1991-2001.* Delhi, Oxford University Press.

9

Collective Bargaining

Collective bargaining may take place at the national, industry or enterprise level. It could be said that collective bargaining is a means of settling issues relating to terms and conditions of employment and has little to do with labour management relations policy formulation. Nevertheless collective bargaining may reflect - sometimes explicitly and at other times implicitly - labour management relations policy e.g., on wage guidelines, termination of employment procedures. It can also be a means of developing policy formulation at the industry level. For instance, arrangements and agreements resulting from collective bargaining may provide ways in which wages could be adjusted to meet increases in the cost of living, in which event they will constitute an agreed policy on this issue. They may link a part of wage increases to productivity increases or provide for productivity gain sharing in other ways, in which event they represent policy on aspects of productivity. Methods of dispute settlement would reflect a desire for the peaceful resolution of disputes.

In a more general sense, collective bargaining (which has its supporters as well as its critics)is a critical element in pluralism. As Harry Arthur's explains:"

> Why does pluralism place collective bargaining at the centre? Because, as adherents and critics agree, in the pluralist vision, labour and management, as autonomous interest groups, can and should jointly fix the rules of employment upon terms which represent an acceptable compromise between their competing interests. But is this process of negotiation and compromise a good in itself? Pluralists believe that it is, although their rationales vary: collective bargaining

> replicates the processes by which conflict is and should always be resolved in a democracy; it projects democratic values into the workplace; it preserves the autonomy of social forces as against the pervasive influence of the state; it is faithful to - but makes more acceptable by its mobilisation of countervailing power - the conventional marketplace techniques of economic ordering in a capitalist economy; it ensures the participation, and thereby the moral commitment, of those most directly concerned with outcomes; it represents a significant advance over abusive and oppressive unilateral employer control."

Collective bargaining, inasmuch as it promotes democracy at the enterprise as well as at the national and the industry levels (depending at which level collective bargaining takes place), is an important aspect of a sound industrial relations system.

Nature of Collective Bargaining

The ILO Convention No. 98 (1949) relating to the Right to Organise and to Bargain Collectively describes collective bargaining as:

> "Voluntary negotiation between employers or employers' organisations and workers' organisations, with a view to the regulation of terms and conditions of employment by collective agreements."

There are several essential features of collective bargaining, all of which cannot be reflected in a single definition or description. They are as follows:

i. It is not equivalent to collective agreements because collective bargaining refers to the process or means, and collective agreements to the possible result, of bargaining. There may therefore be collective bargaining without a collective agreement.

ii. It is a method used by trade unions to improve the terms and conditions of employment of their members, often on the basis of equalising them across industries.

iii. It is a method which restores the unequal bargaining position as between employer and employee.

iv. Where it leads to an agreement it modifies, rather than replaces, the individual contract of employment, because it does not create the employer-employee relationship.

v. The process is bipartite, but in some developing countries the State plays a role in the form of a conciliator where disagreements occur, or may intervene more directly (e.g. by setting wage guidelines) where collective bargaining impinges on government policy.

vi. Employers have in the past used collective bargaining to reduce competitive edge based on labour costs.

A pluralistic outlook involves acceptance within a political system of pressure groups (e.g. religious groups, unions, business associations, political parties and so on) with specific interests with which a government has dialogue, with a view to effecting compromises by making concessions. Pluralism implies a process of bargaining between these groups, or between one or more of them on the one hand and the government on the other. It therefore recognises these groups as the checks and balances which guarantee democracy. It is natural that in labour relations in a pluralist society collective bargaining is recognised as a fundamental tool through which stability is maintained, while freedom of association is the sine qua non without which the interest groups in a society would be unable to function effectively. There can therefore be no meaningful collective bargaining without freedom of association accorded to both employers and workers.

The existence of freedom of association does not necessarily mean that there would automatically be recognition of unions for bargaining purposes. Especially in systems where there is a multiplicity of trade unions, there is a need for predetermined objective criteria operative within the industrial relations system to decide when and how a union should be recognised for collective bargaining purposes. The obvious way would be to recognise the most representative union, but the criteria used to decide it and by whom may differ. It is in some systems determined on the basis of the union needing to have not less than a particular percentage of the workers in the enterprise in its membership. This may be decided by a referendum in the workplace, or by an outside certifying authority (such as a labour department or an independent statutory body), or by reference to "check off". There may be a condition that once certified as the bargaining agent there cannot be a change of agent for a prescribed period (e.g. one or two years) in order to ensure the stability of the process.

Especially in developing countries some of which have a multiplicity of unions, there is sometimes a problem of unions being unable to secure observance of agreements by their members. Where a labour law system provides for sanctions for breaches of agreements, the labour administration authorities may be reluctant to impose sanctions on workers. Where there is frequent non-observance of agreements or understandings reached through the collective bargaining process, the party not in default would lose faith in the process.

Support of the labour administration authorities is necessary for successful collective bargaining, and this implies that they will:

i. provide the necessary climate for it, e.g. provide effective conciliation services in the event of a breakdown of the process, and provide the necessary legal framework for it to operate in where necessary;
ii. not support a party in breach of agreements concluded in consequence of collective bargaining;
iii. as far as is practicable, secure observance of collective bargaining agreements;
iv. provide for the settlement of disputes arising from collective bargaining if the parties themselves have not so provided.

It is an obvious condition for successful collective bargaining that both parties bargain in good faith. Otherwise the process is unlikely to yield positive and enduring results.

Representative and strong unions are necessary to ensure that there is an equality in the bargaining positions of the parties and to ensure the observance of agreements. Where the employer is represented by an organisation which is the other party to the process, such organisation should be similarly effective. Both the management and union should keep their managers and members respectively well informed as a lack of proper communication and information can lead to misunderstandings and even to strikes. Sometimes managers and supervisors who are ill-informed may inadvertently mislead the workers who work under them about the current state of negotiations, the management's objectives and so on. In fact, it is necessary to involve managers in deciding on objectives and solutions, and such participation is likely to ensure greater acceptance - and therefore better implementation - by them.

Advantages of Collective Bargaining

It is sometimes claimed that in non-industrialised countries settlement of wage issues through collective bargaining - especially on a national or industry wise basis - can be an obstacle to a wage policy to promote specific economic objectives because wage rates are not necessarily fixed on criteria designed to promote specific economic and social objectives (other than as compensation for cost of living increases), and that they often tend to reflect the bargaining strength of the parties or the supply and demand conditions of labour. With some exceptions (such as Japan) wage increases through collective bargaining in Asia pay little attention to productivity, individual or group performance and to skills. However, collective bargaining has many advantages which have been claimed for it as a means of resolving differences between management and employees, though it has made little positive contribution to higher productivity and higher earnings by linking pay to performance and skills.

Collective bargaining has the advantage that it settles issues through dialogue and consensus rather than through conflict and confrontation. It differs from arbitration because the latter represents a solution based on a decision of a third party, while arrangements resulting from collective bargaining usually represent the choices or compromises of the parties themselves. Arbitration may invariably displease one party because it usually involves a win/lose situation, and sometimes it may even displease both parties.

Collective bargaining agreements often institutionalise settlement through dialogue. For instance, a collective agreement may provide for methods by which disputes between the parties will be settled. This has the distinct advantage that the parties know beforehand that if they are in disagreement there is an agreed method by which such disagreement may be resolved.

Collective bargaining is a form of participation. Both parties participate in deciding what proportion of the 'cake' is to be shared by the parties entitled to a share. At the end of an agreed term labour again insists on participating in deciding what share of the fruits of their labour should be apportioned to them.

Collective bargaining is a form of participation also because it involves a sharing of rule making power between employers and unions, and this has eroded areas which in earlier times were regarded as management prerogatives e.g. transfer, promotion, redundancy, discipline, modernisation, production norms. However, in some countries such as Singapore and Malaysia, certain subjects such as promotion, transfer, recruitment, termination of employment on grounds of redundancy or reorganisation, dismissal and reinstatement, and assignment of duties within the scope of the contract of employment, are regarded as management prerogatives and outside the scope of collective bargaining. But collective bargaining suffers from the drawback that it seldom deals with how to enlarge the "cake", as the way of increasing the share of each party without eroding competitiveness.

Collective bargaining agreements sometimes renounce or limit the settlement of disputes through trade union action or lock out. Therefore collective bargaining agreements can have the effect of guaranteeing industrial peace for the duration of the agreements, either generally or more usually on matters covered by the agreement.

Collective bargaining is an essential feature in the concept of social partnership towards which labour relations should strive. Social partnership in this context may be described as a partnership between organised employer institutions and organised labour institutions designed to maintain nonconfrontational processes in the settlement of disputes which arise between employers and employees. Collective bargaining has valuable by-products relevant to the relationship between the two parties. For instance, a long course of successful and bona fide dealings leads to the generation of trust. It contributes towards some measure of understanding by establishing a continuing relationship. Once the relationship of trust and understanding has been established, both parties are more likely to attack problems together rather than each other.

In societies where there is a multiplicity of unions and shifting union loyalties, collective bargaining and consequent agreements tend to stabilise union membership. For instance, where there is a collective agreement employees are less likely than otherwise to change union affiliations frequently. This is also of value to employers who are faced with constant changes in union membership and consequent inter-union rivalries, resulting in more disputes in the workplace than otherwise.

Collective bargaining agreements which determine wage rates on a national or industry level, place business competition on a more equal footing as a result of some standardisation of the costs of labour. This is probably a less important advantage today in the face of technological innovations and productivity drives.

Perhaps most important of all, collective bargaining usually has the effect of improving industrial relations. This improvement can be at different levels. The dialogue tends to improve relations at the workplace level between workers and the union on the one hand and the employer on the other. It also establishes a productive relationship between the union and the employers' organisation where the latter is involved in the process.

As between the employer on the one hand and his employees and union on the other, collective bargaining improves relations for the following reasons or in the following ways:

a) It requires a continuing dialogue which generally results in better understanding of each other's views.

b) Where collective bargaining institutionalises methods for the settlement of disputes, differences or disputes are less likely to result in trade union action.

c) It could lead to cooperation even in areas not covered by collective bargaining arrangements.

As between unions on the one hand and employers' organisations on the other, collective bargaining improves the industrial relations climate in the following ways:

a) It acts as a means of exerting influence on the employer or the employee, as the case may be, where the unreasonable position of one party results in a deadlock. The employers' organisation or the union, as the case may be, has an interest in exerting influence on its respective members; the maintenance of the relationship between the two parties is seen as important to issues well beyond the current dispute. Both parties know that the current dispute is only one of many situations which are likely to arise in the future, and that a good relationship needs to be maintained for the overall benefit of their respective members.

b) The entry of a union and employers' organisation into a dispute facilitates conciliation or mediation. Sometimes one or both parties are able to divorce themselves from the main conflict, or from their position as representatives of their members, and mediate with a view to narrowing the differences and finding compromise solutions.

c) Collective bargaining often leads employers' organisations and trade unions to establish links, and to look for and increase areas of common agreement. This in turn ensures to the benefit of their respective members.

As between unions and their members, collective bargaining tends to enhance the stability of union membership. Employees who perceive that their union is able to secure collective bargaining agreements, or obtain concessions through collective bargaining, are less likely to frequently change their union affiliations.

Current Collective Bargaining Trends

In no country can it be said that collective bargaining has been entirely at the industry or enterprise level, since each system has a mix of both, even though not in equal measure. However, industrialised market economies have generally practiced bargaining at the industry level, except in the USA where there has been more bargaining at the plant or enterprise level. Industry level bargaining in the USA has mainly been in specific sectors such as coal, steel, trucking and construction.

During the last decade there has been a move towards more enterprise level bargaining in many countries due to numerous reasons. There has been a decline in union membership in several countries such as the USA, Britain, France, Netherlands and Australia. Increasing unemployment and difficult business conditions have made employers reluctant to commit to wage policies at the industry or national level. The emergence of governments in some industrialised countries more favourably disposed towards private enterprise has resulted in allowing market forces to operate, thus weakening negotiations at the national level. Many employers view centralised bargaining as facilitating a more equal distribution of incomes (which is one reason why many unions prefer centralised bargaining), but as depriving employers of the ability to use pay as an instrument for productivity improvement and to compensate for skills and performance. Strategic compensation systems are workable only if introduced at the enterprise level to match the goals sought to be achieved. In Sweden, which has been an extreme case of centralised bargaining, one of the strategies of the Swedish employers during the last ten years has been to decentralise collective bargaining. Germany, another country well-known for centralised bargaining, is displaying a tendency towards decentralised bargaining. The push by employers for flexibility in the context of increasing global competition has resulted in many flexibility issues such as new working time arrangements, atypical contracts and pay systems being needed to be dealt with largely at the enterprise level.

Compared with industrialised countries, collective bargaining in Asia has been minimal. There has been an increasing tendency towards bargaining on wages and terms and conditions, which has sometimes resulted in some form of arrangements among governments, employers and unions which lay down certain guidelines as in Singapore, and the Accords from 1983 onwards in Australia. Asia has had a mixture of industry and enterprise level bargaining, with the latter predominating. Apart from low unionisation rates in several Asian countries which militate against industry level bargaining, increased competition and the need for flexibility does not make industry level bargaining popular in Asia. The Japanese have demonstrated how a combination of enterprise level bargaining and shopfloor level mechanisms enable enterprises to adapt to rapidly changing business conditions and also to increase productivity.

In most countries, therefore, the tendency is to see the enterprise as the centre of gravity of industrial relations. It is likely that some of the main concerns of employers such as productivity, quality, performance, skills development, the need to be competitive and to make rapid changes to adapt to the global marketplace, will eventually result in less centralised collective bargaining.

Collective Bargaining vs. Bargaining on Employment

The distinction between "collective bargaining" and the wider concept of "bargaining on employment" is blurred. There are many countries in which various species of macro-level corporatism are practised, that is, there are either tripartite negotiations on macroeconomic guidelines or an implicit joint understanding amongst major actors on these guidelines, geared to foster what are expected to be employment-favourable income policies or other measures relevant for employment, such as labour market policies. While these approaches have been practised for decades in many countries, the emphasis within these approaches has changed since the 1980s. Within the framework of the broad move towards supply-side economics thinking and practice, "wage moderation" became the crucial term which embraces the underlying concept of most of these approaches. This trend entailed a move towards "supply-side corporatism" whose forms have differed across countries. Above all, and sometimes intertwined with central bilateral or trilateral frameworks, it included a great deal of decentralisation of collective bargaining. As Ozaki rightly notes, "decentralisation of collective bargaining is above all related to the search for higher competitiveness."

In his overview on the wide range of employment-oriented bargaining practices in Europe, Zagelmeyer makes the useful distinction between "social pacts" between the collective bargaining actors and governments, and "employment pacts" between the collective bargaining actors. It is these "employment pacts" on which the present study will be focused, even though it must be taken into account that in some countries tripartite "social pacts" may influence or even provide a legal or political framework for "employment pacts" between the collective bargaining actors. Further, and even more important, is the close linkage between "employment pacts" and a greater emphasis on decentralised collective bargaining on employment issues within the wider framework of supply-side corporatism. What can be said about clear-cut trend towards decentralisation is that (1) greater attention has been paid to the distinction and diversification of collective bargaining levels, including the company and establishment levels, and within this move, (2) the "nature" and contents of collective bargaining on employment, and employment insecurity, have changed substantially. Following this line of exploration we do refer to industry-level bargaining wherever appropriate, but in most cases it will be the level of firms or individual establishments on which this kind of collective bargaining takes place and on which the emphasis of the present study will be laid.

Looking back at the historical evolvement of collective bargaining on employment insecurity, it may seem confusing that the preferred terms used in the literature aimed at addressing the issue have changed over time. However, the changes in language followed the dynamics in practice. The arguably most important starting point for what has developed over recent decades in this respect was "concession bargaining" in large parts of unionised industries in the U.S., and the automotive industry in particular, since the 1980s.

Things became more blurred once "concession bargaining" spilled over in the 1990s to Europe and in doing so, began to change and expand its contents. As compared to the U.S., and given the diversity of institutional settings across European countries, it is much less obvious in Europe who is responsible or entitled to negotiate with whom at what level and on which issue, and it is equally open to debate which direction negotiations may take.

In centralised corporatist environments, for instance, there may be sectoral or central agreements with the intention of fostering competitiveness at sector or company levels by wage moderation or by facilitating flexibility at company level. At the same time, employment pacts may aim at providing greater leeway for local actors to engage with bargaining on these issues, thus opening pathways to decentralised collective bargaining on a large array of issues directly or indirectly connected with the safeguarding or promotion of employment and employment security. Terms coined in the literature of the late 1990s to capture this multifaceted trend in collective bargaining on employment issues include "framework agreements on competitiveness and jobs", "social pacts", "alliances for jobs", "local pacts for the safeguarding of employment", or simply "pacts for employment and competitiveness".

In the context of these analyses, PECs were defined as "collective agreements at sectoral or company level that deal explicitly with the issues of employment and competitiveness, and with the relationship between them, to either safeguard jobs that are at risk or create new ones". As Sisson pointed out, even though "there is no 'typical' PECs", most of them have two objectives: (1) to minimise employment reductions or to stabilise employment, and (2) to reduce costs of organisations or to improve their ability to adapt.

This approach to conceptualise collective bargaining on employment insecurity clearly evolved within the European context, if taking into account the earlier U.S. experience of concession bargaining. Parallel endeavours undertaken within the framework of the ILO had to agree on a wider concept.

Nevertheless, for the purposes of the present study it appears useful to stick to the narrower term and concept developed in the EU context, i.e. the explicit dealing with employment insecurity. The ambiguous nature of collective bargaining affecting employment as analysed by Ozaki, based on his coverage of negotiations both explicitly and implicitly addressing employment issues, fully applies to the various, if more explicit approaches to PECs in Europe: "Recent developments in collective bargaining reflect the growing ascendancy of enterprise strategies over labour market regulation. While previously labour market regulation aimed at providing equity in working conditions had an important impact on the formulation of enterprise and production strategies, recent collective bargaining outcomes primarily follow enterprise strategies aimed at market performance and competitiveness. As we see it, this general tendency in collective bargaining in the course of the 1990s can best be underscored by more recent and most advanced examples of collective bargaining on employment insecurity. American approaches may regarded as an almost consensual starting point for most current collective bargaining on employment issues, including the PECs in the European context. Therefore, it appears sensible to put the explicit employment pacts at the centre of the present study.

Finally, our more focused, and maybe limited, approach appears particularly justifiable in the light of more recent shifts in both practice and literature on this topic.

This shift in emphasis towards what will be called in the present study "derogations" or "deviant collective agreements" reflects more recent moves in some, if not all, European countries towards local job guarantees in exchange for an explicit undercutting of norms laid down in multiemployer collective agreements on wages, working time or other topics. Looking back at the 1990s, the literature on new trends in collective bargaining on employment had mostly optimistic connotations, particularly in the European context.

A critical scholar like Sisson attributed to PECs the capacity to bring about a combination of decentralised collective bargaining with a substantial enlargement of both range and depth of the issues addressed: "Collective bargaining, it seems, is proving itself to be very capable of coping with the increasing complexities of managing the employment relationship as well as continuing to provide a mechanism for dealing with issues of distribution."

To some extent, there may have been a climate change over recent years, for that matter. As the European Foundation for the Improvement of Living and Working Conditions finds, the follow-up agreements in the current decade seem to be "less acceptable in recent years than PECs were in the 1990s". One major concern connected with recent trends in deviant agreements has been the underlying power shift within the relationships of the collective bargaining actors to the disadvantage of the trade unions, entailing major risks for the future architecture and functioning of existing collective bargaining systems. If this was the case, it might entail repercussions on employment security through the back door.

As becomes obvious in this very brief observation of some major trends in collective bargaining on employment insecurity over recent decades, it is hardly possible to separate the potential impacts of collective agreements on employment security from their sideeffects on the industrial relations systems, and the repercussions of these side effects on employment.

The present study will draw primarily on a review of existing research into the incidence of collective bargaining tackling employment insecurity in Europe and, to some extent, in the U.S. As to other industrialised countries, we refer to the information and assessment given by Ozaki but cannot go beyond it. However, for more recent experience in Europe, the European Industrial Relations

Observatory database of the European Foundation for the Improvement of Living and Working Conditions serves as a valuable source of information. It should be noted, however, that the literature available on collective bargaining addressing employment insecurity is still limited, which may reflect differences in pertinence of this topic in the practice of collective bargaining across countries.

Collective Bargaining and Employment Insecurity

In the wake of the end of the "golden age" of post-war capitalism in the advanced industrialised world, with unemployment rates remaining at unaccustomed high levels in many of these countries, the fight against unemployment and employment insecurity gradually moved centre stage either as an implicit precondition or an explicit issue of collective bargaining. Negotiations on this issue will only take place if labour law in a given country sets limits to the unfettered "commodification" of labour, or if the presence of trade unions and the probability of the social conflicts entailed make negotiations over the containment of employment insecurity a matter of political rationality.

On the other hand, it must be noted that an environment of unemployment and of employment insecurity may limit the potential impact of trade unions. As unions have always proved to be more vulnerable in phases of business slump compared to phases of economic recovery and rapid employment growth, it is more than evident that the post-1970s economic developments have entailed marked shifts in the power relationship to the disadvantage of trade unions. For that matter, the drop in the wage shares of national income in the U.S., and even more markedly in the EU, is an equally significant indicator as the drop in trade union density in most EU countries over recent decades. This power shift is to a large extent based on a fundamental reorganisation of capitalist production systems. Reorganisation makes employers less dependent on unions, but it also makes single employers less dependent on employers' associations as representatives of collective interests vis-à-vis the unions. The beneficiaries of the power shift are not the employers' associations but the single employers, a fact that can pose organisational problems for the employers' associations as well.

Thus, it is fair to assume that while employers in many cases face a need to negotiate on employment insecurity, the balance of powers in these negotiations tends to tip in their favour. This ambiguity involved with negotiations on employment insecurity should be borne in mind as a problematic underlying the whole scale of bargaining issues and approaches discussed in the present study.

Both historically and systematically, there are different reasons and causes behind collective bargaining on employment insecurity. The different causes, in turn, entail different rationales and approaches of the actors involved which impact on the contents of the agreements.

The first, and arguably most "classical", cause behind collective bargaining on employment insecurity are structural shifts and crises in the economy. These crises may include cases like the continuous downsizing of particular industries such as steelworks or shipyards in Western Europe and the U.S. in the process of international redivision of labour. They may also include, within the same process, the loss of competitiveness of major industries in some countries vis-à-vis rising players from other parts of the world in increasingly globalised markets, such as the automotive industry. In the latter case, the gap in labour costs between unionised and non-unionised parts of the same industry within a given country may become ever more important. The latter two problems were the factors that stood at the very beginning of concession bargaining in the U.S. in the early 1980s.

The basic constellation of interests in these cases has always been the objective of employers to cut down on labour costs in general, and on numbers of workers employed in particular, whereas the main interests of employee representatives and unions has been to slow down this very process. Over the years retrenchment has been gradually supplemented by more sophisticated measures such as changes in wage and personnel structures.

A second cause of collective bargaining on employment insecurity, closely related to but different from the first, has been the failure of individual companies within highly competitive markets, in most cases connected to changing fortunes over business cycles. Arguably one of the most prominent cases in this respect was the crisis of Europe's largest car manufacturer, Volkswagen, in the early 1990s. Clearly, the situation was different from the concession bargaining cases in the U.S. motor industry in the precedent decade. The rationale behind collective bargaining at VW was, in the colloquial wording of those days, the "cut-down on hours rather than workers". It resulted in the so-called four-day week which was revised by a return to the 35(+)-hour industry standard only recently.

A third driver of collective bargaining on employment insecurity is the globalisation of business operations in general, and the continuous reshuffling of the division of labour within international value chains in particular. Again, this driver is connected with those indicated before, but it has gained distinctive characteristics over recent years. The flagship terms here are "relocation" of businesses and operations at a global scale and "restructuring" of business units geared to increase profitability. The more traditional aspect within this challenge is the emergence of competitors with lower wage costs, particularly from newly industrialised countries. Most prominently, however, is the transfer of extra-organisational challenges to internal ones within multinational corporations. The "internalisation" of international relocation and the frequent, and in many cases almost continuous, restructuring of organisations have been closely linked with shareholder value oriented corporate governance. Individual establishments may be confronted with the risk of retrenchment or shutdown even if they are in the black. "Global financial markets-driven capitalism has turned shutdowns from an effect of crises and structural change into a 'normal' tool of corporate restructuring".

This move gives rise to new challenges, new topics and new actors when it comes to collective bargaining on employment insecurity. The more the competitive challenge becomes an internal one to be tackled within large companies, and the less the issue at stake is to rescue 'marginal suppliers', the more the full range of measures geared to improve business efficiency beyond the simple cut-down in wages or staff comes into play. As to the actors, the competition amongst locations becomes an issue of negotiation between supranational employee representations and management, and of articulation within these supranational representative bodies.

Interestingly, relocation and restructuring have increasingly been used as role models for upheavals within the public sector in many countries. One strand of activities has been the privatisation of formerly state-owned companies, which in many cases entails major cutbacks on jobs and the deterioration of employment stability. Equally important has been the strive within public services for the adoption of governance techniques such as cost centres developed for the purposes of large private businesses, particularly in health care.

This observation leads us to a fourth driver pertinent to the topic of the present study which goes beyond the three causes and rationales behind collective bargaining on employment insecurity covered in the literature so far. There may be a great deal of political pressure behind moves towards collective bargaining on employment insecurity which should be identified as a driver in its own right.

The direction of this pressure, however, may differ substantially. The government initiative towards the establishment of the statutory 35-hour week triggered a wave of company bargaining activities on the reorganisation of working time, which contributed to a substantial widening of the thematic scope of company bargaining, and gave a boost to the number of establishments involved in company bargaining on all sorts of issues, including employment insecurity, unknown so far in the French context.

Government policy can also play a central role in the development of collective bargaining as an element of an overriding national strategy on employment and labour market issues, as pursued in the Netherlands by the end of the 1990s.

This approach, as the authors conclude, "contrasts starkly with partly politically motivated innovations which merely 'fiddle around' with labour costs." The latter could be very much observed in Germany in the so-called "Agenda 2010" policies in which the Federal government aimed at deregulations in the German labour market. As the government announced that it would change the legal framework of collective bargaining if there was no agreement between collective bargaining actors on the so-called "opening" of collective agreements to local deviations or derogations, it exerted pressure on the collective bargaining actors in general, and on the trade unions in particular, to pave the way for changes in the architecture of the system. It resulted in cracks in the foundations of the collective bargaining architecture. At the company or establishment level it opened the door to bartering temporary job guarantees against the undercutting of industry standards.

Thus, ironically enough, employment insecurity may not just become an issue of collective bargaining because there is such insecurity, it may also become an issue of collective bargaining because major actors utilise employment insecurity as a vehicle to bring about changes in the architecture and the functioning of the collective bargaining system in a given country. It is in this vein that Ozaki rightly holds that, "one of the factors strengthening the pressure is the predominance of neo-liberal economic thinking among policy makers." Even though the incidence differs across countries, which can be attributed not least to the industrial relations practices and systems, the increase in pertinence is beyond dispute amongst observers. Assessments have been based primarily on experts' opinions.

In a very small number of countries, including Spain, France and Germany, these assessments have been supplemented by government statistics on collective bargaining and on surveys amongst establishments or employee representatives. As to the former, according to the collective agreements register of the French Ministry of Labour, five per cent of all firm-level agreements in 2007 addressed the safeguarding of employment, as compared to less than three per cent three years earlier. Thus, it is noteworthy that local agreements on working-time organisation soared after the introduction of the 35-hour week and still was the main topic of roughly one-quarter of all firm-level agreements in 2007.

At the same time, it is interesting to note that in neighbouring Germany the importance of employment and competitiveness pacts exceeded the French practice substantially. As a survey amongst works councils in Germany undertaken in 2003 revealed, almost one-quarter of establishments with works councils had employment and competitiveness pacts of various kinds. Originally conceived as adjustment instruments in crisis situations that threaten jobs and the company's very existence, PECs are fast becoming a new 'normal' regulatory instrument while collective bargaining standards are becoming guidelines that give firms considerable leeway to come to company-specific solutions.

The impact of PECs on competition is setting a trend that other firms find difficult to resist." This assessment underscores the political, rather than just numerical, importance of the drivers discussed here, as they impact directly or indirectly on the contents and outcomes of collective agreements on employment insecurity and equally on the architectures and processes of collective bargaining.

The move towards collective bargaining on employment insecurity began historically as the drive of industries and individual companies towards the loosening of rigidities imposed by earlier collective agreements, which were increasingly regarded as millstones on increasingly competitive international markets. As these new collective bargaining practices evolved and spread abroad to countries with stronger organisational bases in industrial relations than existed in the U.S., they took on a new form. It is true that the shift in power relations to the disadvantage of unions remained a key feature of this process. But it is also true that these dynamics entail a widening of bargaining issues and the involvement of new and more actors, and that they have evolved from primarily defensive agreements to more offensive agreements, addressing a wider scope of topics relevant for the competitiveness of industries and companies. It is this scope in the contents of agreements that will be explored in what follows, before turning to the impacts on the processes of collective bargaining.

Collective Agreements

The distinction between 'defensive' or reactive strategies on the one hand and 'offensive' or pro-active strategies on the other suggested by Freyssinet and Seifert appears useful for the present context. As these authors point out, it would be too narrow to look just at the employment outcome intended. If the link between employment and competitiveness is taken as a framework for categorising collective agreements, the criterion should be whether agreements are geared only towards reducing labour costs, or if they aim at a reduction of labour costs in connection with improvements in work organisation and other factors of competitiveness.

To develop the argument further, the reduction of labour costs is always a key component of collective agreements dealing with employment and competitiveness, and it would be hard to find any agreement which tackles employment insecurity without addressing ways to reduce labour costs. However, the crucial question is how this objective is to be attained. Thus, the distinction between defensive and offensive approaches to collective bargaining on employment insecurity may also be flagged by the commonly used terms of "low vs. high roads" towards business success or towards economic and employment success of socio-economic models.

In what follows, we present key components of collective agreements addressing employment and competitiveness along the lines of a simple typology. Dwelling on and extending typologies developed in earlier studies, we would like to distinguish the following key bargaining contents regarding the instruments designed to curtail employment insecurity:

a) *Employability:* Agreements in firms facing downsizing measures or restructuring may, apart from measures accompanying redundancies, aim at preparing redundant workers for a better fit with internal or external labour markets.

b) *Wage cuts:* Agreements on wage restraint or wage differentiation for either all workers or sub-groups, and the expansion of atypical employment forms. These measures may include an undercutting of industry standards.

c) *Working time redistribution/reorganisation:* Measures to redistribute work including collective reductions of working hours or the promotion of part-time work.

d) *Stabilisation of the workforce:* Training measures, job rotation models, facilitating of non-standard employment but also integration of temporary or agency workers and in-sourcing of formerly outsourced activities.

e) *Process or product innovation:* Measures aimed at reviewing work practices and introducing new forms of work organisation; innovation prospects may also include investment in new products and new technologies.

f) *Voice:* Many agreements include procedural innovations with respect to employee voice such as the involvement of workforce representatives in the process of cost cutting or reorganisation.

Obviously components from one group can be combined with measures from others. However, a more detailed content analysis would reveal typical overlaps of contents, and other combinations which are rather unlikely to occur.

A second observation regarding the contents of agreements is that all components may in principle be combined with either job retrenchment to a greater or lesser degree, including early retirement measures, with the intention of safeguarding core activities of the firm, or in contrast with job guarantees.

Employability

The rationale behind measures aimed at the improvement of employability is to prepare redundant workers for a better fit with internal or external labour markets. Thus, the line between this group of measures and the bulk of agreements dealing with downsizing of organisations and staff reductions is blurred.

As to the content of agreements dealing with this issue, two approaches may be distinguished. The first is the establishment of either internal or external staff pools.

Internal staff pools have been used in other countries too, in most cases without state aid. Prominent examples may be encountered in formerly state-owned companies such as the telecom sector but also in large public hospitals where downsizing or restructuring of organisations may be handled via "internal job centres".

Most likely these approaches will be combined with a variety of measures dealing with training. The importance of training in policies curtailing employment insecurity, however, goes beyond the specific staff pool approach. While training may also be part of collective agreements, in some countries policies aimed at fostering continuous training are most likely to be part of tripartite initiatives. In recent years, this has been the case for instance in Austria and in Denmark. In the latter, further training was combined with "rob rotation" schemes in the 1990s. In job rotation models the company employs substitutes during the period when employees participate in training and educational courses. There are individual agreements similar to the Danish model in some other countries, namely in Northern Europe. As Freyssinet and Seifert note, however, the integration of the job rotation concept in collective bargaining is rare and may be encountered at best in Scandinavian countries. The issue here is not just the curtailing of job losses in the short term. It is also about providing the skills needed in the midterm, i.e. in the economic recovery after the crisis. Thus, "retraining – not redundancy" may become a high profile issue on the collective bargaining agenda in the near future.

Wage Cuts

Wage reductions or, at least, wage "moderation" have been at the core of employment-oriented collective bargaining strategies. Following the guidelines of supply-side focused economic thinking, wage moderation used to be the ultimate rationale behind both explicit and implicit employment pacts at national or sectoral levels. These approaches practised in many countries, most pronounced within corporatist environments of small and open economies such as in the Netherlands, have been described in great detail by earlier studies on employment-oriented collective bargaining strategies. It is true that at the macroeconomic level wages must be regarded both as a cost and as a demand factor, and recent economic debates tend to give more emphasis to the latter than they used to in recent decades, but at the level of individual firms the demand aspect is abstract, while the cost aspect is concrete.

Thus, there is no indication that at this level there could be a reversal of mainstream approaches in the near future. Wage moderation and reductions at firm level can take different forms and they can be either temporary or permanent in nature. Most importantly, they can be the prime instrument for regaining competitiveness, or they can be combined with other instruments, such as process or product innovations and investment decisions.

The classic case of employment pacts focused on wage reductions has been concession bargaining in the U.S. since the 1980s. In his in-depth comparison of concession bargaining in the U.S. and in Germany, Massa-Wirth finds substantial differences between the approaches in these two countries, depending on the power relations, the industrial relations systems, and on the strategic orientations of major actors.

One interesting aspect mentioned by Massa-Wirth is the slowdown of the dynamics of concession bargaining in the U.S. in the 1990s due to the increase in "peripheral" workers. The distinction between core and periphery and the boost in temporary workers and agency staff has been increasingly important in many European countries, too. This, in turn, gave rise to new equity challenges within workforces in the current decade.

In the comparison between the U.S. and Germany, the latter may stand, to some extent, for typical approaches in Europe over the 1990s. The quid pro quo principle in particular has always played an important role in negotiations, even though Freyssinet and Seifert are very cautious when it comes assessing to what extent this principle is actually applied in practice. What continues to be typical for European approaches at any rate are the blurred lines between and the complex mixture of wage cuts and various modernisation measures. What must be stressed here is that traditionally pay levels at VW has been substantially higher than the industry standards.

Another high profile example of intertwined working time extensions and pay reductions or pay moderations was the French subsidiary of the German manufacturer Bosch in 2004. It was paradigmatic both for the relocation challenge within multinational companies and for the questioning of collectively agreed industry standards on pay and working time at the national level. In exchange, management committed itself to investment in a new product line geared to save 190 out of 300 jobs threatened at the Vénissieux plant. The deal was particularly controversial against the background of the statutory 35-hour week in France.

While the deals struck at Volkswagen do not interfere with industry standards, the Bosch deal in France highlights the ambiguous tightrope act between industry standards and employment guarantees. While in some cases this tightrope act proved to be just a temporary deviation from industry standards with standards being eventually reinstated after the recovery of the firm or establishment, there are also examples of breaches in pay or working time standards with only very limited employment effects.

In June 2004, a plan by the German-based electronics group, Siemens, to move 2,000 jobs from Germany to Hungary was cancelled as a result of the conclusion of a 'supplementary agreement' by management and the German Metalworkers' Union at two mobile phone plants. The Siemens deal stipulated that from October 2004 average weekly working hours were increased from 35 to 40 hours for full-time workers without any compensation in pay.

The return to the 40-hour week in these plants, pushed forward as an explicit pilot model in 2004 by one of the largest and most powerful German companies, sparked a controversial debate on the alleged need to extend working hours in Germany in order to regain price competitiveness on export markets and to safeguard jobs in manufacturing. In the course of events, the substantial reduction in pay entailed proved to be an important element in the sale of the establishments to the Taiwanese company BenQ which eventually closed down the two plants in 2007.

Concession bargaining may not just be a challenge to labour standards agreed at national or industry levels, with effects on the employment conditions of workers. The same standards may be part of the regulatory framework and important for ensuring the same competitive conditions for firms. "Deviant agreements" change the conditions under which firms compete. A conflict on wage cuts in Denmark demonstrates the difficulty.

The food processor Danish Crown announced at the end of 2004 that it would close its Tulip meat factory in Ringsted and relocate production to Germany, if a new local collective agreement failed to introduce a cost reduction equivalent to a wage cut of 15 per cent. Such an agreement was accepted by the majority of the plant workers but was rejected by the Danish Food and Allied Workers' Union which argued that it was not in line with the relevant sectoral agreement. The agreement was meant to be part of a special pilot scheme allowing substantial deviations at decentralised level from the conditions set by the sectoral agreement.

Slaughterhouse workers in other factories of the same company went on strike and the employees at the Tulip plant rejected the deal in a ballot. Shortly after, the Ringsted plant was closed and production relocated to Germany. It may have become obvious that clear-cut concession bargaining on wages or working time is highly controversial.

Most importantly, there is a need to combine these wage cuts with measures aimed at improving the efficiency of the organisation. It is this combination which may make concessions tolerable for workers, but also for competitors within the same industry. Finally, as Sisson points out, management needs to obtain the agreement of employee representatives in order to change the terms of existing collective agreements: "Intensifying competition requires management both to minimise costs and promote the cooperation of the workforce necessary for continuous improvement."

Working Time Redistribution

The following discussion focuses on collective agreements which utilise the reduction or reorganisation of working times for the purposes of curtailing employment insecurity. Collective bargaining on working time in general is a subject for a different study. The outstanding, and arguably unique, series of working time agreements involving major moves to either safeguard or increase employment in recent years was triggered by the introduction of the 35-hour week in France. As soon as these agreements stipulated certain provisions on the safeguarding or creation of jobs, the respective companies would receive exemptions from social security contributions.

Following these acts, the number of firm-level agreements soared, and so did working time as a subject of decentralised negotiations. The dynamics triggered by the first act also entailed major evaluations of employment effects. It showed, first, that the economically most successful firms were the first to enter into negotiations and to implement the 35-hour week. Second, and controlled for these differences in turnover growth, it showed that employment growth in these firms continued to exceed that in firms of the same size in the same industry. Evaluations of earlier local working time reductions in France had found that vulnerable groups of workers had benefited most from these redistribution measures as their contracts were stabilised, or as their working hours were extended in the case of part-time workers.

According to a survey commissioned by the Ministry of Labour, almost half of workers hired after these working time reductions had been unemployed before. Next to the employment effects, the boost in working-time flexibility was a major outcome of the working-time reductions in France.

It must be noted that the French case explicitly represented an 'offensive' approach to general working-time reductions and was introduced within an environment of economic growth, thus reinforcing employment growth in this period. The current economic crisis, however, gives rise to a different agenda setting. At present, as far as working-time related initiatives are concerned, it is the safeguarding of jobs on which all endeavours are focused. Earlier experience in working-time reductions geared to safeguarding employment may provide interesting lessons in this respect. One particular and probably unique approach was the 'Collective Agreement for Promoting Employment' concluded in 1998 in one region of the German metal industry.

This arrangement provided for the establishment of a joint association, run by the employers' federation and the trade union, to promote employment in the metalworking industry with a view to creating additional jobs, promoting more part-time work and continuing vocational training, and boosting the chances of employment of disadvantaged young people. The workforce received a certain wage adjustment for a pre-specified period of time, financed out of a fund provided by the employers' federation with minor contributions from the workers. Employees could also voluntarily reduce their weekly working time from 35 hours to a minimum of 17.5 hours for a maximum period of two years. Formerly unemployed people were hired for this period to fill the working time vacated. If, for example, four employees reduced their working time from 35 to 28 hours per week for two years, one unemployed person could be hired for this period. In effect, out of the roughly 80,000 employees in the metalworking industry in that region, more than 1,100 had reduced their working time and as a result about 275 unemployed persons had been employed.

The Achilles heel of the scheme, however, were the bonus payments for workers who reduced their working hours. For a short time, these payments were exempted from taxation and social security contributions. Given that many of the workers involved were women with low pay, the exemptions did matter and made the scheme an attractive choice. When this practice was stopped by Federal law in 2002, the collective bargaining parties decided to end the experiment.

Beyond this unique case, local pacts on working-time reduction and the redistribution of working hours usually include measures which enhance flexibility in working-time organisation. However, there are also examples of local agreements on employment and competitiveness which focus just on flexibility measures, without changing the average number of hours worked per week. Recent examples of this approach range from car manufacturers to financial organisations.

A recent high profile example in the motor industry was a deal struck at Nissan in Spain. In January 2008, the car manufacturer announced its plans for redundancies affecting 450 permanent workers out of a total 4,500 production workers at its Barcelona factory. However, a preliminary agreement concluded in February 2008 provides for more flexible working time schedules in exchange for a partial withdrawal of the redundancy measure.

Given the current crisis, however, most initiatives will address the reduction of working hours, rather than just an increase in flexibility, in order to prevent or reduce mass redundancies.

The company-level collective agreement concluded by Volkswagen AG stipulated a 20 per cent working-time reduction for the company's entire workforce and triggered a broad range of activities aimed at greater flexibility of working-time organisation over the 1990s. It was also the starting point for various other agreements on efficiency enhancement measures in the work processes of the company. At the same time, it has been intertwined from the beginning and even more markedly so in recent years with indirect wage cuts which helped to adapt the wage levels at Volkswagen to the lower standards in the metalworking industry agreements.

Irrespective of these particularities of Volkswagen, any working-time reduction without corresponding wage compensations helps to reduce labour costs. This is even more so when this working-time reduction entails flexibility measures in working-time organisation. Hence the exemplary character of the VW deal which continues to be a model case for "survival/recovery" agreements.

It should be noted, however, that in the case of Volkswagen, while cuts in hours and pay amounted to 20 per cent, monthly wages remained virtually stable. In the negotiations pay issues were crucial. The bargaining actors smoothed the problem by (1) a minor pay compensation conceded by the company, and (2) by a redistribution of annual premia, which had been part of earlier pay agreements, from annual to monthly payments. Thus, monthly wages remained roughly unchanged. It must be noted that the existence of this pay leeway may be expected in above-average flourishing companies or sectors of a given economy only. It cannot be taken for granted that cuts in working hours by 20 or 30 per cent, or even more, accompanied by wage cuts in the same dimensions, can be accepted by a majority of the workers affected by the imminent threat of redundancy. Interestingly, it is in the UK where the "Volkswagen approach" has been revitalised recently. The move will prevent 350 out of 500 job losses planned by the company in light of falling sales due to the global financial crisis. Negotiated – as distinct from imposed – short-time working arrangements are uncommon in the UK. The British Trades Union Congress (TUC) and the Federation of Small Businesses (FSB) have gone further down this road by proposing to introduce short-term working subsidies for around 600,000 workers per year with a replacement rate of 60 per cent of the income lost.

In the present situation, given the need for dramatic cuts both in working hours and pay companies and workers are obviously running into a dilemma. The more the pay cuts are in line with companies' needs regarding survival of the crisis, the less tolerable they become for workers. The only resource for a solution of this dilemma are public subsidies. This need is acknowledged, to a greater or lesser extent, in "short-time working" or "temporal unemployment" schemes existing in some European countries.The German short-time working scheme which has been revised and flexibilised recently may serve as a flagship example here. It stipulates that working time for all or part of the workforce may be reduced by between 10 and 100 per cent. The hours not worked are compensated by the labour administration at 60 per cent. The social security contributions for the hours not worked are reduced to 80 per cent; the 50 per cent share of the worker is paid by the labour administration but the employer's part has to be paid by the employer. The latter payment will be borne by the labour administration, too, if the time slots of short-time working are used for training measures. Moreover, training measures will be subsidised. An extension up to 24 months and further cost reductions for employers are being discussed amongst employers' federations, trade unions and the Ministry of Labour. First, as pay compensation issues are playing a crucial role, it is more likely for work-sharing to become a major policy issue in countries with dismissal protection and unemployment insurance systems than in countries with less developed systems of "decommodification" of labour. This is not to say that it is impossible to strike local deals on work-sharing in countries with – by European standards – lower levels of workers protection, as has been demonstrated by some recent work-sharing initiatives at company level in the UK. Yet, the level of wage compensation will most likely depend on the level of other public allowances such as unemployment benefits and on the costs to be borne by employers in the case of dismissals. The less developed these provisions and opportunity costs are, the less pronounced could be the potential compensatory payment for workers linked with work-sharing agreements.

Second, work-sharing in the current economic situation will in most cases be only feasible in combination with public subsidies. These subsidies will be crucial irrespective of the concrete organisation of work-sharing. It may be organised within a public scheme, as is the case in Germany; it may also be organised within the framework of multiemployer or single-employer bargaining. Thus in current work-sharing activities the borderlines between public schemes and schemes based on collective bargaining may become blurred. Whatever the actual scheme is based upon, however, it will not work without the interplay of collective bargaining actors and the state. Third, it is fair to assume that employers will urge for a reduction of the remaining staff costs, including the employers' social security contributions. The linkage with training makes sense but is not easy to implement in practice. Further training and the continuation of vocational training wherever existent should be regarded as indispensable elements of any work-sharing activity.

Stabilisation of the Work Force

Reviewing the experience with the boost in temporary and agency workers since the "labour market reforms" in many European countries, it is widely accepted today that these categories of workers experience, on the average, less favourable working conditions and compensation than employees with standard employment contracts. Hence the obvious need to put moves to curtail job insecurity amongst these categories of workers high on the bargaining agenda.

Basically, as has been established by recent data analyses in Germany and roughly in line with earlier findings, there continues to exist a positive correlation between job stability and the incidence of collective bargaining. Nevertheless, evidence on collective bargaining aimed at curtailing employment insecurity of temporary or agency workers is scarce, and sometimes paradoxical. In the course of the "flexibilisation" of labour markets which took place in many countries in the 1990s, there were examples of collective agreements, as in Italy, accompanying government initiatives which facilitated the employment of temporary workers as a means to foster employment growth.

In the beginning of the current slump, these workers were the first to be sacked. It is true that there were early examples of agreements, as in the Netherlands, which stipulated that after a certain period of time, temporary workers would be made permanent. However, agreements of this kind continue to be scarce. Interestingly, collective bargaining on this issue tends to benefit from facilitating political frameworks. As part of a new legislative proposal, the Spanish government, employers' organisations and trade unions signed a preliminary agreement in April 2006. It proposed new legislation containing provisions enabling entrepreneurs to reduce their direct taxes on labour and transform some temporary contracts into permanent ones. It remains to be seen to what extent this general tripartite approach will suffer from the current dramatic slump in the Spanish labour market. The same applies to a recent national agreement for temporary agency workers in Italy.

As has become obvious in this short overview the improvement of employment conditions of temporary and agency staff has not yet become an established collective bargaining issue. It remains to be seen whether recent experience in the current crisis will impact future approaches of collective bargaining parties.

Process or Product Innovation

Safeguarding of jobs is tightly intertwined with management decisions on investment, product lines, and organisation of the work process. Given that these decisions are at the heart of management prerogative in any capitalist environment, it cannot be taken for granted that these issues are being addressed by collective bargaining. Nevertheless, negotiations in a number of countries are moving in this direction. High-profile examples of this move widely discussed in the media are often from the motor industry, such as a 'company-level alliance for jobs' agreed in 2006 at Ford Germany between management and the works council. The deal stipulates, in return for wage concessions that dismissals will be banned at German sites until 2011. Three model ranges will continue to be produced at the two German sites, and the investment required for modernisation and adaptation of the production facilities are envisaged.

Given the fierce competition in the motor industry and its current deep crisis, this kind of agreement linking either the retrenchment or the safeguarding of jobs with restructuring and investment plans has become a frequent and periodic experience in Europe.

The Swedish-based electrical appliances company Electrolux and the metalworking industry unions agreed in 2008 on a restructuring plan for the Italian productions sites of the multinational. The deal includes a wide range of instruments, from state-supported short-time working schemes accompanying the sale of one of the plants, internal job pools, to a three-year investment plan for the remaining plant. While it is fair to assume that this kind of complex agreement will spread in the years to come in larger parts of the manufacturing industry, it is important to point to collective bargaining initiatives in the public sector aimed at boosting employment, rather than safeguarding jobs. A noteworthy initiative in this respect was recently developed by the Irish Municipal Public and Civil Trade Union (IMPACT) which launched a gradual and sustained campaign of industrial action against recruitment restrictions imposed by the Health Service Executive (HSE). As part of the action, trade union members employed by the HSE are refusing to cover posts left vacant by the recruitment freeze, as well as stopping non-emergency overtime and out-of-hours work.

The dynamics involved in these approaches, either in the private sector or in the public services, lead collective bargaining parties to new territories. These initiatives may well be "retrenchment" or "survival" oriented. Some of the instruments, however, are taken from the "adaptation" toolbox. One advanced example of this innovative approach is a recent and ongoing initiative launched by the German metalworkers union IG Metall, flagged as a "better, not just cheaper" campaign. It aims at turning the tables when it comes to relocation and undercutting of collective agreements by trying to set product and process innovation on the bargaining agenda within the respective firms.

The Outcomes

Employability-geared measures, as soon as they apply to measures within the respective companies rather than external job pools, will be most pertinent in "survival" and "adaptation" agreements. The same applies in principle to the other three contents described here, though emphases may differ in detail. The stabilisation of workforce measures in particular will depend very much on the political environment, as demonstrated by the example of agreements in Spain. These different thematic emphases across collective agreements on employment and competitiveness have been summarised in earlier overviews as a prevalence of 'defensive' agreements. That is, most agreements "have been aimed principally at avoiding or limiting job losses or mass redundancies, in exchange for a lowering of labour costs and/or an increase in levels of flexibility and length of working time in the organisation.Quite obviously the employment effects to be expected from pacts on employment and competitiveness depend very much on the type of the respective agreement. "Retrenchment" pacts may be at best protective, if temporary, in nature. The protective character of "survival" agreements may consider a slightly longer time horizon. At first sight, "adaptation" agreements appear to yield the most sustainable employment effects.

Unfortunately the assessments based on plausibility cannot be supported by sound evaluations. With the notable exception of the introduction of the 35-hour week in France, there has been, to our knowledge and in accordance with earlier overviews, no technical evaluation of the outcomes of local employment pacts so far. What does exist are assessments of actors involved and individual case studies providing insights into the development of employment figures in establishments covered by PECs. There are good reasons to believe that it will remain difficult to move to safer grounds for that matter.

To begin with, the numbers of staff before and after agreements on employment and competitiveness may reflect contrasting cases.

Many PECs aiming at "survival" include both staff retrenchment and measures geared to avoid further layoffs. Other local deals were struck in firms in the black, but under the threat of relocation. Since the drivers and backgrounds behind PECs can be very different, the scope for quantitative evaluations is quite limited.

Another, maybe more substantial reason for the problems of evaluation is the difficulty in assessing the side effects of local pacts on other firms competing in the same markets, or on the economy as a whole. Interestingly, these side effects may occur in all types of agreements, both the more 'defensive' and the more innovative or 'offensive' ones. Safeguarding of jobs based on wage cuts, but equally on innovations in one firm may be harmful for employment levels in competing firms – hence the possibility of zero-sum games. However, there is a substantial difference between these two kinds of side effects. 'Defensive' agreements drawing primarily on wage cuts may trigger a race-to-the-bottom in the respective market, whereas innovation-oriented agreements may push competitors on the same 'high road'. In theory, the latter rationale has been elaborated and tested within the "varieties of capitalism" approach.

The finding of Auer at al., in their cross-country computation on the positive relationship between productivity and stability of workforce would support this argument. There are substantial implications for industrial relations and collective bargaining systems of the contrasting 'low' vs. 'high road' approaches to collective bargaining on employment insecurity. One fundamental effect of multi-employer bargaining systems is that certain attributes of human labour power, wages in particular, are taken out of the competition on the labour market. In doing so, competition will shift to other aspects, such as efficiency of the production process, or product quality. Thus, the crucial question is to what extent local pacts establish a combination of temporary concessions of employee representatives in terms of wages or working hours on the one hand, and of measures geared to processes and product innovations and to enhancing the employability of workers on the other. In their analysis of firm level agreements on employment and competitiveness in Germany, Büttner and Kirsch observed a set of preconditions for this combination to actually happen. These include the extent to which agreements address:

— sources of sustainable cost reductions;
— potentials for a boost of internal flexibility and staff mobility,
— measures to safeguard and enhance human capital within the firm; and
— the involvement of local employee representatives.

Last but not least, these authors assert the need for "professional work structures" of employee representations.

New Actors and Problem of Articulation

Employment pacts at the enterprise level come along with new and local actors. Depending on the country and the respective industry practice, a PEC can be negotiated (a) by both local actors and actors from higher levels of collective bargaining associations, (b) by the local actors, but has to be also accepted by higher levels of unions or employers' associations, or (c) by the local actors alone. In all these cases local union organisation, works councils and employers become actors of collective bargaining, thus giving rise to the need for articulation of different levels of organisation.

The problem of articulation has at least three facets. One of them is the question of whether local actors are getting support from their organisations in negotiations, and how much. Support can be related to information the actors receive, advice from their organisation, or direct and helpful interventions in negotiations at higher levels. A second facet is, if and to what extent local actors are controlled by higher associational levels in the sense that the processes and results of local negotiations are registered at higher levels, whether there are guidelines developed for negotiations by higher levels or whether higher levels are making binding decisions for local actors to enter or not to enter into negotiation or to accept or not to accept the result of a negotiation. The third facet is related to the question of coordination. The most important question concerning the coordination of negotiations is whether they are interdependent in the sense that one negotiation is stimulating actors in another company also to enter into negotiations on a PEC.

The coordination problem can also become virulent within a company if interdependencies exist between different locations of the company. In this case, coordination – from the employee representatives' perspective – has to prevent inner-organisational competition between plants based on wage cuts. In both cases collective bargaining actors at higher levels have to make sure that local actors do not violate collectively agreed labour standards. In the literature, the views expressed on the problem of articulation are far from unequivocal.

To begin with, it seems quite plausible to expect that the unions' interest in articulation is higher than that of the employers' associations. Whenever unions have been able to implement higher bargaining levels, they defend it as an achievement of struggles and as a public good. Employers' associations normally have an interest in higher level bargaining only if a single-employer bargaining strategy of the unions would yield higher labour costs in important parts of an industry than multi-employer bargaining. Therefore in this situation a decentralisation of bargaining would be favourable at least for those companies that have difficulties in maintaining industry standards, either due to a lack of competitiveness or because the profitability of the firm falls short of the expectations.

Of course the employers' associations could nevertheless opt for the preservation of central collective bargaining to maintain a strong role in wage determination. But doing this would mean opting against the interests of many of their members, and the associations would probably get into trouble because of membership losses. It would be much more reasonable for the employers' associations to arrange their strategies along the interests of their members and also to support decentralisation.

A strong control of actors and agreements to preserve the binding power of higher level agreements is not part of their interests. In this respect the employers' associations can be expected to become less corporatist and more pluralistic in style. The only advocates of strong centralised bargaining and labour standards that remain in this situation are the unions – and maybe the state, depending on its role in industrial relations and the respective cycles of political power.

For the unions the problem of articulation can become more difficult in dual-channel systems of industrial relations. These systems are characterised by the existence of works councils as shop-floor representations elected by all employees and that have certain legal entitlements, such as information or consultation rights. They are an institution in their own right, apart from the unions.

The more independent they are from the unions, the more difficult it is to integrate them into a process of articulation between the organisational levels of the union. If concessions for employment are dealt with by the works councils, the unions have to try to coordinate them, although they are not part of the unions' organisations. However, the situation may be not too different in single-channel systems, as local union organisations will in practice focus on local employee interests in a similar way as works councils. It has to be added that the problem of articulation can become virulent not only for unions but also for employee representatives within a company. In the first case, coordination within the company has to consider the preservation of industry or national labour standards; in the second, local bargaining can foster a regime competition between locations in different countries with different employment standards.

Finally, the need for articulation may be even greater once the employees enter the scene as a third group of new actors besides local employee representatives and enterprise management. Local unions or works councils can involve employees as relevant actors by information, mobilisation and participation. In the case of information, employee representatives try to inform the employees more or less continuously about the reasons for negotiations of a PEC, the development of the negotiations, and the results.

There are also other forms of participation where employees are actively involved in bargaining commissions and the like. Employee involvement can have ambiguous implications for articulation. On the one hand, employee involvement can be expected to increase the legitimisation of local unions bargaining with management and thereby to increase their bargaining power. As well, the union can benefit as a whole if employee involvement brings new members and an increase in union density. We will show later that these effects can be observed in the case of the German metalworking industry. On the other hand, rank and file involvement can also result in a decline of central control, especially if it includes mobilisation and participation. In the case of mobilisation, it is far from clear that the mobilised can be restricted on the role designated to them by their representatives. However, it is fair to assume that in most cases local employee representatives are in close contact with both higher union levels and with employees and will actively try to prevent problems of articulation.

Decentralisation and Derogation

Until the end of the 1990s, the assessment of PECs used to be quite positive amongst actors and observers. Although, or because, PECs contributed to the decentralisation of collective bargaining, they were widely regarded as a positive sum game for both employers and unions. The widening of the bargaining agenda and the promotion of a partnership approach by strengthening the role of employee representatives in companies were regarded as the most important advantages for unions besides employee protection. Even if a local agreement is not widening the agenda very much and is mainly characterised by employee concessions, the dangers of undermining higher level collective bargaining standards is quite low if the concessions made do not affect these standards.

Over the past few years, however, the situation has changed. As Ozaki argues, while "decentralisation may bring some benefits to workers, (...) the arguments put forward by its proponents share many common elements with the neo-liberal economic arguments about macro-economic management. There is often a thin line separating decentralisation and deregulation." In fact, the distinction between decentralisation and deviations from collective agreements has become blurred. To begin with, informal agreements have developed in some countries as a result of "wildcat cooperation" between local actors which violate standards agreed at higher levels. Once wildcat cooperation gains importance, it may entail an erosion of collective bargaining. They allow for local deviations from industry standards in specified cases. In this case deviation becomes formalised, which opens the chance for the unions to organise articulation and control.

The derogation or opting out clauses on which DCBAs are based can have different forms. Firstly, these clauses can define certain procedures and competencies. They can describe obligatory steps to be taken in negotiations, such as the need for employers to consult the local union or to give a detailed analysis of the economic situation of the company. Furthermore, they can specify who is entitled to negotiate an agreement. It may be shifted to the local actors, and/or it may need to be accepted at higher levels of the collective bargaining system. Secondly, these clauses can define the conditions or the scope of local shortfalls of collective bargaining norms.

DCBAs are a specific product of what can be called micro-corporatist arrangements. There are three features of DCBAs that justify their classification as corporatist: they are negotiated by collective actors – unions or works councils on one side, and the companies, maybe supported by employer's associations, on the other; the collective actors are strong enough to legitimise them with regard to third parties like the employees, higher union levels or the employers' association; and the actors are able to guarantee the transformation of norms into social action. The weaker the local actors dealing with DCBA are, the less they are corporatist and the less useful they are with respect to the outcomes expected. The power asymmetry on which DCBAs are based implies an obvious problem for micro-corporatist arrangements. On the one hand, the fact that DCBAs exist indicate a power shift in favour of the enterprises. If the unions are too strong, either centralised bargaining will dominate, or decentralised bargaining will, at worst, deal with temporary deviations from industry standards.

References

Daley, A. 1999. *The hollowing out of French unions: Politics and industrial relations after 1981*, in A. Martin and G. Ross (eds.): *The brave new worlds of European labour: European trade unions at the millenium* (New York, Oxford), pp.167-216 .

European Commission. 2006. *Industrial Relations in Europe 2006*, Luxembourg, Office for Official Publications of the European Communities.

Frege, C.; Kelly, J. 2003. "Union revitalization strategies in comparative perspective", in *European Journal of Industrial Relations*, 9, pp. 7-24.

Freyssinet, J.; Seifert, H. 2001. *Negotiating collective agreements on employment and competitiveness.* Office for Official Publications of the European Communities.

Bibliography

Adams, R.J. 1991. 'An International Survey of Courses in Comparative Industrial Relations', in M. Bray (ed.), *Teaching Comparative Industrial Relations,* ACIRRT Monograph No 2 University of Sydney, Sydney.

Agarwal, S.L., 1978. *Labour Relations Law in India*, Macmillan Company of India Ltd.,New Delhi.

Atkinson, J. 1985. 'The Changing Corporation' in D. Clutterbuck (ed.), *New Patterns of Work,* Gower, Aldershot.

Bailey, E. K. 1995. 'International Compensation', in O. Shenkar (ed.), *Global Perspectives of Human Resource Management,* Prentice Hall, New Jersey.

Bamber, G.J. & Lansbury, R.D. 1993. *International and Comparative Industrial Relations,* Routledge, London.

Bhattacharya, B.B. and Mitra, A. 1993. .Employment and structural adjustment: A look at 1991 census data., in *Economic and Political Weekly*,(Mumbai, Sameeksha Trust, 18 Sep., pp.1989-95.

Boxall, P. & Deeks J. 1992. 'New Zealand' in M. Rothman, D. Briscoe & R. Nacamulli (eds.), *Industrial Relations Around the World: Labour Relations for Multinational Companies,* De Gruyter & Co., Berlin.

Briscoe, D.R. 1995, *International Human Resource Management*, Prentice Hall, New Jersey.

Chakravarty, S. 1974. *Reflections on the growth process in the Indian economy*, Mimeograph. Hyderabad, Hyderabad Administrative Staff College of India.

Clegg H.A. 1960. *A New Approach to Industrial Democracy.* Blackwell, oxford..

Daley, A. 1999. *The hollowing out of French unions: Politics and industrial relations after 1981*, in A. Martin and G. Ross (eds.): *The brave new worlds of European labour: European trade unions at the millenium* (New York, Oxford), pp.167-216 .

Datt, R. 1993. .New economic policy and its impact on industrial relations and employment in India., in *Indian Journal of Labour Economics.* Delhi, Indian Society of Labour Economics, 1, pp. 66-76.

European Commission. 2006. *Industrial Relations in Europe 2006,* Luxembourg, Office for Official Publications of the European Communities.

Fergusson, J. 1997. 'Casual Employment Contracts: Continuing Confusion when Protection and Free Market Clash', *New Zealand Journal of Industrial Relations,* 22/1, pp. 123-142.

Frege, C.; Kelly, J. 2003. "Union revitalization strategies in comparative perspective", in *European Journal of Industrial Relations*, 9, pp. 7-24.

Frenkel, S and Royal, C. 1996: *Globalization and Employment Relations.* Paper prepared for ILO/EASMAT, Bangkok; published under authorization as Centre for Corporate Change Paper No 63, University of New South Wales, Sydney.

Freyssinet, J.; Seifert, H. 2001. *Negotiating collective agreements on employment and competitiveness.* Office for Official Publications of the European Communities.

Government of India, 2002. *The Report of the Second National Commission on Labour* .

Government of India. 1969. *Report of the Industrial Licensing Policy Enquiry Committee.* Delhi.

Indian Law Institute,1987. *Labour Law and Labour Relations Cases and Materials*, N.M. Tripathi Pvt. Ltd, Bombay.

International Labour Organisation 1997. 'Perspectives: Part-time work: Solution or Trap?', *International Labour Review*, Vol. 136, No. 4.

Joshi, V. and Little, I. 1996. *India's Economic Reforms: 1991-2001.* Delhi, Oxford University Press.

Mallick, P.L., 1989. *Industrial Law*, Eastern Book Company, Lucknow.

Mamoria, C.B., and Ganakar, S.B., 2000. *Dynamics of Industrial Relations*, Himalaya Publishing House, Mumbai.

Margerison, C.J., 1969. "What do we mean by industrial relations? A behavioural approach", *British Journal of Industrial Relations*, Vol. 7, No. 2,.

McNally, B. 1999. *Global Managers? An investigation into transnational competencies in the New Zealand Finance Sector'*, unpublished dissertation completed in partial fulfilment of the requirements for an MBA Henley Management College.

Otto Kahn - Freund 1969. "Industrial Relations and the Law - Retrospect and Prospect". Vol. 7 *British Journal Of Industrial Relations*.

Roscoe Pound . 1921. "A Theory of Social Interests" in *Papers And Proceedings of the American Sociological Society*, May.

Salamon, Michael, 1998. *Industrial Relations Theory and Practice (3rd ed.)*, Prentice Hall.

Sharma, B. 1996. *Industrial Relations in ASEAN: A Comparative Study*, International Book Services, Kuala Lumpur.

Shenkar, O. 1995. *Global Perspectives of Human Resource Management*, Prentice Hall, New Jersey.

Vause, G.W. 1992. 'Labour Relations in Thailand', *East Asian Executive Reports*, 14(11) November 15, pp. 14-17.

Verma, A., Kocahn, T. & Lansbury, R. 1995. *Employment Relations in the Growing Asian Economies*, Routledge, London.

Index